Signing the Body Poetic

I0998844

Signing the Body Poetic

ESSAYS ON AMERICAN SIGN LANGUAGE LITERATURE

H-Dirksen L. Bauman
Jennifer L. Nelson
Heidi M. Rose

EDITORS

With a Foreword by William C. Stokoe
and a Preface by W. J. T. Mitchell

Includes DVD

UNIVERSITY OF CALIFORNIA PRESS

BERKELEY   LOS ANGELES   LONDON

University of California Press, one of the most distinguished university presses in the United States, enriches lives around the world by
advancing scholarship in the humanities, social sciences, and natural
sciences. Its activities are supported by the UC Press Foundation and
by philanthropic contributions from individuals and institutions. For
more information, visit www.ucpress.edu.

University of California Press
Berkeley and Los Angeles, California

University of California Press, Ltd.
London, England

Library of Congress Cataloging-in-Publication Data

Signing the body poetic : essays on American Sign Language literature /
H-Dirksen L. Bauman, Jennifer L. Nelson, Heidi M. Rose, editors ;
with a foreword by William C. Stokoe and a preface by W. J. T.
Mitchell.
    p.   cm.
  "Includes DVD."
  Includes bibliographical references and index.
  ISBN-13: 978-0-520-22975-4 (cloth : alk. paper)
  ISBN-10: 0-520-22975-4 (cloth : alk. paper)
  ISBN-13: 978-0-520-22976-1 (pbk. : alk. paper)
  ISBN-10: 0-520-22976-2 (pbk. : alk. paper)
  1. American Sign Language literature.   2. Deaf authors.
3. Deaf, Theater for the.   4. Visual literature—History and
criticism.   I. Bauman, H-Dirksen L., 1964–   II. Nelson, Jennifer L.,
1965–   III. Rose, Heidi M., 1963–

HV2353.S53   2007
890—dc22   2006016236

Manufactured in the United States of America

15 14 13 12 11 10 09 08 07 06
10 9 8 7 6 5 4 3 2 1

This book is printed on New Leaf EcoBook 60, containing 60%
post-consumer waste, processed chlorine free; 30% de-inked recycled
fiber, elemental chlorine free; and 10% FSC-certified virgin fiber,
totally chlorine free. EcoBook 60 is acid-free and meets the minimum
requirements of ANSI/ASTM D5634–01 (*Permanence of Paper*).

. . . Were you thinking that those were the words, those upright lines?
those curves, angles, dots?
No, those are not the words, the substantial words are in the ground and sea,
They are in the air, they are in you.

Were you thinking that those were the words, those delicious sounds
out of your friends' mouths?
No, the real words are more delicious than they.

Human bodies are words, myriads of words,
(In the best poems re-appears the body . . .)

WALT WHITMAN
"A Song of the Rolling Earth"

CONTENTS

CONTENTS OF THE DVD

The main reference to each DVD clip appears in **boldface** in the text.

FOREWORD

When in 1960 it became clear that American Sign Language (ASL) is indeed a language, something more than a language emerged from underground. A language does not just provide a community of users with a way to communicate; it preserves their memories, encapsulates their hopes and desires, and safeguards their values—all the more so when its use involves art. A people's language and culture are inseparable, so this volume exploring ASL literature is doubly welcome.

It brings to the public eye some of the cherished gems of ASL literature, but it does more: it shows how inseparable are a visual language and the role of the body in its expression. Movement as dance is of course linked with music in Western culture, but at the cost of more and more separation from language. ASL poetry reunites dance and artistic utterance; it shows that there is a nonparadoxical meaning in the term *silent music* and reminds us that rhythm stems from movement, not from sound. The present volume helps to explain this phenomenon and much else that make sign language literature unique and able to enrich our cosmopolitan twenty-first-century culture.

William C. Stokoe
1919–2000

PREFACE: UTOPIAN GESTURES

——————

W. J. T. MITCHELL

Although the language of gesture and spoken language are equally natural, still the first is easier and depends less upon conventions. For more things affect our eyes than our ears. Also, visual forms are more varied than sounds, and more expressive, saying more in less time. Love, it is said, was the inventor of drawing. It might also have invented speech, though less happily. Not being very well pleased with it, it disdains it; it has livelier ways of expressing itself. How could she say things to her beloved, who traced his shadow with such pleasure! What sounds might she use to work such magic?

JEAN-JACQUES ROUSSEAU
On the Origin of Language

"Making gestures quotable" is one of the substantial achievements of the epic theater. An actor must be able to space his gestures the way a typesetter produces spaced type. . . . Epic theater is by definition a gestic theater. For the more frequently we interrupt someone in the act of acting, the more gestures result.

WALTER BENJAMIN
"What Is Epic Theater?"

It is a great honor to be invited to write a preface to this pathbreaking book on the poetics of American Sign Language (ASL), the language of the Deaf in most parts of North America. But it is more than an honor. It is also a gesture of openness and generosity to invite a nonsigner like myself, deaf and mute (or blind, illiterate, and bereft of hands), to introduce a book of this sort. In the world of the Deaf, I am a disabled person, incapable of hearing or seeing or reading or listening to what is being said by the people around me.

But this is not a book about disability. It is about poetics—about the movement from language to literature, the moment when language takes flight and creates new worlds out of words and images. Sign language, "speaking" with the hands, has now established a firm beachhead in its long struggle for legitimation and recognition. No serious linguist would now deny that sign is a language in its fullest and most complex sense, not some impoverished form of expressive gesticulation, pantomime, or "drawing pictures in the air." The question remains, however: Now that we know that hands can speak to the eyes and the mind, what are they capable of saying? What sort of thoughts and feelings can they produce?

One answer is obvious. Gesture languages make possible the everyday life of Deaf communities as fully fluent, internally conversant societies.[1] They provide the medium for discursive expressions of all sorts among a community of signers—everything from gossip to business to philosophical arguments to declarations of love. But when language turns to literature, when the word is poetic, it becomes, as Nelson Goodman has observed, a "way of worldmaking." The turn, in fact, may well be in the opposite direction: first the poet creates the world along with language, and then we settle into ordinary life and language. "Language," as Ralph Waldo Emerson observed, "is fossil poetry," a "sort of tomb of the muses."[2] When the poet speaks, the dead metaphors, the forgotten images, the linguistic fossils come back to life and the world is re-created.

What worlds will the languages of gesture create and re-create? And how will those worlds matter to the speaking and hearing community? Why should those who live in the world of phonetic language care about the poetry of the Deaf community? What difference could it possibly make to *us*? What would a gesture of recognition amount to? Would it merely be "lip service"? Or could it lead us to new vistas of apprehension and comprehension, new forms of "prehensibility," literally a grasping of new meanings with a hand as eloquent and labile as the tongue?

Certainly anyone who takes a professional interest in language and literature, and beyond that an interest in visual, verbal, and auditory media, should find something compelling about the contemporary emergence of gesture languages. If I may quote myself reflecting on this matter for the members of the Modern Language Association:

How often do we have the opportunity to witness the maturation of a new language, complete with poets, story-tellers, rhetoricians, scholars, and theorists? If every language requires a great vernacular poet to lay its foundations, the Homer (or Dante) of American Sign Language may well be among us, laying to rest the ghosts of all the "mute inglorious Miltons" who hover around the margins of our militantly oral poetic traditions. "Phonocentrism" has been challenged at the level of theory many times in the last twenty years; American Sign Language makes this challenge concrete, visible, practical, and political, graphically inscribing a "writing of/on the body" that is (in every sense) no figure of speech. The poetry of the Deaf stages for us in the most vivid possible form the basic shift in literary understanding that has been occurring before our eyes in the last decade: the movement from a "textual" model (based in the narrowly defined circuit of writing and speech) to a "performance" model, exemplified by recent work in the semiotics of drama, film, television, and performance art, and the interplay of language with the visual/pictorial field. Even those who never learn to sign a single phrase of ASL must, if they are serious about the relations of the arts and social formations, take the artistic productions and theoretical reflections of the Deaf community into account.[3]

To this I would now add that the emergence of interest in gesture language in our time is not only symptomatic and illustrative of a host of paradigm shifts in the human sciences. It also has an undeniably utopian component, if only because we cannot know in advance what it will produce. We can only speculate, given what we know about language, literature, the senses, the body, and the media, what gesture language can produce.

The first thing a utopian conception produces is an estrangement of the familiar, self-evident terms of existence. All of our standard preconceptions about language and the senses are brought into crisis by the emergence of gesture. The distinctions between word and image, between telling and showing, reading and seeing, writing and speaking, listening and watching, all seem to shimmer and vibrate in the presence of sign language. We don't quite know how to talk about talking anymore when the hand takes over from the tongue; we don't quite know how to look at images when the eye quickened by gestural literacy stands in for the ear. Sign languages are not just another language group among the family of natural languages. They stand outside all the languages based in speech and audition and their rendering in phonetic script, yet they reveal that what Stephen Pinker calls "the language instinct" transcends the physical or sensory organs that serve as its vehicle of expression.[4] Rousseau remarked long ago that "the invention of the art of communicating our ideas depends less upon the organs we use in such communication than it does upon a power proper to man."[5] That is why linguistics is not baffled by the shift from verbal to gestural speech. As Diane Brentari puts it: "Signs made using the arms and body in sign languages and those made using the tongue, velum, glottis, and palate in spoken languages are equivalent from the point of view of grammar."[6] But poetics, which attends to the thickening and heightening of the sensuous materiality of the sign, does not have the Cartesian clarity and abstraction of linguistics. The medium, as Marshall McLuhan noted, is not just the message, but the *massage*. The gesture becomes not just a differentiable sign within an ideal structure but a laying on of hands, a virtual holding of the beholder. If Coleridge's Wedding Guest is "held" by the glittering eye and glib tongue of the Ancient Mariner, what kind of grip can the gestural orator exert on an audience? What difference does it make if the organ that communicates the first words to an infant is also the hand that rocks the cradle?

Poetics must engage, then, with the myths, metaphors, and fantasies about the physical specificity of the medium, not simply with the system that makes communication possible. It adds to the linguistic "instinct" the linguistic *drive*—the compulsions and automatisms, the need-demand-desire circuit that constitutes the human subject. Freud argued that dream images are not directly mimetic or iconic but actually a kind of hieroglyphic script constructed on the principles of the rebus, the visual-verbal pun. What is the mode of representation in the gestural or signed dream? Do scrolls unfold from the hands as in medieval paintings? And if Lacan is right that the unconscious is structured like a language, what difference does it make if that language arises in the scopic (eye/hand) domain rather than in the vocative (mouth/ear)? If we can say more than we mean to, surely we signify in excess as well, and this is where the poetic function arises, flashing forth from the very hands that try to get a grip on the world and the word. When does the intentional gesture slip into the magical motions of the conjuring hand, parting the waters or loosing them like the sorcerer's apprentice?

Consider the role of hands in Walter Benjamin's reflections on "The Work of Art in the Age of Mechanical Reproduction." The painter is like the magician, working with gestures and a "laying on of hands"; the photographer is like the surgeon who cuts into the patient's body, penetrating appearances to lay bare an "optical unconscious."[7] This simile needs to be updated in our time to reckon with a new figure of the healing hand and a new art form. "Virtual surgery" is now being developed in which the surgeon wears data gloves and operates on the patient's body, manipulating the laser scalpels by remote control from a different room. This procedure allows a precision of significant hand movements capable of performing microsurgeries that would be impossible for the "natural" hand of the surgeon. Similarly, the evolution of gesture languages offers new resources of precision, complexity, and eloquence across the full range of media (live and virtual performance, video and cinema) in which they can be archived. There is no writing system for gesture language, but in the age of the data glove and digitized image sequence that may have the effect of transforming a handicap to a new form of handiness.

There is a temptation, while giving in to these utopian gestures, to sentimentalize sign language, to idealize it in a way that may be counterproductive. Our imaginary sign may begin to sound like the language of Milton's angels, providing immediate, intuitive, and transparent communication (just like the sex of his angels, which transcends genital fixation to achieve an unobstructed commingling from head to foot). Rousseau suggests that gesture language is "easier" and "depends less upon conventions," that it is more varied, expressive, and quick-acting, thus invented (along with the art of drawing) by Love before speech was perfected. Sign is positioned in our mythic histories of language as both the first and the last, oldest and youngest, the original language before speech and the newest language on the planet, coming into its own in the age of the digital image, another medium of expression that deconstructs the boundary between word and image. Sign is liable to be overestimated in a time (like ours) when "the Body" and "Visual Culture" have become reigning cliches and transcendental signifiers. It will be important, therefore, to remember the long history of the denigration of gesture language, its association with savagery and animality, stupidity and disability. The utopian gesture is shadowed at every turn by its dystopian counterpart. This double movement of over- and underestimation is, in fact, precisely what constitutes the mythologizing and fetishizing of gesture by oral cultures, a process that will have to be worked through as gesture language explores its worlds of literary possibility and reaches out to engage the world of the hearing.[8]

What gesture languages offer, then, is not only a utopia but what Foucault called a "heterotopia," the "disorder in which a large number of possible orders glitter separately." Utopias, Foucault notes, are crucial to the literary enterprise: "[U]topias permit fables and discourse: They run with the very grain of language and are part of the fundamental dimension of the *fabula;* heterotopias dessicate speech, stop words in their tracks, contest the very possibility of language at its source; they dissolve our myths and sterilize the lyricism of our sentences."[9] If a language is a way of world making, it is also a way of unmaking the world and producing a revolutionary shock. It is impossible not to be reminded here of the theory of gesture elaborated by Berthold Brecht and Walter Benjamin, a notion of gesture not as a vehicle of communication but as a kind of interruption in the flow of meaning.[10] Brecht's "epic theater" was designed precisely to counteract organic, naturalistic modes of acting and dramaturgy by constantly interrupting the action with self-consciously theatrical gestures—songs, subtitles, metacommentaries, and ironic acting styles. The *gestus* was designed to produce an "alienation effect" that would dispel the theatrical illusion and put the audience in a critical, testing, and experimental posture. *Gestus* was also, as Benjamin noted, "the restoration of the method of montage decisive in radio and film, from an often merely modish procedure to a human event."[11]

In a similar way, the traditional understanding of gesture as a silent handmaiden to speech, an emphatic supplement to oral expression, is disrupted by the revelation of gesture as full speech in and of itself. As gesture approaches language, it becomes citable and re-citable, with the potential to interrupt discourse the way a citation intrudes as a foreign body or specimen in the linear flow of a text.[12] One could imagine a bilingual performance in which speech and gesture had a contrapuntal or even contradictory, ironic relationship.[13] In written language, we see this most literally in the way a "block" quotation serves to "block" the reader's progress, framing off a string of words as a detour, a change of speaker: "[I]n contrast to the actions and undertakings of people [gesture] has a fixable beginning and a fixable end. This strict, framelike closure of every element in an attitude *(Haltung),* which at the same time is entirely inserted in a living flux, comprises one of the fundamental dialectical components *(Grundphänomene)* of gesture. . . . The retarding character of interruption, the episodic character of framing *(Umrahmung)* are what endow gestural theater with its epic quality."[14]

If gesture interrupts discourse, it also interrupts actions, precisely by restaging the relation between words and deeds, words and things. We do things with our hands, but what happens when we also say things with them? Can we do and say at the same time, saying something by doing something, or doing something by saying something? Gesture is, in one sense, suspended action, like a feint in boxing, the simulation of an action. The no-look pass in basketball is a gesture of the eyes deliberately designed to contradict and distract from the accompanying action of the hands. But the gesture is also the framed action, the citable move, the summarizing account of what an action "amounts to." We say that it is a "nice gesture" to give a gift or remember to telephone a sick friend. The thing done may involve statements, but it is also framed as a statement in itself. It is not the gift, or what is said on the phone, but "the thought" (that is, the gesture) that counts. Perhaps gesture is best understood as the moment when thought becomes visible, tangible, or palpable, staged and framed as *form*—something to be held and to hold us in mutual prehension. What will philosophy become when a thought, an argument, a system can be framed as a citable gesture, held out to the beholder in the signing space of the human body? How might the movements of abstract ideas, of Kantian categories such as space and time, the noumenal and the phenomenal, or the motions of dialectical reasoning itself take on new valences in the space-time of performative demonstration?

For Benjamin, gesture takes the place of Hegel's "negation" in the operations of the dialectic. Instead of the abstract antithesis, determined by a logical antinomy to a thesis, the contradiction is unpredictable, even accidental. Like montage, like the shocking collision of disparate elements in surrealist and dadaist collage, gesture disrupts the smooth flow of "business" (and discourse, politics, aesthetics) "as usual." In Brecht's aesthetics, it is the key to the alienation effect, which positions the actor and the beholder in a critical (not empathic) relation to the dramatic action. Aristotelian drama— the organic unfolding of an action with a beginning, middle, and end, the purging of the spectator's emotions with the tragic plot—is to be replaced by an "epic theatricality" of gestures to be critiqued. Are these modernist, vanguardist gestures relevant to the public emergence of a gestural poetics in our time? What will the thought of them look like when they are translated into the full language of gesture? Like the use of visual and optical metaphors to explain perception, cognition, understanding, memory, reflection, and imagination, the metalanguage of hands, arms, and body is woven through the entire vocabulary of the human subject as a beholding, form-shaping, grasping, prehensile creature. What will happen to human consciousness when this figurative metalanguage is literally realized in the gestures of the eloquent signing body?

These questions can be posed by a nonsigner like myself, but they can be answered only by those who think and speak with their hands. Just as gesture interrupts phonetic language, it also disrupts phonetic literature, conjuring up the spectacle of a new poetics and aesthetics that rewrites the expressive and receptive human body and the spaces it inhabits. Gesture languages do not simply provide instruments for new ways of "getting a grip" on a reality that is already available to us. They are more like a way of groping in a darkness that we did not even know was there, a series of probes into the unknown, and (equally important) a way of letting go, relaxing our grasp in order to permit new experiments with perception and expression to occur. Blake's prophecy that "Visionary forms dramatic" will become the lingua franca of a renovated human civilization may yet come true in the convergence of the newest minority language on the planet with new technologies adequate to the codification and dissemination of its literary/artistic productions:

> And they conversed together in Visionary forms dramatic which bright
> Redounded from their [Hands] in thunderous majesty, in Visions
> In new Expanses, creating exemplars of Memory and of Intellect
> Creating Space, Creating Time according to the wonders Divine
> Of Human Imagination . . .
> . . . .
> . . . & every Word & Every Character
> Was Human.[15]

We are privileged to be in a position to behold this process of human imagination.

NOTES

1. I am well aware that the term *gesture language* is a highly controversial usage and that some in the Deaf community may hear in it an unpleasant reminder of "a history of linguistic oppression," as H-Dirksen L. Bauman puts it (pers. comm., June 2, 2000). I have no wish to offend anyone who associates negative connotations with the term, but I feel compelled to use it for two reasons: (1) poetics has to take into account the materiality of the linguistic medium, and for sign language that is unavoidably the visible gesture of the

hands, along with the signer's body and face; (2) an engaged poetics of sign cannot afford to ignore the history of the denigration of gesture, any more than African American studies can afford amnesia about negritude, or feminism can forget about misogyny. These histories of prejudice are part of whatever poetry can be made from the human suffering they entailed. On the "militant oralism" that has underwritten the speaking community's denigration of gesture, see Oliver Sacks, *Seeing Voices* (New York: HarperCollins, 1990).

2. Ralph Waldo Emerson, "The Poet," in *Essays* (New York: Franklin Watts, 1970), 303.

3. W. J. T. Mitchell, "Gesture, Sign, and Play: ASL Poetry and the Deaf Community," MLA Newsletter, Summer 1989, 13–14.

4. Stephen Pinker, *The Language Instinct* (New York: HarperPerennial, 1995).

5. Jean-Jacques Rousseau, *On the Origin of Language,* trans. John H. Moran (Chicago: University of Chicago Press, 1966), 10.

6. Diane Brentari, *A Prosodic Model of Sign Language Phonology* (Cambridge, MA: MIT Press, 1998), 1.

7. Walter Benjamin, "The Work of Art in the Age of Mechanical Reproduction," in *Illuminations* (New York: Schocken Books, 1969), 233.

8. See W. J. T. Mitchell, "The Surplus Value of Images," chapter 4 in *What Do Pictures Want?* (Chicago: University of Chicago Press, 2005), 76–106.

9. Michel Foucault, *The Order of Things* (New York: Pantheon, 1970), 48.

10. See Sam Weber, "Citable Gestures," in *Mediated Drama/Dramatized Media,* ed. Eckart Voigts-Virchow (Trier: Wissenschaftlicher Verlag, 2000).

11. Berthold Brecht, "The Author as Producer," in *Reflections* (New York: Harcourt Brace Jovanovich, 1978), 235.

12. It is worth noting here that cognitive scientists have linked what they call "gesture-speech mismatch" to "transitional knowledge states." When children's gestures seem "out of synch" with their speech, it is a reliable sign that they are about to learn something new. See Susan Goldin-Meadow, Martha Wagner Alibati, and R. Breckinridge Church, "Transitions in Concept Acquisition: Using the Hand to Read the Mind," *Psychological Review* 100, no. 2 (1993): 279–97. I am grateful to Bill Brown for suggesting this reference.

13. Such a bilingual performance would be something like the illuminated poetry of William Blake, a multimedia "composite art" in which image and text, gesture and voice are woven in complex counterpoint, and mere "illustration" of text by image, voice by gesture, is resolutely avoided. See W. J. T. Mitchell, *Blake's Composite Art* (Princeton: Princeton University Press; 1977), for further discussion.

14. Benjamin, "Work of Art," 521, quoted in Weber, "Citable Gestures," 8.

15. William Blake, *Jerusalem* 98:28ff, with "Hands" substituted for "Tongues."

ACKNOWLEDGMENTS

This project was conceived after the 1996 ASL Literature Conference in Rochester, New York, when we participants recognized both the close interconnection of our respective researches and the need for a substantive text on the fledgling field of ASL literary theory and criticism. The idea for an edited volume was developed to achieve widespread Deaf/hearing collaboration and to include research from multiple disciplines and theoretical approaches. We had a great deal of assistance along the way, without which we could never have accomplished this project.

We are grateful for the financial support provided by the National Endowment for the Humanities–Collaborative Research Division, the Gallaudet Research Institute, and Villanova University. The Gallaudet University Television and Media Production Department, including Jim Dellon, Gary Brooks, and Barry White, generously donated studio time, equipment, and expertise to complete videotaping for the DVD. We also thank Cindy King, director of Gallaudet University Academic Technologies. Facundo Montenegro and Rene Visco contributed greatly to the filming of the DVD.

In addition, for their insights and inspiration we thank Elizabeth Abel, Benjamin Bahan, Michael Barnett, Nicole Salimbene Bauman, Bernard Bragg, Joseph Castronovo, Peter Cook, Michael Davidson, Lennard Davis, Steve Goldsmith, Mario Hernandez, Lynn Jacobowitz, Ella Mae Lentz, Stanley Matelski, Walt and Kay Nelson, Jaine Richards, Carol Robinson, Jerome Rothenberg, Daniel I. Slobin, Jennifer Smith, and Paul Wapner. These individuals provided invaluable support and consultation in the development and execution of this project.

We are grateful to Linda Norton for being the first editor to believe in this project. We thank Randy Heyman, Rose Vekony, and Elisabeth Magnus of the University of California Press and Becky Ryan and Joe Dannis of DawnSignPress for their patience and efforts in seeing this bilingual and bitextual collaboration through to completion. Joseph Josselyn also is to be thanked for the production of the DVD.

Finally, we wish to acknowledge the late William Stokoe, whose pioneering efforts ultimately made this volume possible, and the late Joseph Castronovo, whose vision and artistry are deeply missed. We dedicate this volume to their memories.

Below we provide a few guidelines and clarifications to assist your navigation through this combined book and DVD.

First, you will see the words *deaf* and *Deaf* throughout the volume. The distinction between upper- and lowercase usage has become an accepted practice in Deaf studies and is used to denote differences between physiological and cultural aspects of d/Deafness. Lowercase *deaf* refers to the physiological condition of profound hearing loss, while uppercase *Deaf* refers to a culture—the linguistic minority of [in this case] Americans who use ASL as their primary language. When authors in this volume use *deaf* they typically refer to an individual or population that both cannot hear and identifies with the majority of people who use spoken-written language; for example, a reference to an "oral deaf person" means that this person without hearing has been raised to speak and lip-read rather than sign. When authors use *Deaf* they typically refer to an individual or group identified by his or her primary use of ASL and thus identified with a community of signers who define themselves as a linguistic and cultural minority rather than disabled group.

Second, to assist nonsigning viewers, we provide English captions and voice-over for most of the DVD, but you will notice that not all texts are translated. Some ASL artists prefer that their poems stand alone without English translation. For these texts we provide a synopsis in the chapter so that you may follow the story while viewing the text in its original visual and spatial form. For the sections of the DVD that *do* include captions and/or voice-over, we encourage nonsigning viewers to turn these features off after using them for translation purposes. This will allow you to focus your attention on the visual, spatial, and performative features of ASL that are discussed across all chapters of this volume.

Finally, you will frequently see references to signs in all capital letters, for example POETRY; this form denotes the gloss of a particular sign, the meaning of a sign written using English words.

ONE

Introduction

H-DIRKSEN L. BAUMAN

JENNIFER L. NELSON

HEIDI M. ROSE

For an ASL version of this introduction, see DVD **clip 1.1.**

Before you embark on this volume of essays on American Sign Language (ASL) literature, we invite you to see it in its natural habitat, the body-turned-text. Rather than read this page *about* sign literature, insert your DVD, sit back, and "read" this short poem, "Let There Be Light" (**clip 1.2**).

We begin with this poem because it is a type of creation myth of sign literature. The signing persona is a sign poet at the origins of this new field of human creativity. Within the first fifteen seconds, the poem embodies the fundamental thrust of this book: a remapping of the field of literature to include an emerging body of literature composed not for the ear but for the eye.

The poem opens with the sign LIMIT, imposing itself in front of the body, then moving mechanically to the ear and placed like a box, locking our attention on this single parcel of the body. This LIMIT-ON-THE-EAR sign does not imply that the limitation is deafness; rather, the limitation is that of *phonocentrism,* the unquestioned orientation that speech and hearing are the only fully human modalities of language. The sign poet knows better. He pushes, heaves, and coaxes LIMIT-ON-THE-EAR sign around to the eyes where it transforms into an open portal, a lens through which to peer deeper into a new visual landscape of language, a new literary cosmology under a vast dome of STARS.

At this point, the fundamental shift has taken place: from the ear to the eye. But this is only the beginning. In a wild Promethean gesture, the sign poet sweeps the light from the sky, condensing the stellar firmament into a few drops, the pure light of language dropped into the hands of this Deaf bard, who rubs his hands together, conjuring the signs BECOMING and MOTIVATION.[1] Once the poetic work is undertaken, the attar of starlight catalyzes into FIRE-GROWING-OUT-OF-FIRE, visually echoing the sign for SIGNING. As the hand-fire grows, out fly SPARKS, lighting tiny fires in this new field. They at first burn in isolation, then grow, unite, and SPREAD until the entire landscape is afire and AGLOW. The poet watches in satisfaction. This literary practice now lights up the landscape.

Indeed, recognition of ASL literature is spreading, as is its practice. With the growth in recognition of ASL as a foreign language in high schools, colleges, and universities, it is only natural that awareness of this emerging body of literature is increasing. We hope this volume will aid in introducing and exploring a new dimension to the field of literature.

Clearly we are in the presence here of something different from traditional literature. *Poetry* often conjures images of lines not quite reaching the right margin and the musical incantations of the speaking voice, whereas *prose* evokes images of justified margins, indented paragraphs, chapters, and books held by silently engrossed readers. But in sign literature, the same hands, face, and whole body used for everyday eating, sneezing, and lifting are transformed into the kinetic shape and skin of the poem. Here, reading becomes viewing, books become videos, and paper becomes a performing body. In a most literal sense, this is a form of "writing-the-body"; the poet's body becomes a palimpsest over which course the three-dimensional kinetic images of sign. Rather than hearing word after spoken word, or reading from left to right, we follow three-dimensional, kinetic images, an experience perhaps more akin to watching cinema than reading a book.[2]

Yet the experience is still very much like reading a book or listening to a poem. Like works of written and spoken literature, creative works in sign open wide enough for the imagination to move around in, to play and conjure its own images. Whether the tale is recited by a blind Homer wandering the Grecian hills in the eighth century BC, an eighteenth-century Ghanan griot, a nineteenth-century British novelist, or an emerging Deaf poet in a dormitory room late at night, the impulse to create and pass down stories and poetry lives on. Whether the work of literature is written, spoken, or signed is of little consequence. What is of consequence is the way the Deaf/ASL literary movement has developed over the years into a vibrant literary tradition that engages the current literary scene in significant ways and poses a fundamental and radical critique of the traditional notion of literature.

In this introduction we first explore the critique that the emergence of sign literature warrants and then consider how the Deaf/ASL literary movement relates to contemporary poetics. As W. J. T. Mitchell points out in the Foreword to this volume, the emergence of sign literature presents a host of implications for the wider category and practice of literature itself. Indeed, sign literature forces us to rethink the whole notion of literature as it has evolved within the assumption that human language is exclusively spoken or written. Even in the early years of the twenty-first century, this assumption is still quite common. Only as recently as 1996, for example, the Modern Language Association International Bibliography changed its classification of manual languages from the "Invented Languages" category next to Klingon and Esperanto to give them a status similar to that of Indo-European languages. Within this profoundly phonocentric belief system, the discovery by William Stokoe ([1960] 1978) that manual languages are replete with all the linguistic properties of spoken languages is a paradigm shift, forcing a fundamental redefinition of language. Over four decades of linguistic research have forever altered our understanding of the human language capacity to include manual as well as spoken languages. We now know, for example, that upon birth the human mind may just as easily acquire a manual as a spoken language; whether the infant is hearing or deaf is of little consequence.[3] Sign, then, is as much a part of the human language instinct as is speech.

Had we realized this all along, we might have ended up with a term other than *language,* which derives from *langue,* or tongue, and a term other than *literature,* which originates from *littere,* or letter. Clearly, it is too late to change the terms *language* and *literature,* so we must open them up to encompass what has been a part of them all along—sign languages. Just as the linguistic term *word* now encompasses manual signs, the terms *language* and *literature* may also include the manual-visual modality. But more is at stake here than simple redefinition. The addition of sign to the body of literature warrants a rethinking of such fundamental notions as textuality, genre, performance, and body as they have been constructed within a decidedly hearing model. As Michael Davidson has written, "The time seems right for extending this critique of the literary along a Deaf axis, not simply to add a new constituency to literature, but to re-think the entire edifice of literary production from the ground up" (pers. comm., Spring 2002). This volume represents the first such attempt at radically rethinking literary practices in light of sign.

One such redesigning of the literary landscape has been reflected in the evolution of the sign POETRY. The original sign was formed by the signed letter P moving over the outstretched and slightly bent arm. This sign was originally derived from the sign MUSIC or SONG, which has the same hand movements and arm position but uses a flat hand instead of the signed letter P (**clip 1.3**). That poetry is a form of verbal music served as the initial default setting that informed this sign; further, the substitution of the letter "P" for "poetry" indicates the alphabetic, scripted dimension of hearing-centered poetics. During the 1989 international Deaf Way conference, however, a group of Deaf poets expressed the need for a sign that would not be derived from MUSIC or from phonetic writing but would instead reflect the embodied nature of sign poetry. They decided on a sign based on the sign EXPRESSION (**clip 1.4**). This sign begins with both hands on the chest, opening up and moving outward. The current sign for SIGN-POETRY, then, is conveyed through one closed hand at the chest, moving outward and opening up. This sign suggests that poems emerge directly out of the body as offerings from the chest, heart, and lungs, unmediated by speech or writing. Depending on the speed and tension of the sign, poems can shoot, flow, or ooze out into the world. The music-based POETRY signifies written or spoken poetry, while the new sign refers to the unique corporeal, nonphonetic nature of sign poetry.

This new sign—as well as all of sign literature—offers a new critical lens through which to identify the phonocentric bias underlying all literary and linguistic production. This signed etymology is a further example that poetry is not a stable and elite practice handed down through the ages among a privileged few but rather a complex terrain of ideological production that favors certain practices and attempts to discourage others. Now we can bring to light what has been a hidden factor within the evolution of literature all along—that the marginality of sign has itself helped to draw the boundaries that fortify speech's primacy. The fact that deafness and sign languages have been relegated to the margins of literary production becomes especially evident when one considers the centrality of blindness in the Western literary imagination. Homer, the ur-poet of the West, is reputed to have been blind. As Lennard Davis (1995) has written, "The point is that blindness is no bar to creating oral narrative. Blindness may in fact be synonymous with storytelling in an oral culture, while deafness would be the opposite of such a tradition. It is hard to imagine Homer as a deaf bard" (107). Through the reification of blindness through Homer, Oedipus, Milton, and others, we have a symbol of language in its unadulterated oral medium; at the same time, blindness precludes, physically and symbolically, any recognition that sign could just as easily produce narrative and poetry. Sign and deafness, then, become the Other of language and literature: muteness and silence.[4]

While poetry may have begun with the figure of the blind poet, now, over two millennia later, a host of Deaf bards are anything but mute and silent, and their live vernacular has coaxed sign literature from the shadows of speech and writing. We now recognize how the margins have informed the center: how the very absence of sign has helped to de-sign the literary landscape. While speech and writing have reigned supreme as literary media, there have always been some poets and writers who have sought to move beyond the phonetic, linear structure of language; they have sensed that speech could be made more visual and writing more kinetic, and, what's more, that literature could become visual and kinetic *at the same time.* It is as if poets and writers have experienced a type of phantom limb phenomenon as they went groping about for a literary medium much like sign without ever laying their hands on it. Now that a Deaf/ASL literary movement has emerged into its own, we may note how it stands at the intersection of historical trajectories that push literature, poetry in particular, beyond its linear conventions. One trajectory is the desire to resituate poetry's original connection to the body through performance, and the other is to make poems increasingly visual through experimentation with the written form.

One of the great ironies of sign literature is that it may be considered a form of "oral literature" insofar as it has no traditional written form and is passed on through a face-to-face performance tradition. Clearly, *oral* here refers, not to oralism, the pedagogy of teaching speech to deaf persons, but to the similarities between sign and oral literature. This new form of "orality" requires its own sign, just as sign poetry required its unique designation. When signing the title of a class by the Gallaudet University professor Ben Bahan entitled "Oral Traditions in the Deaf Community," Deaf students have begun to substitute STORYTELLING for "Oral," while still mouthing the word *oral* (**clip 1.5**). (See chapters 2 and 3 of this volume, by

Bahan and Krentz respectively, for further exploration of "oral traditions" in the Deaf community.) Yet sign poetry not only resembles ancient literary forms but also engages the current literary practices of oral, performance poetry.

The impulse to perform has surely waxed and waned through the centuries, depending on pressures of printing and reading practices at any given historical moment. For quite some time we have been witnessing a widening and deepening of the impulse to coax poetry off the page and back into the performing body. Consider the widespread popularity of poetry slams, where poems come to life in breathing, sweating bodies; before that, the Beat poetic tradition of reciting poetry to improvisational jazz; David Antin's semi-improvisational "talk poems"; Charles Olson's midcentury call for an orally based, "projective verse"; the body of multicultural "ethnopoetics" collected by Jerome Rothenberg and others; the vibrant oral poetry of Amiri Baraka and Ntozake Shange; the feminist performances of Carolee Schneemann and Anne Waldman; and the techno-poetic performances of Laurie Anderson. To all this, add the more "mainstream" poetry business (po-biz) of university-supported poetry readings, lectures, and workshops where poets like Galway Kinnell, Mary Oliver, W. S. Merwin, and Stanley Kunitz pack campus auditoriums. This urge to free poetry from the page to take a physical, human form is a desire for immediacy and embodiment.

In this resurgence of oral poetry, there have been only a few moments of crossover between Deaf and hearing poets. The most notable was a meeting between Allen Ginsberg and Deaf poets in Rochester, New York, arranged by the hearing poet Jim Cohn. During the 1984 gathering, Ginsberg asked for volunteers to translate the image of "hydrogen jukebox" from his famous long poem "Howl." Deaf poet, actor, and teacher Patrick Graybill was summoned to attempt the translation. Graybill performed the image of a man putting a coin in the jukebox, the record moving into place, the needle touching down, and the record spinning faster and faster to the beating music until finally whipped into the fury of a hydrogen explosion of music (**clip 1.6**). As Graybill finished his image, Ginsberg exclaimed, "That's it! That's what I meant!" In Graybill's rendition, the explosive, musical nature of "Howl" and the image of a hydrogen jukebox quite literally come to life. Life is what the Beats, as well as many contemporary poets, were after, and that is what sign poetry inherently has, without being sought out. As Jim Cohn (1986) has written: "What deaf people DO with language is what hearing poets try to MAKE their language do" (263). In this performance-based age of poetics, sign poets have an "oral" language that remains largely unwritten and embodied.

Sign poetry may also be recognized as a moment of synthesis in the long-standing drive to wed poetry with the visual arts. As far back as Simonides of Keos's fifth-century BC formulation that "Poetry is speaking painting, and painting is mute poetry," artists and poets have sought to fuse the visual and the literary aspects of human creativity. Even the most cursory search of the history of art and literature supports this claim. Dick Higgins (1987), for example, traces the "ongoing wish to combine the visual and literary impulses" (3) in his study of "pattern poetry" that spans the globe from 300 BC to the present. Once could also cite the enduring interplay of "the Three Perfections" (poetry, calligraphy, and painting) in China, the formidable output of ekphrastic poetry, the accumulation of illustrated books over the centuries, and modernist and postmodernist poetic forms—Futurism, Dadaism, concrete poetry, L = A = N = G = U = A = G = E poetry, and multimedia cyberpoetry—as testimony to the fundamental impulse of integrating the visual and literary arts. Such output of visual forms of poetry signifies not a minor tradition but a profound preoccupation with pushing a linear, phonetic language beyond its conventional limitations to form an alternative linguistic perceptual field.

Such an enduring phenomenon has, of course, meant different things to different ages, but, as Wendy Steiner (1986) points out, the desire to fuse poetry with visual arts— through either analogy or practice—reveals a prevalent aesthetic desire to find an art form that approximates the full visual-spatial-kinetic dimensions of nature and human experience. "In both cases," writes Steiner, "the arts approach each other by appropriating a crucial feature from the other that it lacks—visuality in poetry, motion in painting" (12). Not until the advent of sign poetry could the physical material of the poem be at once visual and kinetic. While oral poetry foregrounds movement and performance, and writing foregrounds the visual text, neither of these modalities unites vision and movement as fully as sign poetry.

Now that we have entered the digital age, visual and performance poetic traditions continue to evolve, widening the variety of textual media. As Christopher Beach (1999) writes, "American poetry has abandoned its rarefied position as the print genre epitomizing high literary culture, and has increasingly defined itself as a dialogic cultural mode exploiting forms of popular media from public television to MTV, from sound recordings to CD-ROM" (170). Surely there is no reason why poems cannot be loosened from the page and set free to assume what media they want for the moment. The entire notion of "reading" a screen as opposed to a page, for example, takes on new meanings. "Screen-space," writes William Marsh (1999), "implies a quasi-new location for the activity of poetry" where practitioners of cyberpoetics celebrate the dynamism of writing. "*Things happen* on the screen that quite simply do not happen on the page." While Marsh is referring to cyberpoetic techniques that allow words to spin, dissipate, disappear, and morph, the same holds true for the screen space of sign poetry. Three-dimensional kinetic images *happen* on the screen. Works of poetry are less beholden to the pre*scribed* form of the page, the line, the voice. When the poetic impulse rises inside the body of a sign poet, it is released from the flat-land of the page and given an arena in which it can fashion poetic texts. The emergence of sign literature, then, can be seen as emblematic of the larger transformation toward visual-digital technology. As a result, sign literature may be considered a type of postmodern bardic phenomenon; it is akin to ancient literary forms in that it has no traditionally written form, yet it engages the current digital transformation of reading, language, literacy, and literature. In a sense, one could say that while literature is reputed to have begun in a state of blindness (that of Homer), it has also been expanding to include the state of deafness by assuming an increasingly visual, kinetic, and embodied textual form. As such, the Deaf/ASL literary movement should not be seen simply as a derivative art form, a minority cultural practice, or something that children do during the "Star Spangled Banner" before the Super Bowl. Sign poetry deserves to be recognized in its full literary and historical significance: as a culminating moment in the inextinguishable desires to make poetry *alive* and to make it *visual.*

TRACING THE EMERGENCE OF ASL LITERATURE

The existing body of published ASL literature can trace its origins to the early nineteenth century, after the founding of the first residential schools for deaf children.[5] These schools established a cohesive American Deaf community and a standardized language, what is now called ASL. Story-telling and language games such as ABC and number stories became the foundation of the Deaf "oral" literary tradition and continue to be a vital part of Deaf culture to this day (discussed by Christopher Krentz and Ben Bahan in chapters 2 and 3 of this volume). While live performance in ASL was no doubt a hallmark of Deaf social gatherings in the first half of the twentieth century, two key events in the 1960s mark a major shift in the texts emerging from Deaf literary artists—linguistic research on ASL and mainstream use of videotape technology.

In the forty years since William Stokoe pioneered the research that began to uncover the linguistic complexities of ASL, and since the advent of videotape technology, ASL literature has expanded to include a growing range of artists and widening innovations in style and structure. Since many ASL texts are performed live and go unrecorded, it is of course impossible to identify every artist who has influenced the art form's development. Only a select few have achieved national recognition through video publications, and only a handful travel the country performing and/ or leading workshops. It is these few whose work is the focus of the currently small body of sign literary criticism.[6]

As with most literary movements, it is impossible to trace the ASL poetry movement to a single point of origin. Signed translations of written poetry and stories have been around since the earliest filmed recordings of sign language, from M. Williamson Erd's recital of "The Death of Minnehaha," to Charles Krauel's footage of high school girls performing an Anne Hathaway poem at the Illinois School for the Deaf, to Joe Velez's version of "Jabberwocky."[7] Something distinctly different, however, began to occur among the various artists affiliated with the National Theatre of the Deaf, especially in its groundbreaking performance of *My Third Eye*.[8] As Padden and Humphries (1988) note, in the performance of *My Third Eye* a major change took place in the way Deaf performers thought about and used their language (79). While many parts of this performance are still English based, several performers created original poetry and storytelling in ASL without recourse to English. In the 1970s, then, sign literature had begun to unmoor itself from the continent of English and set sail into its own realm.

Like all pioneers, however, early ASL poets carried deeply ingrained notions of what constituted literary standards. It is as if these adventurers began with a compass whose magnetic north pointed to the standards of phonetic languages but soon found that there was another compass whose magnetic north pointed toward a "different center"[9]—that is, toward the unique visual, spatial, and kinetic dimensions of sign. As Ben Bahan writes, these artists "were schooled in literate form[s] of poetry growing up bilingual; so naturally, being exposed to literate forms of poetry becomes deeply imprinted; but when they create work in ASL, it is visual and spatial; it is fundamentally different" (pers. comm., Sept. 2001). Surely it would have been impossible to shake the influence of spoken and written poetics, yet, as Bahan points out, it was the very fact that they were *not* writing in English that was so riveting, exciting, and new.

The initial revelation of sign's literary potential has become an often repeated story among these early Deaf poets and storytellers. For example, Ella Mae Lentz and Clayton Valli tell similar stories of the initial discovery of the "different center" of poetic practice. These poets come from opposite sides of the country, Lentz from Northern California and Valli from New England; both wrote poems in their youth, and it never occurred to either of them that their sign language could produce poetry. Yet after the advent of sign linguistics, a much-needed validation encouraged their poetic impulses to be diverted into sign.

After these poets began to create original works in ASL, they gradually found eager Deaf audiences that appreciated their poems full of intricate linguistic patterning and rich visual-kinetic imagery. There was a certain *jouissance* (the sheer pleasure of the interacting with a text) as audiences saw their language of everyday discourse lifted into such well-crafted poems. The numerous reminiscences and personal narratives that allude to this *jouissance* suggest that artists had played informally or privately with the creative possibilities of their language before but that sign linguistics gave them license, affirmation, and a vocabulary from which to explore ASL's "different center."[10]

At the same time these poets were producing their work throughout the 1980s, another locus of the poetry movement was underway in Rochester, New York, where the hearing poet Jim Cohn organized the "Bird Brain's Society," which featured evenings of "open mike" nights. Here young poets like Debbie Rennie and the Flying Words Project (Peter Cook and Kenny Lerner) would perform original works. This poetic scene was especially galvanized when, as described above, Jim Cohn arranged for a meeting between Allen Ginsberg and Deaf poets (see clip 1.6). The work of Beat poets was to strongly influence the performance poetry of Peter Cook. Cook, who was raised orally and who began to sign in college, fused a Beat aesthetic with a fascination with the Deaf actor Bernard Bragg's technique of "visual vernacular" (for more on this technique, see clip 5.5). After pairing up with the hearing poet Kenny Lerner, Cook began to take sign poetry in a new direction, creating alternative or even avant-garde poetry accessible to both hearing and Deaf audiences.

For some critics, the work of Flying Words Project is more akin to the avant-garde literary tradition of Ezra Pound, Charles Olson, and Allen Ginsberg, while Valli and Lentz represent a more formalist approach akin to Robert Frost's (Bauman 1998; Cohn 1999; Ormsby 1995). The suggestion of emerging traditions is helpful, especially for hearing audiences familiar with those traditions, in sketching out the landscape of ASL poetic practices. However, the notion of a formalist versus a Beat tradition is borrowed from hearing literary traditions and does not represent absolute categories. Poets who appear to be grounded in formalism use visual vernacular techniques, while poets who may be likened to the Beats often use such formalist techniques as rhyming and metrical patterns. Further inquiry is needed to more accurately identify traditions and lineages.

While ASL poetic practices have been evolving, Deaf storytelling has also been a growing cultural and literary phenomenon. For an in-depth inquiry into the various narrative traditions that have evolved within the American Deaf community, see Ben Bahan's chapter in this volume (chapter 2). Bahan identifies numerous subgenres within the wider category of "storytelling" that are akin to oral or, more accurately, "face-to-face traditions." In keeping with the domain of oral-formulaic traditions, there seems to be something more than an individual author or teller at work; indeed, a whole community and tradition are funneled into these narrative practices.

Consider, for example, the story of "Eyeth" as retold by Sam Supalla. It begins on a Friday afternoon at a school for deaf children, with a child who is found crying on the steps by his hearing teacher. When asked why he is crying, the child answers that he does not want to go home for the weekend to his nonsigning, hearing family. The teacher tells him of a far-away planet called "Eyeth" where everyone signs and says he can go there someday. The child grows up, studies rocket science, and becomes an astronaut. He travels to Eyeth and becomes a teacher of sign at a school for hearing children. One Friday afternoon he comes upon a child crying because she does not want to go home to her nonspeaking, deaf family. The teacher comforts her and tells her that one day she can travel to Earth where almost everyone hears. Here, powerful images of parallel universes, themes of identity and belonging, are expressed through the pun on *ear-th* and *eye-th*. Sam Supalla notes that he grew up seeing this story and then incorporated it into his repertoire. While he may be the performer, he is not the "author" per se.

This is not to say that all stories are culturally shared. There are numerous productions of original works in ASL storytelling. Take Ben Bahan's

"Bird of a Different Feather," for example. In this story of a straight-beaked bird raised by a family of eagles, Bahan creates an allegory that speaks to the misunderstanding and oppression experienced by deaf children of hearing parents. In addition, the Live at SMI! videotape series features such acclaimed storytellers as Bill Ennis, MaryBeth Miller, Patrick Graybill, Eric Malzkuhn, Gilbert Eastman, and Elinor Kraft. Most of the stories in these tapes are original works performed in front of a live audience that feature a wide range of storytelling techniques and styles.

From the preceding discussion readers might conclude that poetry and prose/narrative are clearly distinguished in sign literature. Not so. The question of genre in a visual, spatial literary form remains a problem to explore; we cannot presume that qualities associated with genres of a written literary form will translate to a visual and spatial mode in the same ways. It should be clear from our discussion thus far that certain ASL artists clearly identify themselves as poets or storytellers, but it could be argued that the distinctions derive unnaturally from comparisons with the hearing literary world. We need to ask if language modality (speech versus sign) influences genre; to answer this question, we may need to break away from the vocabulary of spoken-written literature. Rose (1992a), for example, has suggested employing modal analysis (lyric, epic, dramatic) as a more useful categorization than genre. Bahan also explores a new taxonomy of oral traditions in ASL in his chapter in this volume. As with any form of literature, genre boundaries are contested and fluid domains.

Sign criticism has only begun to reflect on the wider implications of the emergence of sign poetry for the category of "literature" and of "poetry" itself.[11] This volume recognizes the importance of the existing trends in ASL literary criticism as well as offering new possibilities. By exploring wider literary theory and criticism, as well as other art forms related to ASL literature, it attempts to open up the study of ASL literature to new perspectives that will both further elucidate sign as an aesthetic medium and expand connections among other art forms.

BOOK OVERVIEW

This volume aims to create connections between sign literature and a number of areas in the humanities and fine/performing arts, including literary theory, comparative literature, performance studies, film, and education.

Because of the interdisciplinary appeal of sign poetry, existing publications on sign literary criticism and performance are widely dispersed. In designing this project, we intended to include as many disciplines and perspectives as we could, although there are by necessity some gaps in our coverage. As we juxtapose Deaf, hearing, and interdisciplinary perspectives in one space, many of these "voices" are able to interact for the first time.

The first section, "Framing ASL Literature," deals with the initial textual and theoretical questions raised by the recognition of sign as a legitimate medium for language and literature; this section focuses on issues relating to the continuum of signed texts, from face-to-face to film and video. Ben Bahan's chapter, "Face-to-Face Tradition in the American Deaf Community: Dynamics of the Teller, the Tale, and the Audience" (chapter 2), traces the development of the poetic, "oral" art of Deaf storytelling via ASL narratives and A–Z (or alphabet) and number stories, among others, and ends with cinematic techniques as they are transformed by a manual medium. Chris Krentz's chapter, "The Camera as Printing Press: How Film Has Influenced ASL Literature" (chapter 3), investigates the impact of videotape technology on the traditionally "oral" nature of sign language literature by drawing parallels with the advent of the printing press and its impact on written literature. Krentz notes that videotape has become the form of ASL literary "writing" for the Deaf community, a phenomenon that has both positive and negative consequences for ASL literature and the Deaf community. Cynthia Peters's chapter, "Deaf American Theater" (chapter 4), uses Bakhtin's concept of carnival to discuss the evolution of original ASL drama.

The second section, "The Embodied Text: 'Writing' and Vision in ASL Literature," approaches the body itself as the creative medium in ASL and discusses the implications of embodied artistic and literary expression. Dirksen Bauman's chapter, "Getting out of Line: Toward a Visual and Cinematic Theory" (chapter 5), extends Valli's notion of the line in ASL. Bauman's investigation moves away from phonocentric criticism and toward a more politically aware and visually centered poetics through comparisons with visual and cinematic arts. Jennifer Nelson's chapter, "Textual Bodies, Bodily Texts" (chapter 6), considers sign in relation to the Derridean, non-essentialist notion of "writing" and textuality. She argues that the body as a medium for literature is a valid form of "writing" in the Derridean sense as long as the body produces referential signs that have meaning created by a community. Heidi Rose's chapter, "The Poet in the Poem in the Performance: The Relation of Body, Self, and Text in ASL Literature" (chapter 7), explores the implications of bodily production as text, highlighting the performative nature of ASL literature. Rose argues that performance quality exists as part of literary quality, as the text emerges from the idiosyncratic style of the particular artist's performing body. Liz Wolter's chapter, "ASL Literature Comes of Age: Creative 'Writing' in the Classroom" (chapter 8), explores sign literature creation in praxis and includes an interview with the poet Peter Cook on the philosophy of sign poetry as creative "writing."

Section Three, "The Political Text: Performance and Identity in ASL Literature," examines the political and rhetorical ramifications of sign literature. Kristen Harmon's chapter, "'If there are Greek epics, there should be Deaf epics': How Protest Became Poetry" (chapter 9), uses the notion of the subaltern peace epic to write about the emerging genre of the ASL epic as initiated by Gilbert Eastman's "Epic: Gallaudet Protest." Harmon situates the Deaf epic within a postmodern, postcolonial theoretical tradition, as a genre emerging from a culture whose body and language are controlled and appropriated by a hearing, speech-based society. Carol Robinson, in "Visual Screaming: Willy Conley's Deaf Theater and Charlie Chaplin's Silent Cinema" (chapter 10), explores various rhetorical constructions and manifestations behind the use of the "visual scream" through a semiotic analysis of playwright Willy Conley's *FALLING ON HEARING EYES—a museum of sign languish for people with communication disorders.* Michael Davidson's chapter, "Hearing Things: The Scandal of Speech in Deaf Performance" (chapter 11), extends the focus of this book to explore the multivalent aspects of speech and writing in the work of the British deaf performance artist Aaron Williamson and the deaf visual artist Joseph Grigely. While Davidson's chapter explores ASL poetry, it also opens up a cluster of issues that revolves around wider questions of speech, writing, and sign in d/Deaf performance and art.

Taken together, these chapters represent a wide diversity of scholars and artists who have begun what promises to be a long journey of exploring the uncharted terrain of ASL literature.

FUTURE DIRECTIONS

While this collection aims to introduce new methods of analyzing ASL literature, no such collection can possibly be complete. This book is more an inquiry, a seeking, a pushing of boundaries, a testing of theories. More work is needed, for example, on ASL narrative and drama. There is also a necessarily limited range of artists and performances in this book. As a whole new generation of Deaf performers develops its literary skills, unpublished performers abound; as W. J. T. Mitchell (1989) has said, there could be a Homer somewhere in the Deaf community right now. Further, while this book may be bicultural (i.e., hearing/Deaf), it is not multicultural. Narratives and poetry from all Deaf populations, not just from published white performers, need to be explored and celebrated.

In addition to the limited scope of ASL performances represented in this volume, there is a necessarily limited number of critical approaches. Further work could explore sign literature via, for example, Marxism, phenomenology, narrative analysis, reader (or viewer) response theory, and feminist theory and criticism. Lane (1992), Wrigley (1996), Corker (1997), and others have already utilized Foucauldian discourse as power analysis, but certainly more remains to be done in applying the work of Foucault to ASL literature.

Finally, disability studies is another ripe arena for exploration. As W. J. T. Mitchell points out in his Foreword, *Signing the Body Poetic* is not a book about disability per se. It does not directly attempt to theorize disability or the relations between deafness and disability. Rather than focusing on what Deaf people do not have, the contributors focus on what Deaf people do have—a burgeoning literary tradition with implications that extend to the very foundations of literature.[12] That stated, however, clearly the literature from Deaf and disabled persons may speak out in tandem against the hegemony of ableist ideologies, and further studies can investigate this important aspect of sign literature.

NOTES

1. Such a condensation recalls Emily Dickinson's

> Essential Oils—are wrung—
> The Attar from the Rose
> Be not expressed by Suns—alone—
> It is the gift of Screws—
>> (1997, no. 675, lines 1–4)

2. See Bahan's and Bauman's chapters in this volume (chapters 2 and 5) for further exploration of the cinematic poetics of ASL literature.

3. See Petitto and Marentette (1991). They demonstrate that, "contrary to prevailing accounts of the neurological basis of babbling in language ontogeny, the speech modality is not critical in babbling. Rather, babbling is tied to the abstract linguistic structure of language and to an expressive capacity capable of processing different types of signals (signed or spoken)" (1493).

4. Yet who is to say that there was never a Deaf bard prior to recent times? One can only speculate that Deaf, signing communities have existed throughout history. Plato, for example, mentions that there was a signing community in fifth-century BC Athens. Why couldn't there have been a creative use of language among deaf persons around the pillars of the Acropolis? Because there is no written document, one can only speculate.

5. Refer to Appendix A in this volume, "Time Line of ASL Literature Development," for a detailed presentation of the events, artists, and publications that have contributed to the evolution of ASL literature.

6. See Appendix A for additional information on influential artists and publications.

7. For the "Death of Minnehaha," see *The Preservation of American Sign Language* (1997); the performance of "Jabberwocky" appears in *Tyger, Tyger,* a film originally produced by the National Theatre of the Deaf (Velez 1967).

8. A brief history of the National Theatre of the Deaf can be found in Appendix A.

9. The image of a different center is explored further in Padden and Humphries (1988).

10. See Lou Fant's and Gilbert Eastman's essays in *Sign Language and the Deaf Community: Essays in Honor of William C. Stokoe* (1980).

11. For examples of more contemporary sign criticism, see Bauman (1997a, 1997b), Brueggemann (1999), and Rose (1992b, 1994, 1996, 1997).

12. Mairian Corker deals extensively with the issue of tensions and relations between Deafness and disability at length in her book *Deaf and Disabled, or Deafness Disabled* (1997); see also Lennard Davis's *Enforcing Normalcy* (1995).

REFERENCES

Bauman, H-Dirksen L. 1997a. "Beyond Speech and Writing: Recognizing American Sign Language Literature in the MLA." In *Profession 1997,* 168–79. New York: Modern Language Association.

———. 1997b. "Toward a Poetics of Vision, Space and the Body: Sign Language and Literary Theory." In *The Disability Studies Reader,* ed. Lennard J. Davis, 315–31. New York: Routledge.

———. 1998. "American Sign Language as a Medium for Poetry: A Comparative Poetics of Sign, Speech, and Writing." PhD diss., State University of New York, Binghamton.

Beach, Christopher. 1999. *Poetic Culture: Contemporary American Poetry: Between Community and Institution.* Evanston, IL: Northwestern University Press.

Brueggemann, Brenda Jo. 1999. *Lend Me Your Ear: Rhetorical Constructions of Deafness.* Washington, DC: Gallaudet University Press.

Cohn, Jim. 1986. "The New Deaf Poetics: Visible Poetry." *Sign Language Studies* 52 (Fall): 263–77.

———. 1999. *Sign Mind: Studies in American Sign Language Poetics.* Boulder, CO: Museum of American Poetics.

Corker, Mairian. 1997. *Deaf and Disabled, or Deafness Disabled?* Buckingham: Open University Press.

Davis, Lennard. 1995. *Enforcing Normalcy: Disability, Deafness, and the Body.* London: Verso.

Dickinson, Emily. 1997. *The Complete Poems of Emily Dickinson.* Ed. Thomas H. Johnson. Boston: Little, Brown.

Eastman, Gilbert. 1980. "From Student to Professional: A Personal Chronicle of Sign Language." In *Sign Language and the Deaf Community: Essays in Honor of William C. Stokoe,* ed. Charlotte Baker and Robbin Battison, 9–32. Silver Springs, MD: National Association of the Deaf.

Fant, Lou. 1980. "Drama and Poetry in Sign Language: A Personal Reminiscence." In *Sign Language and the Deaf Community: Essays in Honor of William C. Stokoe,* ed. Charlotte Baker and Robbin Battison, 193–200. Silver Springs, MD: National Association of the Deaf.

Higgins, Dick. 1987. *Pattern Poetry: Guide to an Unknown Literature.* Albany: SUNY Press.

Lane, Harlan. 1992. *The Mask of Benevolence: Disabling the Deaf Community.* New York: Knopf.

Marsh, William. 1999. "Virtual Skin: A Brief Look at Visual-Kinetic Poetics in Context." *YLEM Newsletter* 19, May/June. Accessed July 23, 2005, from http://warnell.com/syntac/ylem.htm.

Mitchell, W. J. T. 1989. "Gesture, Sign, and Play: ASL Poetry and the Deaf Community." *MLA Newsletter,* Summer, 13–14.

Ormsby, Alec. 1995. "Poetic Cohesion in American Sign Language: Valli's 'Snowflake' and Coleridge's 'Frost at Midnight.'" *Sign Language Studies* 88:227–44.

Padden, Carol, and Tom Humphries. 1988. *Deaf in America: Voices from a Culture.* Cambridge, MA: Harvard University Press.

Petitto, Laura Ann, and Paula F. Marentette. 1991. "Babbling in the Manual Mode: Evidence for the Ontogeny of Language." *Science* 251:1493–94.

The Preservation of American Sign Language: The Complete Historical Collection. 1997. Videocassette. Burtonsville, MD: Sign Media.

Rose, Heidi. 1992a. "A Critical Methodology for Analyzing American Sign Language Literature." PhD diss., Arizona State University.

———. 1992b. "A Semiotic Analysis of Artistic American Sign Language and a Performance of Poetry." *Text and Performance Quarterly* 12:146–59.

———. 1994. "Stylistic Features in American Sign Language Literature." *Text and Performance Quarterly* 14:144–57.

———. 1996. "Inventing One's 'Voice': The Interplay of Convention and Self-Expression in ASL Narrative." *Language in Society* 25:427–44.

———. 1997. "Julianna Fjeld's 'The Journey': Identity Production in an ASL Performance." *Text and Performance Quarterly* 17:331–42.

Steiner, Wendy. 1986. *The Color of Rhetoric: Problems in the Relation between Modern Literature and Painting.* Chicago: University of Chicago Press.

Stokoe, W. C. 1978. *Sign Language Structure.* Silver Spring, MD: Linstok Press. (Original pub. 1960.)

Velez, Joe. 1967. "Jabberwocky." In *Tyger, Tyger,* prod. National Theatre of the Deaf. Videocassette. Indianapolis: Captioned Films for the Deaf, Inc.

Wrigley, Owen. 1996. *The Politics of Deafness.* Washington, DC: Gallaudet University Press.

PART ONE

Framing ASL Literature

TWO

Face-to-Face Tradition in the American Deaf Community

Dynamics of the Teller, the Tale, and the Audience

BEN BAHAN

INTRODUCTION

The brief DVD clip with which this chapter begins (**clip 2.1**), showing a duo performance of a "song" whose signs are arranged to a rhythmical cadence, is only one short moment in a long history of storytelling and performance in the American Deaf community. As long as Deaf people have congregated in schools, clubs, and homes, they have passed down cultural patterns, values, and beliefs in the DEAF WORLD[1] from one generation to the next in something very much like an oral tradition. According to Goody (1992), "[T]he oral tradition consists of everything handed down (and ipso facto created) through the oral channel—in other words, virtually the whole culture itself" (13). As James Paul Gee (1983) recognizes, "[I]t sounds paradoxical to say so, but ASL [American Sign Language] exists in an 'oral' culture, a culture based on face-to-face signed interaction, with writing and middle-class literacy playing little or no role in much of the heart of the community. Like many other such cultures, it has an active tradition of folklore and performance-centered 'oral' (signed) narrative, encapsulating traditional values, and passed down from generation to generation" (232).

While similarities abound between signed and oral traditions, the Deaf community is not a purely oral community; rather, it exists along an oral-literate continuum. In many parts of the world, oral subcultures exist within a literate majority culture (Ong 1982; Edwards and Sienkewicz 1990; Goody 1992). In these communities, it is not surprising to find an oral-literate continuum (Edwards and Sienkewicz 1990). There are people who thrive on oral traditions when among members of their subculture but who can also behave as members of the literate majority culture. Those people are likely to be bilinguals. In such cross-cultural contact situations, the notion of "pure" orality is probably nonexistent. "Moreover, elements of the oral tradition, like folktales, inevitably get written down, whereas elements of the written tradition are often communicated orally" (Goody 1992, 13). The DEAF WORLD is obviously a minority culture situated within a majority culture, so the notion that it is primarily an oral culture—without any influence from literate culture—is misleading; however, the situation is more complicated than it seems.

There is no widespread use of a written form in the primary face-to-face language of the community—ASL.[2] In addition, most, if not all, members of the DEAF WORLD are ASL-English bilinguals to varying degrees (see Grosjean 1996), so there is some access to literate cultural knowledge. Moreover, because Deaf people are also members of the majority culture (i.e., American culture), they interact on a daily basis with English-speaking people by communicating with them in a variety of ways: speaking or writing. Although literate knowledge is accessed in a language (English) that is not primarily used in face-to-face situations among members of the DEAF WORLD,[3] we cannot ignore the relationship between the two cultures and their influences on each other. It is safe to say, then, that many of the patterns of oral and signed face-to-face traditions are similar and that only the medium is different. To be more precise in reflecting this difference of medium, this chapter will use the term *face-to-face tradition.*

The synthesis of thoughts and observations reported in this chapter sprang from my role as a storyteller and lifelong participatory member of the DEAF WORLD. I have had the opportunity of exchanging insights with other storytellers, poets, and performers over more than twenty years. From these exchanges, I have come to recognize distinct patterns in our literary practices, themes, and genres. Here I offer an overview of these literary patterns in the DEAF WORLD.

The Face-to-Face Tradition in Deaf Culture

To gain some insight into the sociohistorical environment of the face-to-face tradition of Deaf culture, let us turn to the experience of Gilbert Eastman (professor emeritus at Gallaudet University and one of the founding members of National Theatre of the Deaf) (pers. comm., June 1999). He remembers being exposed to the types of stories discussed in this chapter while growing up at American School for the Deaf (ASD) in Hartford, Connecticut, in the 1940s. He vividly remembers watching with awe as older kids performed various stories, especially when he was a Boy Scout. His troop would go camping every year, and at night the boys would gather around the campfire and share stories. The older Scouts would tell and retell mystery stories, ghost stories, scenes from movies, Deaf-related experiences, jokes, sign play, and ABC stories. Bear in mind that the "older tellers" in Eastman's childhood memories were boys who were enrolled in school in the early to mid-1930s. They must have learned the craft of storytelling and tales from someone before them. One might wonder: Just how far back did those ASL story performances at ASD go? Interestingly, we are fortunate to have one of the earliest records of a signed performance captured in a film project by the National Association of the Deaf (NAD) that was produced between 1910 and 1920.[4] The film series contains various lectures, performances, poems, stories, songs, and narratives of personal experience. One storyteller in this series, John B. Hotchkiss, a professor of English and history at Gallaudet, was an ASD graduate. In one of his performances, a narrative of personal experience entitled "Memories of Old Hartford," he reminisced about his days at ASD as a child (in the early 1860s) and his encounter with the famed French Deaf educator Laurent Clerc.[5] He recounted various stories about Clerc, who was already retired but living nearby at the time Hotchkiss was at ASD. In one instance, he portrayed Laurent Clerc lecturing about how the subtle difference in English word order makes a big difference in meaning, focusing on the meaning difference between the two phrases "eat to live" and "live to eat."[6] In any case, we know that since Hotchkiss's time Deaf storytellers have been passing on their stories, culture, and identity through a tradition that has been kept alive through face-to-face events. We don't know exactly which ASL literature genres existed in the early days, but we know from the NAD films that at least the following genres go back to the turn of the twentieth century: narratives of personal experience, lectures, and translated songs, poems, and stories.

According to Gilbert Eastman, the environment of sharing stories was not limited to those inside a school for the deaf. There were opportunities for contact among regional schools for the deaf through interscholastic meets (e.g., in football, basketball, and track).[7] He recalls many evenings, before or after the games, when students from different schools would share stories in a snack bar or dance hall. Thus it is apparent that stories were disseminated across a region of several states. It was not uncommon for people to learn new stories from such gatherings and bring them back to their local school. These gatherings also gave budding storytellers the opportunity to try out their craft with a new audience and to establish a reputation as storytellers. Eventually these signers would graduate and enter local Deaf clubs and different associations in the region, such as the American Athletic Association of the Deaf, currently known as USA Deaf Sports Federation, NAD, and the National Fraternal Society of the Deaf. At these regional affairs, they would encounter Deaf people they had met at interscholastic meets and be prompted into performing.

So in essence all these places—schools, interscholastic meets, Deaf clubs, Deaf associations, and regional or national tournaments or conferences—have served as settings that perpetuate face-to-face cultural transmission. Often performances have sprung up at these locations as a by-product of the gatherings. Sometimes the performances themselves have been the goal of the gatherings (as in literary societies and theater groups).

THE TELLER, THE TALE, AND THE AUDIENCE

Everyone in the DEAF WORLD can tell stories and share ideas and personal experiences. However, only a few can do so with such skill that they are often called upon to perform. Those with this special talent are often called "smooth signers." A smooth signer is someone who as a language artist can weave a story so smoothly that even complex utterances appear simple, yet beautiful.

Often these smooth signers end up becoming the community's storytellers and/or poets and are encouraged by the culture to show their craft in a more formalized manner. The culture often dictates, through its encouragement and requests for repeated performances, the kinds of stories/poems that the smooth signers will end up spinning. The three components of the face-to-face tradition —the teller, the tale, and the audience—are so intertwined that it is almost impossible to describe one without the others. The following sections will address each component and show how all the components complement each other.

THE TELLER

The Making of a Storyteller / Poet

One might wonder how "smooth signers" or storytellers and poets develop in oral cultures. According to Edwards and Sienkewicz (1990), some people are apparently born with the gift of being a good talker: "Good talkers have particular expertise; they have a knowledge of a specialized language and body of information and have often undergone a lengthy process of learning and preparation. Yet this training can be of little value if the apprentice has no basic aptitude" (17). Okpewho (1992) similarly states that "[o]ne's mind or nature has to be predisposed toward art before the skill can successfully take root" (21). With this predisposition in place, storytellers still have to be "made"; they must go through an apprenticeship to learn the craft. There are two general ways in which one can be apprenticed: formal training or informal training. Formal training involves a more structured approach toward apprenticeship: one is selected to attend a "school" that has master storytellers as teachers who provide specific training and guidance for future storytellers. In other communities where storytellers are developed informally, apprentices learn and work alongside master storytellers (Okpewho 1992), and apprentices undergo a longer period of training or long-term exposure to experienced storytellers/performers than they would in formal training. In the course of learning through either approach, apprentices "inherit" and learn various specialized techniques: controlling the pauses and tempos in stories, using parallelisms, repetitions, and digressions effectively, and so on. They also learn from master storytellers a core of narratives that employ basic themes or combinations of themes that are meaningful and central to the culture and audience. Master storytellers pass down technical and artistic uses of language that were learned from storytellers before them. In sum, smooth signers undergo a period of preparation.

ASL storytellers appear to show patterns of the kind described above. From a very young age, they tend to be exposed to various adult signers in their community (including their parents) and to have the opportunity to observe various smooth signers performing stories, monologues, and, in some cases, poems. Once they go to school, most of them have the opportunity to interact with smooth signers employed at their school. More importantly, they have the opportunity, from a very young age, to play out the role of a storyteller and retell the stories they have heard to their peers. Their peers probably beg them to tell more stories. To do that, they have to become more active in remembering stories and/or inventing stories on the spot. In their telling, they experiment with various techniques that they have absorbed from watching adult smooth signers in action. This cycle goes on until they reach adulthood. Then they begin testing their work with a larger audience outside the school, at clubrooms, associations, and various Deaf social events.

In essence these storytellers become the culture's historians, teachers, and entertainers (Okpewho 1992; Lane, Hoffmeister, and Bahan 1996). They pick up various styles and nuances that go into telling a story from Deaf adults who have picked it up from Deaf adults before them. Their work combines elements of various other signers, picked up along the way, and, more importantly, their own "signature." All artists borrow ideas, some of which can be traced, yet each artist adds his or her own personal flair. They are also passing down the culture's heritage by sharing the stories they have heard from the adults in their communities, even if they modify the story by adding their own personal touch. In this sense, they are recording life histories of Deaf people and themselves in particular.

Storytellers also teach Deaf people by giving them a sense of identity and a sense of belonging, as well as providing ways of interpreting and comprehending the world collectively, thereby perpetuating the survival of their culture. Each tale has embedded within it messages for ways of behaving and strategies for surviving as a member of a minority culture in a world surrounded by others with different cultural values and world knowledge (see, e.g., Padden and Humphries 1988; Lane, Hoffmeister, and Bahan 1996).

Finally, storytellers' primary goal appears to be to use their gift as language artists to entertain members of the audience. Their role as performers is tied to how they bring the story to the audience. This puts the tellers in the position of controlling how they want the stories to unfold.

A good storyteller needs to be adept at synthesizing different kinds of controls, such as the control of language, of paralinguistic cues, of selection of tales, and, finally, of the audience (Bahan 1994; Lane, Hoffmeister, and Bahan 1996). Control of the first two—language and paralinguistic cues—falls in the domain of language use. In the control of language, a teller must attend to a wide spectrum of linguistic elements, from the smallest units, such as handshape or eye gaze location, to those on the grammar and the discourse level. The teller deploys linguistic units by controlling various paralinguistic elements, including the rhythm, tempo, and pause mechanisms of the story. The teller also exploits facial expressions and nonverbal expressions (which may be used for imitation, among other things) to convey additional messages in an attempt to control the mood and trigger emotions from the audience for various episodes in the story. In essence, these two types of control enable the teller to pay attention to the aesthetic use of language.

However, the task does not end there. The teller has to select an appropriate story. Each teller has a repertoire of stories (and, for some, poems). Some of these stories are suitable only for particular members of the audience and particular locations. Some of the stories are still in various stages of development and have not yet been fully disclosed. There are risks of releasing these stories to an unreceptive audience. The teller has to evaluate the situation he or she is facing (e.g., the audience and location) and proceed to select the stories and tell them. For example, a storyteller would risk inappropriate story selection if he told a detailed story of hunting down and skinning a bear to an audience filled with animal rights advocates.

Tellers also need to monitor the members of the audience from time to time to see if they are engaged in the performance before venturing into disclosing work under construction. If their story selection is irrelevant for the audience/location or simply not good, then they are bound to fail.

There have been instances where a teller reportedly misjudged an audience by assuming that most of the people in the audience were fluent signers, able to follow a high-speed montage composed of rapidly produced signs. Especially in a mixed audience of Deaf and hearing people, and of signers and nonsigners using interpreters, gauging the audience's ability to follow the work may be difficult. The teller may realize upon gauging the audience in the middle of a story that they are not following him or her and then digress in order to work the audience back into the performance.

As the above story illustrates, tellers need to exert some type of audience control. This involves captivating and holding onto the audience's interest. Various linguistic and paralinguistic cues work to hold onto the audience, such as effective use of pause mechanisms (the teller must pause for the right amount of time, not too long or he or she may risk losing the audience), quickly scanning the room to evaluate the audience's involvement while using such devices, and effectively using digression at particular points of the story to hold onto the audience and then woo them back into watching the completion of the performance.

In fact, if any of the four types of control mentioned above (i.e., the control of language, paralinguistic cues, selection of tales, and audience) is missing or unsuccessful, then the teller's work is judged to be ineffective. Good storytellers can adeptly juggle all of these controls to create a fine-tuned, deftly synchronized performance.

THE TALE (AND SOME SELECTED GENRES)

A wide variety of performances/stories are passed along in the Deaf community. Some of these stories have been around for a long time and are comparable to the type of stories that appear in every culture, such as the narrative of personal experience. Some are original tales created by the tellers for members of their cultural audience. Some tales originated in other cultures (i.e., stories in print that appeared in literate cultures) and have been translated or adapted for the Deaf audience.

For the purpose of this chapter, I will cover only three genres: narratives, songs, and stories with constraints.[8] Narratives are further subcategorized into narratives of personal experience, cinematographic stories, folktales, translated works, and original fiction. Songs are also further subdivided to include translated songs and percussion signing. Stories with constraints include ABC stories, number stories, set handshape stories, and worded handshape stories.[9]

Narratives

Narratives are stories that relate various events in chronological sequence. Each type of narrative described here—the narrative of personal experi-

ence, the cinematographic story, the folktale, the translated work, the work of original fiction—unfolds events in a sequence in its own way.

Narratives of Personal Experience

Narratives of personal experience are probably the most common type of storytelling in the Deaf community. These are real-life accounts of various events, including those that are humorous or tragic and those of struggles to overcome various odds. In some of them, "the speaker becomes deeply involved in rehearsing or even reliving events of his past" (Labov, 1972, 354). One commonly retold humorous story in the DEAF WORLD involves a Deaf person being asked by a hearing person, maybe a stewardess, if he can read Braille. A tragic story might involve a story of Deaf person being struck by a train while walking on the track; this is usually followed by comments or instructions on how one should avoid walking on train tracks. In recounting a struggle to overcome odds, a Deaf person might talk about her persistence in finding a job despite mounting discrimination from various potential employers.

Many real-life accounts are vignettes that focus on a single event. For example, the teller might describe how he needed to get a Deaf friend's attention while that friend's doorbell was not functioning and how he tried different strategies until he finally got the friend's attention. Life histories, on the other hand, may be composed of multiple narratives of personal experience. They are works that cover the span of a life or some major aspect of life (e.g., relations with parents, marriage, child rearing, career) or milestone (e.g., meeting a spouse or getting a first job). (See Linde 1993 for more information on life stories in general.)

Each personal experience or life history is unique in its own right, but many personal experiences and personal histories overlap in the Deaf community. Consequently, stories of shared experiences promote bonding among members of the DEAF WORLD and extend beyond the personal to become stories of the life of an entire culture.

Cinematographic Stories

Another popular form of narrative involves using cinematographic technique in the creation of stories. Although cinematographic technique can appear in any genre of narrative performance, a cinematographic story

foregrounds this technique and uses it extensively throughout the work. Cinematographic stories may be attempts to retell or re-create scenes from (or sometimes entire) movies to an audience. But even stories that have no connection with any motion picture may extensively use various filmlike techniques, such as close-ups, panning, zoom in, zoom out, medium shots, far shots, and even the morphing of objects while telling stories (for more information, see chapter 5 of this book).

The way the language is structured makes it possible to engage in this form of storytelling. Tellers do that by taking particular advantage of one aspect of the linguistic system: classifiers, a set of predicate signs that are used to describe the state, shape, and action of the noun signs.[10] With classifiers, tellers are able to utilize the three-dimensional space and use their body and hands in various ways to depict the motion and location of various objects, as well as their salient physical properties. They can also coordinate different classifiers to change the scale of objects, describing activities or states from the microscopic to the cosmic.

Some stories, called classifier stories, consist entirely, or almost entirely, of classifiers. By the use of this linguistic system they would automatically shift across various kinds of classifiers.[11] Each kind of classifier involves a different use of scale and reference frame, so different classifiers can employ the various shots seen in film (e.g., close-up, medium, and long shots) (T. Supalla 1982).

Clip 2.2 shows a simple classifier story I created for children that also involves the manipulation of rhythm. In this story, a scientist inadvertently creates a ball after an explosion in his laboratory. The ball expands and contracts and then bounces out of the room, followed by a boy on a bicycle and eventually by a dog, a girl, an old man, his parrot, and a heavy-set woman. Each of these figures is represented by a distinct classifier. They all join the chase around corners, up a hill, and down a hill and eventually tumble into the lab, where they see the ball smile at them.

Another example of a classifier story is "Durassic Park," told by Manny Hernandez (**clip 2.3**). Adapting scenes from the movie *Jurassic Park,* it clearly depicts the use of cinematographic techniques as it recounts the story of a group of boys who ask their father to take them camping. After packing and loading the car, the coffee-drinking father takes them up a mountain road. When he gets out of the car to relieve himself, the boys find themselves accosted by a Tyrannosaurus Rex, whose giant head and

three-clawed feet are vividly embodied through a cinematic use of classi-fiers. The viewers' experience of this film-inspired story is very much like watching the film itself as Hernandez splices together a sequence of scenes—the boys' reaction, the stalking dinosaur, and the father comfort-ing his son, who has been dreaming the whole scene.

Cinematographic stories ranging from G to X rated can be told in "live action" or "animation" style. Some tellers are better at one style and some at the other. The "Durassic Park" story is a good example of "live action" style. An example of animation style can be seen in a signer's exaggeration of a shocking reaction by signing "eyeballs popping out of their sockets, while the mouth gapes open, allowing the tongue to roll down to the floor," as illustrated in **clip 2.4**. The influence of animation can also be seen in the popular technique of personification, or transforming part of one's body into an object. The most common transformation is turning one's head into various balls, such as a golfball, baseball, or pinball. A teller would, for exam-ple, personify a golfball by making his entire head the ball and then going through various stages of action while empathizing with the golfball, such as grimacing when golf club swings down to the side of its "head."

Given that almost all storytellers incorporate cinematographic tech-nique into their repertoire in some way, we might ask whether this genre originated from or predated movies. It is hard to determine the extent to which movies or filming technique have influenced the way ASL stories are told. Nonetheless, some specialized techniques have obviously been influ-enced by film—such as panning and slow zooming into a scene, as in Supalla's opening segment in *For a Decent Living,* which vividly sets the scene of a vast bleak snow-covered country landscape and depicts the blow-ing snow that comes to a halt in a drift at the side of a farmhouse (**clip 2.5**).

Folktales

Some scholars might categorize the entire body of work discussed here (nar-ratives, poetry, etc.) as Deaf folktales. In this chapter, however, I distinguish folktales as a body of work whose origin is lost but that have been shared in the community for a long time. We should bear in mind that many stories whose origins have been lost may have begun as narratives of personal expe-rience and subsequently been passed around. There have been few studies in the area of Deaf folktales, with the exception of those by Susan Rutherford (1993) and Simon Carmel (1979). Rutherford (1993) has catalogued various types of tales, among them legends, tall tales, and traditions.

Legends, tall tales, fables, and traditions are deeply ingrained in the consciousness of the culture. For example, there is a legend of an encounter between two Deaf rival soldiers during the Civil War who became friends in the middle of a battle and were suspected by their superiors of being spies (clip 2.6). It is not known whether this story is true, yet its message is powerful because it tells of Deaf people bonding in the midst of war. One particularly popular tall tale is about a Deaf scientist's escapade to a distant planet called "Eyeth," where everyone uses sign language as the primary language. A particular community tradition that we often hear about involves an annual rite of passage at Gallaudet University, where freshmen (especially those in the former preparatory program) conduct a rat funeral in the spring to ceremoniously mark the end of their first year (Rutherford 1993). Such folktales carry subconscious cultural messages and reinforce the need for maintenance of tradition to connect the present and the past. It is comparable to professional ball players of today realizing they are part of a rich American tradition that connects them to the Ted Williamses of yesterday. For more information, see the excellent work in the area of American Deaf folktales by Rutherford (1993).

Translated Works

Since many members of the DEAF WORLD are also bilingual speakers of ASL and English, they have access to stories that appear in print. There have even been literary organizations/societies in the DEAF WORLD that have encouraged discussions and translations of these printed works. Translations of printed works into face-to-face interactions have been well documented and preserved in various archived films and videotapes over the years. One of the earliest efforts was a series of films produced by the NAD that featured a variety of performances ranging from Edward Miner Gallaudet telling the story of "The Lorna Doone Country of Devonshire, England" (c. 1913) to Joe Velez performing Eric Malzkuhn's translation of Lewis Carroll's "Jabberwocky" in 1968.

Often in the process of translation, Deaf cultural behavior, values, or norms find their way into the work, whether the translator is aware of this or not. For example, in telling "Little Red Riding Hood," a translator may unconsciously make the characters "Deaf" by assigning them behavior and discourse that are visually based, akin to those in the DEAF WORLD (such as waving one's hands to get attention of another character). An example of conscious translation (i.e., adaptation) of this story might involve making the mother, girl, and grandmother Deaf and the Wolf hearing, to set up a dichotomy that reflects conflicts in the culture.

Original Fiction

In the past twenty years we have seen a burgeoning of original ASL fiction being created in the DEAF WORLD: short stories, novellas, even novels. We can speculatively tie this to the growing communal awareness of ASL as a language and the growing sense of identity among members of the DEAF WORLD (Padden and Humphries 1988). Two original works, for example, appear in the ASL Literature Series by Bahan and Supalla (1992). Although they were videotaped and created in 1992, they developed in the 1980s and have undergone development over the years as they received exposure and were "tested" by interactions with countless audiences in the United States. My own "Bird of a Different Feather" is an allegorical fable of an eagle family into which a straight-beaked bird is born. The narrative of the family's various attempts to turn that bird into a crooked-beak eagle like the rest of the family suggests parallels to issues and events related to the lives of Deaf people (S. Supalla and Bahan 1994; Kettlehut and Bahan 1991a). Supalla's ASL "novella" *For a Decent Living* focuses on various obstacles that a Deaf protagonist overcomes in his journey to earn a decent living (Kettlehut and Bahan 1991b). In the end, his triumph becomes Deaf people's triumph. These two stories are examples of fictional works created in ASL for an ASL-signing audience.

Songs

Because the DEAF WORLD functions as a linguistic minority community within a majority English-speaking culture, members of the DEAF WORLD are predominantly ASL-English bilinguals, to varying degrees. This means many Deaf people are also members of the majority culture (i.e., American culture) and may have acquired, through their interaction with English on a daily basis, some appreciation of various genres that appear to have originated in the oral medium, such as songs.

What is most interesting, however, and what I focus on here, is how signers modify this genre to fit or blend in with the visual discourse that is essential to the face-to-face nature of the DEAF WORLD. Some elements of vocal songs are transposed into the signed modality, such as fluidity of words/signs and the rhythm. The cadence of songs usually springs from the structural way signs are formed (e.g., phonology/morphology) and is visually pleasing.

Two common types of songs used in the DEAF WORLD are translated songs and percussion signing.[12] Although it is difficult to prove, percussion signing may have originated in the DEAF WORLD rather than being modified from the oral medium. However, given the contact of the two worlds, it is difficult to rule out the possibility of influence.

Translated Songs

Translated songs have been around in the DEAF WORLD for a long time. In this genre, the lyrics of various songs are translated into ASL and performed for an audience.[13] They may involve some ritual like singing the "Star Spangled Banner" before various sports events. Note that the pacing of these songs is at the artist's predisposition; he or she is likely to modify the pace so that it fits the visual modality of ASL, as seen in **clips 2.7 and 2.8** of two artists performing the "Star Spangled Banner." Mrs. Washington Barrow's performance was captured in Charles Krauel's film in 1940 (T. Supalla 1994); the other clip features Ella Mae Lentz about fifty-five years later (Lentz, Mikos, and Smith 1996).

Also popular in the DEAF WORLD during the early to mid–twentieth century was the performance of "Yankee Doodle" (see Padden and Humphries 1988 for some discussion on the disappearance of this song). Winfield E. Marshall performs the song in *The Preservation of American Sign Language: The Complete Historical Collection* (1997), and examples of other renditions appear in the film *Charles Krauel: A Profile of a Deaf Filmmaker* (T. Supalla 1994).

Percussion Signing

Percussion signing involves arranging signs to certain beats.[14] There appear to be three types of cadences: "one, two, one, two," "one, two, one-two-three," and a mixture of the first two. It is not unusual to see this type of performance accompanied with a drummer who keeps up with the cadence, hence the use of the term *percussion signing.*

Perhaps the earliest recorded performance of this type is found in Charles Krauel's film (T. Supalla 1994). It is a duo between an unknown signer and George Kannapell, who are entertaining and leading a group with a percussion performance to the cadence of "one, two, one-two-three" (see clip 2.1).[15]

BOAT	BOAT	
1	2	
BOAT-BOAT-BOAT		
1	2	3
DRINK	DRINK	
1	2	
DRINK-DRINK-DRINK		
1	2	3
FUN	FUN	
1	2	
FUN- FUN- FUN		
1	2	3
ENJOY	ENJOY	
1	2	
ENJOY-ENJOY-ENJOY		
1	2	3

Songs like Kannapell's are sometimes performed spontaneously and are often done in social gatherings to "incite a crowd to good cheer and a sense of unity" (Padden and Humphries 1988, 78).

Another group song that is widely known is the Gallaudet University fight song called the "Bison Song" (see T. Supalla in press for further insight into the history of this song).[16] Several schools for the deaf have adopted their own fight songs, perhaps modeling after Gallaudet's fight songs, but it is not known which schools still use them today. In **clip 2.9,** Freda Norman gives an example of a fight song using the cadence of "one, two, one-two-three."

Some people have observed that the tradition of percussion signing appears to have altogether vanished, except for the "Bison Song" (Padden and Humphries 1988). But I have seen several people, perhaps out of nostalgia or a desire to revive this genre, perform original percussion songs—for example, at the Deaf Way conference of 1989. Several years ago I had the opportunity to view a home video of an Easter service performance at a Deaf church in the Midwest in which two members did a brief percussion signing. The performance, translated below, involved a mixed cadence of "one, two, one-two-three" and "one, two." Some description of the signs may be needed in order to follow the translation. The pronoun *he* was presented using an honorific third-person handshape in which the whole hand with an open palm (as in the "B" handshape) points upward to the heavens. The sign for *Lord* involves two contact locations—for a right-hand signer, the first contact begins the left shoulder area and the sign ends at lower right side of the torso. The signer in this performance broke up the sign LORD, assigning "beat 1" to the first contact location and "beat 2" to the second contact location (transcribed as LORD-1 and LORD-2).

CLAP		CLAP
1		2
CLAP-	CLAP-	CLAP
1	2	3
HE		MY
1		2
LORD-1		LORD-2
1		2
HE		MY
1		2
LORD-1		LORD-2
1		2
CLAP		CLAP
1		2
CLAP-	CLAP-	CLAP
1	2	3

Percussion signing may not be as widespread as it used to be in the early part of the twentieth century, but it is far from gone, and it may be reviving in situations that involve the need for sense of unity among a group. A service of worship, such as the one described above, is one particular event where we would expect this type of song to surface.

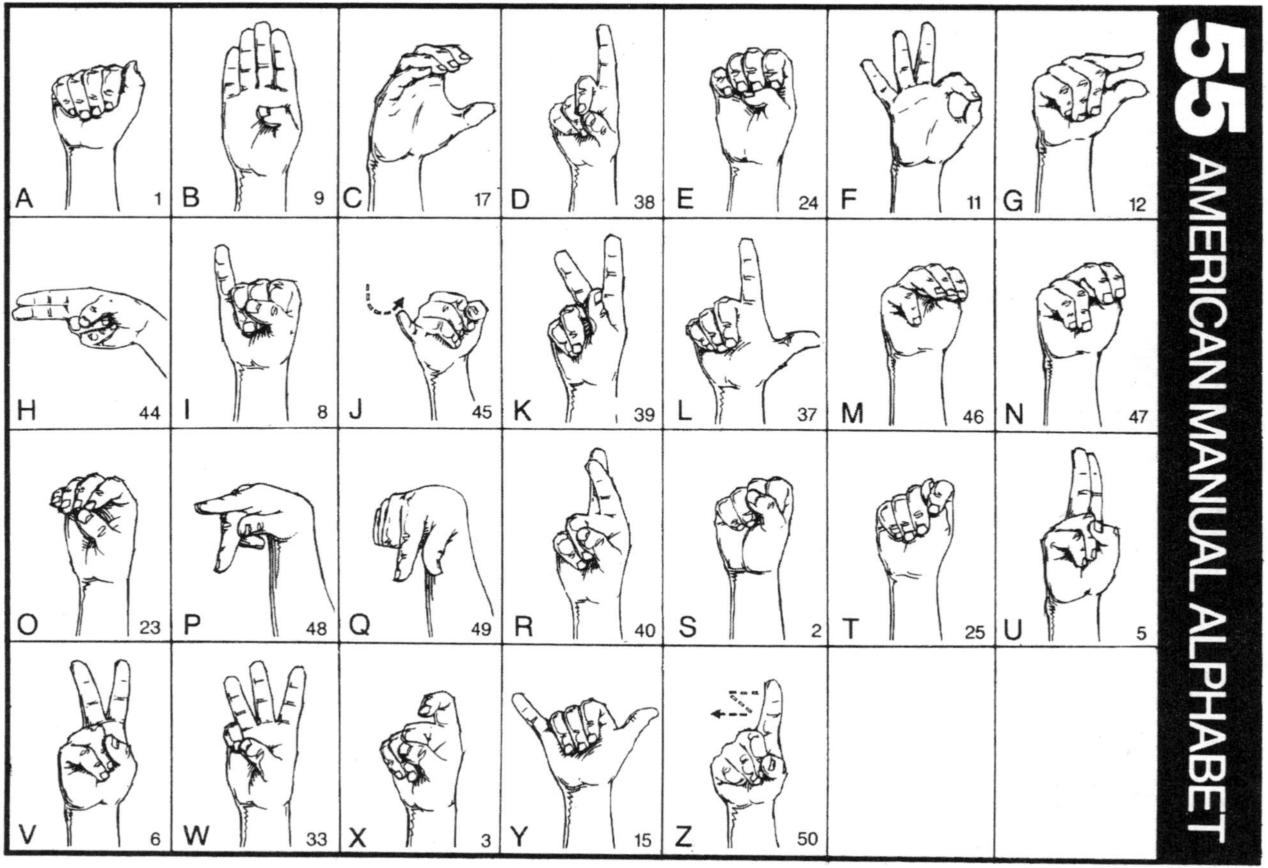

FIGURE 2.1. Alphabet handshapes, reprinted by permission of the publisher from *ASL Handshape Game Cards*, by Frank Allen Paul and Ben Bahan, San Diego, CA: DawnSignPress.

This interplay needs to be taken into serious consideration in examining ABC stories. Some letters in the manual alphabet have basically the same handshape but different movement or orientation. For example, the two sets "K"/"P" and "U"/"H"/"N" have similar handshapes but differ in the orientation of their hands. The letters "I" and "J" differ in their movement (Rutherford 1993). Signers of ABC stories are "allowed," through creative license, to just focus on the handshape and create signs despite their actual orientation and movement in the manual alphabet (Rutherford 1993). There is also a certain amount of flexibility in how the handshapes can be modified, but the handshape used must be close to the form of the original handshape (Rutherford 1993). One may notice that some ABC storytellers have used the gesture for TIME-OUT (as seen in various sporting events) for the letter "T." This violates rules number two (stated above) because the use of this gesture deviates too much from the T handshape. Rutherford noticed in her collection that there was a frequent interchange among the two-fingered handshapes "N," "H," "U," and "V," as well as interchange between the three-fingered handshapes in "M" and "W" (see Rutherford 1993, 38, for a table showing acceptable interchanges).[21] It has been observed that a good ABC storyteller would be able to stay within the acceptable limits of deviation.

Another item in ABC stories that appears problematic is the limited number of signs that come with certain handshapes, such as "E" and "M." Unless signers borrow from manually coded English systems such as Signing Exact English, there are not enough ASL signs with these handshapes. It is predictable that, in the next ABC story we encounter, for "'E'" the signer may well sign "EEE" (comparable to a screech or a whistling sound) and, for "M," "MMM" (used to convey a humming noise).[22]

On the issue of paralinguistic cues and discourse mechanisms, Lon Kuntze (Gallaudet University Distance Education Program 1997) points out that ABC stories are limited not only in terms of how to come up with signs for each letter in sequence but also in terms of how to deal with what is between the letters. That is, the artful use of these mechanisms enhances the story and story line and is essential to a successful ABC story. According to Kuntze, a skillful ABC storyteller would be able to handle these cues effortlessly, to the point that one might not even realize he or she was telling an ABC story.

ABC stories have several classical opening motifs. Although various storytellers may have modified the story line, the opening line with the letters

"A," "B," and "C" is usually maintained, as in these segments from "haunted house" and "race" stories (**clips 2.11 and 2.12**):

A: KNOCK-ON-DOOR
B: DOOR-SWINGS-OPEN
C: SEARCH

A: RACE
B: Classifier B (signing includes a "B" handshape—"wide-bodied object [car] rolling to stop line")
C: Classifier C (signing includes a "C" handshape—"wide tires vibrating with the engine")

This genre has been around in the Deaf community for a long time. Gilbert Eastman remembers seeing ABC stories in the 1940s[23] and is sure that they were around in the 1930s. There is a remote possibility that this genre may have existed around the 1900s at the Ohio School for the Deaf, as reported by one of Rutherford's informants (see Rutherford 1993, 55). Its existence as far back as the turn of the century shows that there is a long history of the interplay between the two languages of ASL and English.

NUMBER STORIES AND PLAYS ON FINGERSPELLED WORDS

Two more story types that build on handshape sequencing constraints are number stories and plays on fingerspelled words. Basically, they follow the same principles described in the ABC story above. The story unfolds based on handshapes that follow the sequence of either the numbers (e.g., 1–15) or any fingerspelled word, including, for example, names of people, activities, and states.

Number stories are self-explanatory: they are like ABC stories, but the story utilizes the number handshapes in order. The play on fingerspelled words may be rather intriguing. Rutherford (1993, 56), using a different label, "fingerspelled/ASL word characterizations," explains that the story content of this type of play usually revolves around "illustrating some aspect of the word." If the word in play were *golf,* then the handshapes for each letter in the word would be used in succession to create a brief story about golfing (see Barwiolek 1984), as in the following example taken from Rutherford (1993, 57):

(right hand)	G : a tee is placed on ground
(left hand)	O : a ball is placed on the tee
(right hand)	L : a club swings at the ball
(left hand)	F : the ball becomes airborne

In such a short sequence (four signs), we have an overall impression of what golfing is about.

Stories with Handshape Type Constraints

Some stories, rather than following a specific sequence of handshapes, use a limited set of handshape(s)—ranging from one (e.g., a handshape used to signal the number 5) to a set of handshapes (e.g., using the three handshapes "1," "A," and "5"). In using this kind of constraint, a teller will still need to comply with two of the three rules stated in the section on handshape/sequencing constraints: the handshape(s) used need(s) to comply with the original intent (if there is deviation, it needs to be within acceptable limits), and the story needs to make sense.

An example of this kind of story is Freda Norman's work "A Full Hand" (**clip 2.13**) in the videotape *Signing Treasures* (Lentz, Mikos, and Smith 1996). In the story, Norman chooses to use two particular handshapes ("B" and "5"), and we can see as the story unfolds that there is some deviation from the handshape. Yet the deviation remains within acceptable boundaries. It involves bending the spreading fingers in "5" and the bending fingers in "B." The story's theme is about a man and a woman who meet and get married. They give birth to a child who grows up and is eventually called off to war. Upon returning home from a long war, he becomes depressed when he learns of his mother's death. His father, who tells him his mother has gone to heaven, comforts him. The way the story unfolds help create a sense-making mechanism that viewers identify.

Ownership of Stories

Tellers may invent their own stories (e.g., telling a narrative of their own personal experience), but in many cases stories are passed down (or passed along) within the community. Even if a story is original, the question of ownership is unclear because unlike stories that are written down, which the writer can write for himself and never share with others, stories in the face-to-face tradition are told to an audience and shared with members of the community.[24]

In my discussions with storytellers, I found that most of them are facing this interesting paradox. As in much of the oral tradition, the notion that the "community" owns the story remains, in some sense. The teller may own only his or her style and perhaps the process of rebuilding the story after acquiring a "story-skeleton" from the culture. But since the 1990s, with the advent of video technology, the ownership question has been undergoing further re-evaluation. When one's performance is "printed" on videotape, it is like having one's work written down. Even the purposes of writing down and videotaping one's work can be similar: going back and correcting the work, fine-tuning some parts of the story until a point of satisfaction is reached, and then creating a permanent document. (For further discussion of this point, see chapter 3 in this volume, by Christopher Krentz.)

THE AUDIENCE

The audience, and the culture they represent, play a crucial role in shaping the work of the tellers and in developing the various tales. They often dictate, through their encouragement and, in some cases, indirectly through requests for repeated performances, the kind of stories and/or poems that the tellers will end up performing. If that is true, then who is governing the story? Okpewho (1992, 45) reports that "in most narrative traditions across the African continent, the storyteller simply has the bare outlines of the story and is expected to make the appropriate adjustment to the details in accordance with the interest of the audience." That is, there has to be a shared mind-set between the audience/culture and the teller to make the tale work. This reiterates the interwoven nature of the triad. The way tellers conduct their work reflects their perception of the culture, and the desired outcome of their work depends on the culture's perception of the way they conduct it.

Tales in a Clubroom: Audience Participation at a Deaf Club

Some Deaf clubs have "open mike nights" where, as part of the program, everyone is free to jump on stage to tell stories, ABC stories, jokes, and poems.[25] At first a line of people wait for their turn, but after a while the audience "weeds out" weak tellers by asking specific persons to come back and tell another story/joke. In this process they are also telling this person what particular genre to cover (e.g., another dirty ABC story). Near the end of the program, the selection process has reduced the line to two to three people, who may just specialize in, for example, dirty stories or cinematographic stories. The point here is that the audience has determined the course of events for that night at the club. They have determined (or in some cases predetermined) who is the best storyteller of the club. And if that storyteller decides not to stand on line but to sit by the bar and watch, he or she will eventually get encouraged by the audience to "get up on stage." Marie Philip (pers. comm., June 20, 1994) recalls the following event at a Deaf club where she grew up. At one open-mike night, a couple of members, not satisfied with the way the event was unfolding, scanned the room and, spotting a fabled local storyteller over by the poker table, publicly urged her to go on stage. In this, we see the role an audience assumes in selecting their teller. It is also not unusual for an audience in a Deaf club to play a role in selecting what tales will be told: to dictate, for example, that the teller tell a funny story instead of the sad one that he or she is telling at the moment. But in a less intimate setting, such as a staged performance, we would not expect to see this type of rapport.

The Changing Audience

One elder storyteller with over seventy years of storytelling experience mentioned to me in passing that he had seen the composition of his audience change rapidly over the past ten to fifteen years. For many years he had been invited to perform at various Deaf-related events and had known what to expect from the audience because he had grown up in the culture and had Deaf parents and grandparents. It was as if the audience was in him and he was in the audience. Lately, however, he was finding it not unusual to encounter a mixed audience containing people who were not part of his culture—that is, hearing people.[26] He reported that this change had had some effect on the way he would present his work. For a while, he was unsure if he should sign the way he normally did, and he would ask himself, "Should I slow down my signs so that these people can understand me?" He even modified his stories so that they would not offend hearing people. But then he found himself going back to the way he normally performed because he had grown accustomed to this mix.

Problems of Mixed Audience

According to Okpewho (1992, 58), "[A] good storyteller is also expected to exercise discretion in the structuring of his stories before a variety of audiences." But what if the audience contains both "insiders" and "outsiders" to the teller's culture?[27] To whom should the storyteller pay attention?

There have been reports of tellers who pay so much attention to the hearing audience that it affects their performance. It is not unusual to find Deaf members of the audience saying that a performer was "too English." Those tellers who decide to be more concerned about the hearing members of the audience may do so for two reasons. First, they may be considering economics: many, if not most, of the paying members of the audience will be hearing people. Second, they may mistrust interpreters and choose to sign in English so that the interpreters will have an easier time following the performance.

In this situation, if a teller focuses on the Deaf audience and tells tales that favor Deaf people and portray hearing people in a somewhat negative light, he will draw protest from hearing members in the audience. As one teller recalled, "I remember after one performance where I was telling various stories about Deaf people overcoming odds and portraying hearing people as ignorant and sometimes as losers, several hearing people would come up to me and remark that I hated hearing people." He maintained that this was not true and that he was only sharing stories he normally shared among Deaf people and Deaf audiences. "So, these stories do upset some hearing people," he told me. "I can easily decide to drop telling these stories and modify my stories to make them happy, but I will not do that, because my stories are from my culture. I will tell it as it is whether they like it or not."

Since everything in a face-to-face tradition is dynamic, we should expect some influence from this mixed audience on the selection of tellers and tales in the future.

CONCLUSION

Since the face-to-face tradition is alive and dynamic, we are currently see-ing several changes. The increasingly diverse makeup of the audience is already having an impact on the selection of tellers and tales. Also, the rap-idly growing use of video technology has already begun to influence the composition as well as the ownership of stories. Because this technology replaces the face-to-face encounter that has been a dynamic force in the community for years, the audience no longer sees tellers demonstrate their ability to construct and perform stories on the spot, showcasing their abil-ity to think quickly on their feet. These changes are an inevitable conse-quence of a contemporary world where cultures and technologies cross borders. Hence the literary traditions in the Deaf community will continue to change as the nature of performance changes.

NOTES

I am grateful to the following people who have over the years shared their insights, discus-sion, and input, some of which eventually found its way into this chapter. They are H-Dirk-sen Bauman, MJ Bienvenu, Bernard Bragg, Simon Carmel, Gilbert Eastman, Leo M. Jacobs, Judy Kegl, Bonnie Kraft, Lon Kuntze, Robert G. Lee, Ella Mae Lentz, Ernest Mar-shall, Marie Philip, Susan Rutherford, Sam Supalla, Clayton Valli, and Janet Weinstock. I am also grateful to Dirksen Bauman, Carol Neidle, and Robert Lee for their editorial assis-tance. Any errors are solely my own. Funding for this work was provided in part through a grant from the National Science Foundation (#SBR-9729010).

1. The capitalized DEAF WORLD is used to reflect how it is signed in ASL. As used in Lane et al. (1996), it roughly translates as a way of life for those who are oriented visually.

2. Several written systems have emerged in recent years, among them Sign Font (Newkirk 1987) and Sign-Writing (Sutton 1981).

3. There are, however, some Deaf bilinguals who are more proficient in English than ASL, and this shows up in the way they converse. The fact that the community acknowl-edges this by labeling this group of people as "English signers" suggests some deviation from the expected face-to-face norm.

4. Charles Krauel has made a collection of films of various Deaf social events, such as weddings, schools, and conventions, from 1925 until the 1970s (see *Charles Krauel: A Profile of a Deaf Filmmaker,* T. Supalla 1994). In fact, the intention of Krauel's and most likely of NAD's films was to serve as medium of disseminating information using the face-to-face language of the community.

5. Hotchkiss enrolled at ASD in 1859 at the age of fourteen and graduated in 1865. Lau-rent Clerc, who co-founded ASD in 1817, died on July 18, 1869.

6. It is highly probable that Clerc was basing his lecture on word order from a famous French saying dating back to Molière in the seventeenth century, *Il faut manger pour vivre et non pas vivre pour manger* (One must eat to live and not live to eat). I am grateful to Carol Neidle for pointing this out.

7. The interscholastic sports conference to which ASD belonged was at that time called Eastern Schools for the Deaf Athletic Association. The conference included the following schools in the mid-Atlantic states and New England: Maryland School for the Deaf, Pennsylvania School for the Deaf, New Jersey School for the Deaf, New York School for the Deaf (Fanwood), and St. Mary's School for the Deaf (Buffalo, NY).

8. Some of the genres in ASL not discussed here are poetry (which is discussed elsewhere in this volume), group narrative, and "sign play" (which might include puns, riddles, jokes and so on; see Rutherford 1993). There are more genres, but few researchers besides Rutherford (1993) have systematically categorized the various genres.

9. Many of these categories are taken, with modifications, from Rutherford (1993).

10. The genre of cinematographic stories could well be called "classifier stories" instead, since the use of cinematographic technique requires sophisticated manipulation of classifiers.

11. There are several types of classifiers, such as semantic, instrument, locative, descriptive, and body and body-part classifiers (see Lentz, Mikos, and Smith 1989 for further description of these types).

12. It should be noted that some members of the DEAF WORLD have created their own lyrics and performed them. Such original songs are performed in the same manner as translated songs, with a sense of fluidity and rhythm. Examples of original songs are David Supalla's "Ballad in Honor of the USA Flag" (C. Supalla and D. Supalla 1992) and Bill Ennis's "Backwards All the Way to Birmingham Alabama" (Ennis 1993).

13. Also, signers (usually those who are hearing or those who have residual hearing) sometimes play a tape or CD of popular songs and sign out the words of the song while keeping in pace with the beat of the music. Such interpreted songs do not seem to be particularly popular with Deaf audiences. I would not categorize them as part of the genre of translated songs because the pace of the discourse is primarily geared to the auditory modality.

14. The label of this category is taken from Ted Supalla (in press).

15. Translated by T. Supalla (appearing in Padden and Humphries 1988 and T. Supalla in press).

16. This song involves a mixed cadence of "one, two" and "one, two, one-two-three."

17. I am grateful to Lon Kuntze for some insights in this section.

18. It is also possible to reverse the sequence, going from Z to A, or to set up a formula of repeating the handshape twice before moving on to the next handshape (i.e., A, A, B, B, C, C, and so on). It is also possible to create a rhythm of 2, 1, 2, 1 with this sequence of handshapes: A, A, B, C, C, D, E, E, F, and so on. However, the sequence must be maintained, one way or the other.

19. These four rules seem to be an unwritten code in the Deaf community; there has been consensus about this among the people I have talked with (e.g., Lon Kuntze, MJ Bienvenu, Ella Lentz, and Clayton Valli) over the years.

20. Peters (2000) points out that in written form ABC stories appear to be analogous to "acrostic" poems. (The plays on fingerspelled words provide an even closer parallel.)

21. It should be noted that the list of allowable deviations proposed by Rutherford is only a beginning effort; further scrutiny is needed. For example, it is questionable whether the "Y" handshape can be interchanged with the "I_I" handshape (opening of index finger and pinkie while the rest of the fingers and thumb remain clenched). Furthermore, the handshapes used in classifiers appear to allow more flexibility with respect to modification.

22. Sometimes, however, tellers will use the "M" handshape to signify signs that ordinarily employ the "flat-O" or "bent-B" handshape: for example, they will use the "M" handshape for MONEY (ordinarily signed with "flat-O") and CHEWING-TOBACCO (ordinarily signed with "bent-B").

23. Simon Carmel, a Deaf folklorist and anthropologist, confirms this observation from his field notes (pers. comm., July 1, 1999).

24. Some tellers will say about their original work: "I feel I own the story because I created it, yet there is another part of me telling me that the story is not mine and it belongs to my people." As storytellers, they seem to feel they owe the culture something for making them who they are and that giving their audiences stories is a way of repaying their debt.

25. I want to particularly acknowledge the late Marie Philip for first bringing this up. Much of what is stated here comes from her observations of one local Deaf club in New England. Similar phenomena have been observed elsewhere.

26. They come from various backgrounds: many of them are sign language students, with skills ranging from beginning to advanced, and interpreters.

27. Deaf performers are not the only ones who are confronted with this issue. For example, a similar situation arises when a black performer who draws on material from black culture (e.g., a comedian like Chris Rock) addresses an audience that contains whites.

REFERENCES

Bahan, B. 1994. "Analysis of ASL Stories and Storytelling." Paper presented March 29, 1994, at Gallaudet University and June 22, 1994, at "Storytelling, Storytellers and the Literary Tradition of ASL," National Theatre of the Deaf Summer School.

Bahan, B., and S. Supalla. 1992. *"Bird of a Different Feather" and "For a Decent Living."* Videocassette. American Sign Language Literature Series. San Diego, CA: Dawn Pictures.

Barwiolek, A. 1984. G-O-L-F. In *Deaf Folklore,* dir. R. Mocenigo, video 2 of *American Culture: The Deaf Perspective.* Videocassette. San Francisco: San Francisco Public Library.

Baynton, D. 1998. *Forbidden Signs: American Culture and the Campaign against Sign Language.* Chicago: University of Chicago Press.

Carmel, Simon. 1979. "Deaf Folklore." Lecture given at Gallaudet University, Washington, DC, May.

Edwards, V., and T. Sienkewicz. 1990. *Oral Cultures Past and Present: Rappin' and Homer.* Cambridge, MA: Basil Blackwell.

Ennis, B. 1993. *Bill Ennis: Live at SMI!* Videocassette. Burtonsville, MD: Sign Media.

Gallaudet University Distance Education Program. 1997. *Telling Tales in ASL: From Literature to Literacy with a Focus on Deaf and Hard of Hearing Children and Youth.* Videocassette. Washington, DC: Gallaudet University.

Gee, J. P., and Walter J. Ong. 1983. "An Exchange on American Sign Language and Deaf Culture." *Language and Style: An International Journal* 16:231–33.

Goody, J. 1992. "Oral Culture." In *Folklore, Cultural Performances, and Popular Entertainments: A Communications-Centered Handbook,* ed. R. Bauman. New York: Oxford University Press.

Grosjean, F. 1996. "Living with Two Languages and Two Cultures. In *Cultural and Language Diversity and the Deaf Experience,* ed. I. Parasnis. Cambridge: Cambridge University Press.

Kettlehut, C., and B. Bahan. 1991a. "The Eagle Fable: A Literary Analysis." Unpublished manuscript, Center for the Study of Communication and Deafness, Boston University.

———. 1991b. "*For a Decent Living* by Sam Supalla: A Literary Analysis." Unpublished manuscript, Center for the Study of Communication and Deafness, Boston University.

Labov, W. 1972. *Language in the Inner City: Studies in the Black English Vernacular.* Philadelphia: University of Pennsylvania Press.

Lane, H., R. Hoffmeister, and B. Bahan. 1996. *A Journey into the DEAF-WORLD.* San Diego, CA: DawnSignPress.

Lentz, E., K. Mikos, and C. Smith. 1989. *Signing Naturally: Teacher's Curriculum Guide—Level 2.* San Diego, CA: DawnSignPress.

———. 1996. *Signing Treasures: Excerpts from Signing Naturally Videos.* Videocassette. San Diego, CA: DawnPictures.

Linde, C. 1993. *Life Stories: The Creation of Coherence.* New York: Oxford University Press.

Newkirk, D. 1987. *Architect: Final Version Sign Font Handbook October 1987.* San Diego, CA: Emerson and Stern Associates.

Okpewho, I. 1992. *African Oral Literature.* Indianapolis: Indiana University Press.

Ong, Walter J. 1982. *Orality and Literacy: The Technologizing of the Word.* London: Routledge.

Padden, C., and T. Humphries 1988. *Deaf in America: Voices from a Culture.* Cambridge, MA: Harvard University Press.

Peters, C. L. 2000. *Deaf American Literature: From Carnival to the Canon.* Washington, DC: Gallaudet University Press.

The Preservation of American Sign Language: The Complete Historical Collection. 1997. Videocassette. Burtonsville, MD: Sign Media.

Rutherford, S. 1993. *A Study of American Deaf Folklore.* Burtonsville, MD: Linstok Press.

Supalla, C., and D. Supalla. 1992. *Short Stories in American Sign Language.* Videocassette. Riverside, CA: ASL Vista Project.

Supalla, S., and B. Bahan. 1994. *"Bird of a Different Feather" and "For a Decent Living": Teacher's Guide and Student Workbook.* American Sign Language Literature Series. San Diego, CA: DawnSignPress.

Supalla, T. 1982. "Structure and Acquisition of Verbs of Motion and Location in American Sign Language." PhD diss., University of California, San Diego.

———. 1994. *Charles Krauel: A Profile of a Deaf Filmmaker.* Videocassette. San Diego CA: DawnPictures.

———. In press. *Film and Deaf Folklife: Charles Krauel and His Time.* San Diego, CA: DawnSignPress.

Sutton, V. 1981. *Sign-Writing for Everyday Use.* Boston: Sutton Movement Writing Press.

THREE

The Camera as Printing Press

How Film Has Influenced ASL Literature

CHRISTOPHER B. KRENTZ

When George W. Veditz, the president of the National Association of the Deaf (NAD), initiated a campaign to preserve sign language in 1913, he turned to a new medium to achieve this goal: film. "There is but one known means of passing on the language: through the use of moving picture films," he said.[1] Veditz pointed to an important truth: before the advent of film technology, people had no effective way to record American Sign Language (ASL). One certainly could not represent ASL through writing. As the Deaf author John Burnet put it in 1835: "To attempt to describe a language of signs by words, or to learn such a language from books, is alike to attempt impossibilities" (24).[2] Deaf Americans passed on stories, poetry, and folklore in ASL by "sign of hand," without the intervention of recording equipment. In this way, sign culture resembled oral cultures (i.e., cultures without writing), as James Paul Gee and Walter J. Ong pointed out in 1983. All communication through ASL had to happen live and face to face. The arrival of film technology in the early twentieth century changed this dynamic: it enabled people to capture and preserve what had once seemed transitory. In the process, film began to alter ASL literature.

In many ways, the advent of film has striking parallels to the invention of the printing press in the fifteenth century. The press helped gradually to change European culture from largely oral to largely literate. The publication of the Guttenberg Bible in 1455 led to a trickle of other printed volumes, which grew into a flood of type, so that society became inundated with books, pamphlets, and newspapers. Along the same lines, the early black-and-white NAD films were followed by several other sign language motion pictures, which have given way in recent decades to an outpouring of videos and DVDs; now hundreds of ASL videos, featuring everything from ASL storytelling and poetry to Deaf history to ASL instruction, are available to consumers.

Of course, print and film differ in important respects. For example, ASL performances on film are not written; they exist in the same mode as they originally appeared. Moreover, while the printing press provoked sweeping changes across Europe and the globe, I am primarily interested in the impact of film on a relatively small population: American Deaf people, who communicate largely through ASL. Still, research on the printing press, oral cultures, and literacy helps to illuminate how film has affected ASL storytelling and poetry. Just as print transformed written literature, so film technology has changed works in ASL. Both print and film have increased dissemination, made their literatures more static, complex, and commercialized, and altered the way people compose and receive texts. In *The Printing Press as an Agent of Change* (1979), Elizabeth Eisenstein discusses how print affected the way people thought and interacted, contributing to such seismic movements as the Reformation and the Renaissance. ASL films have also produced cultural ferment, transforming the way people think about not just sign literature but also Deaf culture itself. Video has made Deaf individuals less of an isolated "oral" community. It has lifted the veil from ASL and, for better or worse, pushed Deaf culture more into mainstream, capitalist America.

ORALITY AND SIGN

Before the arrival of print and film, both hearing and Deaf cultures were "oral" in that they were based on live, face-to-face communication. My use of *oral* in this context may run up against objections, and with good reason. First, the very term *oral* seems a misnomer in connection with the Deaf community. After all, ASL is quite different from speech. *Oral* also echoes *oralism,* the movement spearheaded by Alexander Graham Bell to eradicate sign language, stop deaf intermarriage, and in effect quash Deaf culture. Perhaps *manual* better indicates how Deaf people passed on their stories, folklore, and poetry through sign. In addition, both medieval European and nineteenth-century Deaf cultures had writing, which seems antithetical to an oral/manual society. We surely would be mistaken to call them *purely* oral or manual, for writing did affect communication. Yet it normally played a secondary role to oral/manual exchange. In Europe before print, formal writing was often in Latin (a language unknown to most citizens) rather than in the vernacular. As Walter J. Ong (1982) points out, even when vernacular writing was employed, it often recycled information back into the oral domain, as in sermons or reading of literary or other texts to groups (119). Similarly, writing played an important but peripheral role in Deaf culture. Many nineteenth-century Deaf Americans were bilingual, using both ASL and written English. They favored ASL for personal interaction, as the Deaf author Laura Redden pointed out in 1858. "Writing may be used in [a Deaf person's] intercourse with others, but when conversing with those who are, like himself, deprived of hearing and speech, you will always find that he prefers sign to every other mode of intercourse," she observed (178). Deaf people used written English when they were separated by time or distance, or when they wanted to communicate with nonsigners. Sometimes people translated written English accounts into the manual domain, as when signers reported information from newspapers to assembled Deaf club members. Literature in English or ASL thus did not develop in isolation; it was undoubtedly influenced by the written word, even if that word was in another language. Ruth Finnegan (1988) reminds us that orality and literacy exist on a continuum: "Orality and literacy are not two separate and independent things; nor (to put it more concretely) are oral and written modes two mutually exclusive and opposed processes for representing and communicating information" (175). Writing in Deaf and medieval European cultures influenced but did not obviate their strong manual/oral aspects.

MAKING TEXTS STATIC

Of all the ways that the printing press and film affected their respective literatures, perhaps making language static is the most significant. They arrested texts that had been elastic in the "oral" domain. Before the advent of print and type, both cultures passed on most stories, poetry, and folklore through dynamic live performances. In medieval Europe, people may have heard such renditions by going to a cathedral, town square, or festival. In Deaf culture, individuals frequently saw them by visiting a Deaf club, school, or fair. These events were never the same twice. Performers usually interacted with the audience, making each rendition different, a living, kinetic experience unique to that time and place. Such performances were seldom recorded. The English epic *Beowulf* is a rare exception. The poem was probably first composed sometime in the eighth century and was passed on orally for years. It was likely not written down until the tenth century, and we know it today only because of a single surviving manuscript. How many other oral performances were not transcribed at all or were written down only to be damaged and lost? We can only guess.

Similarly, we have little direct record of nineteenth-century performances in ASL. Contemporary Deaf publications contain frequent references to signed lectures. For example, in 1869 the *Deaf-Mutes' Friend* reported that William B. Swett gave a presentation to the Fanwood Literary Association in New York: "His lecture was replete with incident, accident, adventure, and wit, and was highly relished by all present. He was loudly applauded, and many a mute will look forward with eagerness to the time he will come to lecture again" (Kouponeti 1869, 379). That Swett's signing was entertaining and eloquent, we have no doubt; but we also have no concrete sense of his ASL or the nature of his performance. Along the same lines, we can read English translations of Laurent Clerc's remarks to his Deaf former students in 1850, or John Carlin's lecture at the inauguration of the National Deaf-Mute College (now Gallaudet University) in 1864, but their actual signs, and the flavor of their interaction with the audience, are forever lost.

The invention of print and film made it possible to capture such performances. They moved their literatures away from the oral/manual mode by making them invariable or even "petrified," to use a term of Albert Lord (1963, 193).

FREEING LITERATURE FROM THE CONSTRAINTS OF TIME AND PLACE

In the process, print and film made their literatures much more accessible. We no longer need to go see the performer in person. We can read by ourselves volumes of poetry and prose that were published centuries ago, their messages saved through the powers of print. Similarly, we can view Veditz signing elegantly in 1913; Charles Krauel's footage of ASL songs and festivals from the 1920s to the 1950s; Ernest Marshall's movies with sign language, produced near midcentury; the National Theatre of the Deaf's 1973 play *My Third Eye;* and a host of other ASL plays, stories, and poems, all in our own homes, on our own time, simply by putting a video into our video-cassette recorder, or a CD or DVD in a computer. People living as far away as the Ukraine or Australia, who might not have had much access to ASL performances before, can now view them through video. The signs and expressions will always be the same, faithfully recorded by the camera's eye.

PRESERVATION AND INSTITUTIONAL MEMORY

Print and film not only increased accessibility to their respective literatures but also made it possible to preserve performances that previously had disappeared almost as soon as they were over. In Europe, the printing press produced many copies of definitive texts, which altered the nature of collective memory by providing an authoritative historical record. Whereas before people had to remember things in their heads or depend on those with written manuscripts, now, through books and libraries, they could have much greater access to information. Typography allowed serious students to learn a much larger body of material than would have been humanly possible before (Eisenstein 1979, 72).

In the same manner, film technology played an important role in preserving ASL literature and Deaf history. As mentioned above, Veditz turned to film in 1913 to help save ASL. He was alarmed over the spread of oralism and saddened that many illustrious nineteenth-century signers had passed away without being recorded. Veditz arranged for himself, Robert P. McGregor, Edward Miner Gallaudet, and four other masters of ASL to appear in the NAD films. "We want to keep and preserve the signs as these men now use them to keep and pass on to future generations," he said (quoted in Padden and Humphries 1988, 56). With these films, he succeeded in his goal. Together with subsequent movies, Veditz's films provide a historical record of how the language has grown and changed. In a video called *The Preservation of American Sign Language* (1997), Brian Malzkuhn shows how Veditz's signs for such concepts as "memory," "every year," and "love" compare with current ASL signs. In *Charles Krauel: A Profile of a Deaf Filmmaker* (1994), Ted Supalla discusses old footage of Deaf people performing "one, two, one-two-three" routines and other rhythmic signed songs, an art form that has largely disappeared today.[3] Supalla (1998) has also analyzed early Deaf motion pictures to try to reconstruct the evolution of ASL since 1817. In this way, film provides a valuable record of signed performances and Deaf people's past. Libraries at Gallaudet, the University of Virginia, and elsewhere now have collections of Deaf-related films and videos, creating a canon of literature in ASL.

DISTANCING PERFORMERS FROM AUDIENCES

By making performances static, print and film also changed the way audiences and performers relate to each other. As noted above, one can only see oral/manual performances live; they are interactive and variable. Each piece of oral/manual literature is realized in its actual performance, before a particular audience. The audience, as well as the performer, influences and shapes the work. "In oral cultures an audience must be brought to respond, often vigorously," Ong (1982) says (42). The members of the audience are usually united, with each other and with the artist. Oral/manual performances thus tend to bring people together in close-knit groups.

However, print and film often have the opposite effect, driving English and ASL literature from the public to the private realm. After the invention of the printing press, Europeans had less need to assemble to get information; with books and newspapers, they could read it by themselves. Similarly, video technology decreased Deaf people's need to frequent Deaf clubs and events by making it possible for them to watch a wide assortment of ASL tapes alone whenever they wanted.[4] Print and film disrupt the tension between performer and audience by increasing the distance between the two. We routinely read books without knowing the author, just as we can watch videos of Ella Mae Lentz, Patrick Graybill, and other Deaf entertainers although we have never met them. This breach creates what E. D. Hirsch (1977) has called a "context-free" language, an autonomous discourse to which one cannot directly respond (21–23). We cannot participate in filmed ASL performances as we would in live ones. We are cut off from the performer, watching an act where the audience is silent and invisible, implied rather than involved. Most ASL videos show the performer standing alone. Some artists try to connect with their imaginary audience by addressing the camera directly. In his ASL story *For a Decent Living,* Sam Supalla's narrator occasionally asks for our reactions: "Do you remember?" he asks, or "Can you imagine?" Yet these questions remain rhetorical, rather like Holden Caufield's "If you want to know the truth": no answer is expected. The narrator will continue with his tale no matter how we react. One video series that does give a little flavor of true manual performance is the invaluable *Live at SMI!* collection, which features Deaf storytellers in front of live audiences. For example, Mary Beth Miller (1992) calls on the audience to make requests for impromptu skits, while Gilbert Eastman (1991) coaches the crowd to say the strange word *savaba* (which, he says, Deaf people everywhere use to represent hearing people's indecipherable speech). Even here, however, the viewer of the video is separated from the performance, able to watch but not to participate.

Still, we should be careful not to overstate the case. Just as European society retained oral elements after the invention of the printing press, so Deaf culture continues to have a thriving manual component that video has not come close to eclipsing. Artists like Bernard Bragg and Trix Bruce are well known to Deaf Americans for their live shows as well as for their videotaped work. Most Deaf artists develop and hone their performances in front of audiences before recording them; they also continue lectures and shows after their videos are made. This seems more dynamic and flexible than going on book tours and reading selections from one's published writing. Perhaps a better comparison is to modern music groups, who will record a compact disc in the studio but continue playing live shows in which the music changes a bit each time. Why did fans of the Grateful Dead faithfully follow the band around the country, if not for the precious uniqueness of each live show? Similarly, even if one owns a video of the Deaf storyteller Bill Ennis, that does not diminish the excitement of seeing a live performance in person. The two modes are different and not mutually exclusive. While video has the potential to fragment the Deaf community and to cause Deaf people to assemble less often, it also can spread ASL literature and attract more spectators to live events. The interplay between video and live performance can enrich the quality of both formats. Video, like the printing press, is finally a tool, with many possible uses; it depends how people choose to employ it.

COMMODIFYING LITERATURE

After the advent of print and video, many other persons beside the artist became involved in the production of a work. The printing press eventually gave rise to publishers, typesetters, graphic designers, copy editors, and agents; film led to movie and video executives, directors, producers, lighting experts, and camerapersons. These professionals further separate the performer from the audience. They play an essential mediating role, overseeing production and dissemination and shaping the manner in which texts finally appear on the market. In this way, the publishing and film industries have wrested some control from the artist (Ong 1982, 118; Feather 1990, 851). Publishers have the power to accept or reject manuscripts, much as video entrepreneurs choose which ASL performances to produce. They are primarily motivated by money, which makes literature less an artistic than a profit-making enterprise, governed by the dictates of supply and demand. Publishers often devote substantial resources to popular romances and celebrity memoirs because they know that such titillating, easy-to-read books will sell; meanwhile, authors of more serious poetry and fiction may find little interest from publishers. Similarly, the majority of ASL videos on the market today are aimed at hearing people who are learning sign language rather than Deaf audiences. For DawnSignPress, Sign Media, Sign Enhancers, and other such companies, this practice makes good business sense. After all, hearing consumers vastly outnumber Deaf ones and have more buying power. Such instructional tapes perform a valuable service, helping parents and friends of Deaf people to learn sign. Yet they have skewed the selection of ASL videotapes. For every *Live at SMI!* or American Sign Language Literature Series tape with vintage ASL performances, we see countless other basic videos for beginning signers. This leads to a "dumbing down" of recorded ASL works; it is equivalent to publishers' production of simplistic books of English writing for people who are not readily fluent in English, rather than literary works by authors like Twain, Woolf, Faulkner, and Morrison, who push the language in new directions and confront themes central to our lives. The most eloquent and experimental signers would benefit from more opportunities to record and market their performances. Under the current laws of supply and demand, they probably will not get such chances until more consumers want advanced ASL pieces. Perhaps this is one area where nonprofit university presses, such as Gallaudet or California State University at Northridge, could step in.

INCREASING OUTPUT: REACHING A MASS AUDIENCE

Not surprisingly, the advent of print and film also sparked a marked increase in production. Michael Clapham suggests that, in the first century of print, more books were published than "all the scribes of Europe" had produced since AD 330 (Eisenstein 1979, 45). In the same way, film and video have dramatically increased output and dissemination of ASL performances. Thousands of people must now have seen Veditz's 1913 filmed speech, more than ever could have been assembled conveniently in one place at the time. The explosion of ASL videos in recent decades has had an even broader impact. Today, multiple copies of a video can easily be produced. DawnSignPress reports that it has sold over half a million copies of the *Signing Naturally* instructional videos since 1988 (Cynde A. Hale, pers. comm., Oct. 30, 1998). This is an astonishing figure, considering that experts usually estimate that between five hundred thousand and two million deaf people reside in the United States. If we factor in other instructional materials, this number means that we have approximately as many students of ASL as ASL users in the nation.

Not only can many copies of each tape easily be made, but also more videos than ever are being produced. Sign Media, Inc. has offered over 350 ASL video titles since 1980. These tapes range from ASL storytelling and poetry performances, to Deaf history lectures, to tapes about learning ASL or sign language interpreting—a library for any neophyte or expert. The growing number of recordings that are relatively inexpensive and easily available to any consumer has made ASL and Deaf culture much more accessible to mainstream America. Deaf children attending public schools can see videos of Deaf role models and adults, thus tempering the sense of isolation they frequently feel. Hearing people who in the past may have had reservations about going to a Deaf club or event can now view ASL performances in private, without even meeting a Deaf person. Film has taken ASL from the living realm of signs and expressions to the cinematic domain of videotape. Again, this has both perils and benefits. Film has helped to bridge cultural gaps, to foster understanding, and to make the riches of Deaf culture more available to outsiders. At the same time, it has blurred cultural boundaries, taking ASL performances from the public space of Deaf clubs and festivals to the private world of film.

INCREASING RECOGNITION OF INDIVIDUAL ARTISTS

Before print and video, performers mattered less than performances. We do not know who the narrators of *Beowulf* were; it is the epic poem itself that remains. Similarly, we do not remember many of the Deaf artists who passed on the ASL legends, jokes, signplay, ABC stories, and other folklore that we have today.[5] Such works belong to the community rather than to individual performers. These "singers of tales," as Lord calls them, are merely the anonymous agents who repeat and pass on stories and poems from generation to generation. Print and video changed this, making individual artists inseparable from their works. Just as *The Faerie Queene* is Spenser's, *Romeo and Juliet* Shakespeare's, and *Paradise Lost* Milton's, so now we associate Veditz with his "Preservation of Sign Language" lecture, George Kannapell with "one-two, one-two-three" songs, and Eric Malzkuhn with his distinctive rendition of "Jabberwocky" (Padden and Humphries 1988, 33–36, 77, 84–86). Print and video have provided a new sense of private ownership over specific literary works. Still, oral/manual elements remain. Sam Supalla based parts of his *For a Decent Living* narrative on stories he had seen his Deaf father relate as he was growing up. Even as he makes use of film, he continues the manual tradition by passing on his father's stories to a new generation. Clayton Valli, in his last video of ASL poetry (1995), has different native signers, ranging from children to older adults, perform his poems. Valli no doubt coached each of these people on how to sign his works, much as master performers in oral cultures sometimes mentor apprentices. While his name is prominently displayed on the video box and the poems are all his, Valli distances himself somewhat from the works in the tradition of earlier manual performances. By having other Deaf people sign his poems, he seems to suggest that the works belong not just to him but to the entire Deaf community. Yet the video also has striking nonmanual features. It not only records performances but also encourages viewers to sign the poems themselves. Valli's video helps us to sign his works "out loud," just as we may declaim Milton or Eliot's poetry by reading from a book. As we can see, ASL videos often feature a complex mix of manual and nonmanual elements.

A NEW SELF-CONSCIOUSNESS:
MAKING ARTISTS MORE EXPERIMENTAL

In the first century after the invention of the printing press, writers produced a remarkable amount of innovative work that helped to usher in the Renaissance. Similarly, during the first century of film, Deaf people have recorded a number of groundbreaking works in ASL. By increasing individual recognition, print and video made artists become more experimental and self-conscious. Now audiences have less need for repetition of classic works; they can easily access the originals through books or film. Instead, the challenge becomes to innovate, to add to literary history by pushing language, style, and themes in new directions. In *The Anxiety of Influence* (1973), Harold Bloom says that poets, especially after Milton, struggle to escape from the shadow of past greats, to be original and autonomous, to find their own voice. We can discern a similar trend among Deaf artists. For example, in the last fifty years we have seen a gradual evolution in ASL poetry. Some of the first recorded ASL poets, such as Eric Malzkuhn and Bernard Bragg, performed ingenious signed renditions of well-known poems in English, such as Lewis Carroll's "Jabberwocky" or Robert Frost's "Stopping by the Woods on a Snowy Evening." In the 1980s, a new generation of ASL poets, including Ella Mae Lentz and Clayton Valli, began producing original poems in ASL that make brilliant use of handshapes, rhythm, movement, and space. Such works often directly address Deaf-related themes, including the suppression of ASL or hearing parents' attitudes toward their deaf children. More recently, performers such as Peter Cook and Kenny Lerner, the Deaf-hearing tandem who make up the Flying Words Project, have developed playful, circular poems that often blur the boundary between ASL, mime, and performance art. Their works touch on such diverse topics as Einstein, space travel, the Civil War, and natural disasters. We can see ASL poets consciously building upon each other's efforts, testing the bounds of the language, and experimenting with new forms of poetic discourse.

Artists have become more deliberate in other ways as well. The power of print and video to freeze performances and disseminate them to thousands of people necessarily makes artists more self-conscious in composing their work. Any lapse or weakness, once preserved on type or film, cannot easily be effaced. After the advent of the printing press, some writers began to produce draft after draft, refining their work in privacy until it was suitable for publication. Similarly, ASL performers now can develop their performances with video. Before video, Deaf artists had no way to see themselves performing. In addition, it could often be difficult to remember complicated texts. "It is so easy to write an idea down on paper [in English] but forget an expression or feeling," says Kenny Lerner, of the Flying Words Project. "The whole poem is there but something is missing. Having video allows us to capture those things in our rough drafts" (pers. comm., Aug. 31, 1998). Video allows performers to review their work and to remember exactly what they have done, to revise and refine until it meets their artistic vision. Ironically, print and video have prompted artists to work more in privacy, to develop their texts in isolation so that they can be shared with thousands (Ong 1982, 101). This new self-consciousness, together with the commercialization of literature, has raised standards and has made audiences expect more polished, sophisticated works.

CHANGING LITERARY FORMS

Print and film have affected the presentation of literature in other important ways. Once English poetry and fiction began to be published, the actual type became an integral part of the work. Sterne could include his famous page of solid black type in *Tristam Shandy* (1759–67); Faulkner could employ italics to show time shifts and interior thought; and modernist poets like William Carlos Williams and e. e. cummings could experiment with using print to create visual images on the page. Similarly, video has added a new dimension to ASL literature. In Mary Beth Miller's *Live at SMI!* performance, she appears to change outfits magically by snapping her fingers; it is a trick possible only through camera and film. Ella Mae Lentz, in *The Treasure,* takes advantage of the medium to go into the domain of performance art. She relates each poem in a different setting, wearing different clothing; often the camera moves, looking down at her from above, panning slowly in and out. It creates an effect that would be impossible to achieve live.

William Stokoe has pointed out that sign language itself has cinematic attributes: "The essence of sign language is to cut from a normal view to a close-up to a distant shot to a close-up again, and so on, even including flashback and flash-forward scenes, exactly as a movie editor works. . . . Not only is signing itself arranged more like edited film than like written narration, but also each signer is placed very much as a camera" (quoted in Sacks 1989, 89). ASL performers resemble camerapersons, directing how and what we see. It seems likely that since the advent of film technology, ASL performers have become even more visual, borrowing techniques from Hollywood films and television programs. In the mid–twentieth century, children at schools for the deaf would often attend uncaptioned movies on weekends and then report the plots to their Deaf friends, creatively filling in the gaps when necessary. Gilbert Eastman and Sam Supalla are two storytellers who developed their skills this way. In his *Live at SMI!* performance, Eastman includes several humorous summaries of movies, expertly re-creating the scenery, different characters, and action before our eyes. In one sequence, he depicts American and German soldiers tensely meeting in a tavern; in another, he evokes a doctor standing over a dying woman's bed. We can also discern the effects of cinema in Supalla's *For a Decent Living.* He begins by describing a farm covered with white snowdrifts. The wind blows the snow up against a house. We approach a window, look in, and find the main character sitting in a room, painting a picture. Supalla borrows from the generalized opening sequence of many a Hollywood movie; all that is missing in these first moments is the credits. In this way, film has added new aspects to ASL performances, even as it has complicated others, such as the crucial performer-audience rapport.

Printing contributed to the rise of the novel, which, as John Feather (1990) points out, is "the only literary genre to be invented after the invention of printing itself" (853). The press begat such voluminous eighteenth-century works as *Clarissa* (1748–49) and *Tom Jones* (1749). Oral performers, limited by time, simply could not deliver a piece anywhere as lengthy as these. Novels did not become popular until several centuries after the invention of the press; it will be interesting to see if film technology leads to comparable new genres or longer works in ASL.

MAKING AUDIENCES MORE ANALYTICAL

Print and video also changed the way audiences were expected to respond to texts. In manual/oral cultures, performances often have a circularity, a repetitiveness that gives the works structure and helps both artist and audience remember messages (Edwards and Sienkewicz 1990, 147). Type and film lessen the need for repetition in performances, since the reader or viewer can revisit them at will. We can reread poems and books, just as we may watch ASL works over and over. This encourages artists to make their work more "literary," to add subtle layers of meaning that might not immediately be apparent the first time around. Thus James Joyce and T. S. Eliot could comfortably publish such challenging works as *Ulysses* (1922) and "The Waste Land" (1922), knowing that their readers could study and argue over their esoteric messages.

Similarly, ASL performers are producing more demanding works. Before film became widespread, many ASL songs and performances had a certain engaging simplicity. These manual traditions often are ingenious and satisfying but only occasionally contain multiple levels of meaning. Similarly, in Krauel's films of Deaf festivals in the early twentieth century, people perform versions of "Yankee Doodle" and other pieces in ASL. Here, again, the emphasis is not so much on literary weight as on bringing Deaf people together in enjoyable, easy-to-sign group songs. In contrast, postfilm and especially postvideo ASL performances are more complex. Ben Bahan's narrative "Bird of a Different Feather" is a subtle allegory in the tradition of *Animal Farm* (1947) and *Watership Down* (1972). Through his story of a straight-beaked bird born into an eagle family, he explores the predicament of a deaf child born to hearing parents. Valli's elliptical poem "Hands" combines Whitmanesque celebration of language and nature with sophisticated use of space, handshapes, and rhythm—and it is over in a matter of seconds. Such works cannot be fully appreciated in one viewing; they require multiple readings and thoughtful, analytical responses. "Video gives me comfort that people can see things that are not obvious the first time through," says Lerner (pers. comm., Aug. 31, 1998). Artists now ask more of their audiences. They expect them not just to enjoy performances but also to wrestle with their nuances and challenging meanings.

This new density helped to move literature into the classroom. Although people have been writing about English literature for centuries, it did not become a widespread major in universities until around 1900. The study of English has grown into a sizable enterprise. Just as print helped to commercialize literature and professionalize the author, so it has commodified and professionalized audiences as well. English departments are often the largest on university campuses, and students pay to have professors (yet another intermediary between performer and audience) teach them how properly to read, analyze, and understand great texts. This system has numerous benefits: it introduces students to classic works they probably would not otherwise read and makes them better readers, thinkers, and writers. But it has also distanced literature further from everyday life.

The advent of video has produced a similar dynamic in ASL literature. In the last two decades, a growing number of universities have founded American Sign Language and Deaf studies programs. Bahan, Valli, Sam and Ted Supalla, and several other notable ASL performers are now affiliated with universities. While ASL video companies offer tapes to the general public, the majority of their sales are to university students, faculty, and libraries. Again, this trend has both positive and negative consequences. The academization of ASL literature spreads appreciation of ASL works, helps to legitimize and preserve ASL, creates rewarding jobs for Deaf people, and provides financial revenue for more ASL productions. However, it also nudges ASL further from the Deaf clubs and schools that used to be the center of the community and toward the ivory tower.

Print and film provide the impetus for such academic study of literature. By freezing literary texts, type and video open them to analysis. It is no coincidence that almost all of the ASL performances discussed in this volume are available on video. Yet it is not without paradox: to write in English about videotaped ASL performances is to examine them from several removes. First, as we have seen, video disrupts the essential tension between the performer and audience. Second, to write meaningfully in English about specific ASL performances is difficult. This anthology, with its accompanying DVD, offers perhaps the best solution to a challenging situation. It represents a groundbreaking step forward for ASL literary criticism. Still, both critics and readers would do well to keep the inadequacies of such an approach in mind.

STANDARDIZING LANGUAGES

The fourteenth-century poet Geoffrey Chaucer once complained that English had so much variation it was hard to know how to write it correctly. At the time, English was still largely in the oral domain and highly changeable. Scribes usually wrote in Latin, which learned people throughout Europe could read. Most books continued to be produced in Latin until the early sixteenth century (Febvre and Martin 1976, 224–33). However, as printing took hold, new books were increasingly published in vernacular languages, including English. As a result, English spelling and usages became more standardized. The eventual publication of dictionaries, grammars, and other reference materials made the variations diminish still further. Finally, print brought the work of such distinguished authors as Shakespeare and Wordsworth to thousands of people, enriching and expanding the vernacular English language.

We can observe a similar trend with ASL. Before film, sign was as changeable as other unwritten languages, and because it was oppressed for many years it often developed locally, with little coordination. Even today, Deaf signers will discuss the California sign for a concept versus a New York or Pennsylvania sign. For example, there are at least six variations of the sign for "birthday" in ASL. Just as the press helped to standardize English, film may well make ASL more nationally uniform, even as it preserves past variations.[6] Moreover, some signers never had the opportunity to learn ASL properly and at times mix up its grammar with English. Film may help in this area as well. We now have many reference-type videos of ASL, which show appropriate grammar, facial expressions, phrases, sign vocabulary, and the like. Recordings of master signers like M. J. Bienvenu and Ella Mae Lentz should help to enhance people's ASL usage further.

INCREASING POPULAR LITERACY

In addition to all its other effects, the printing press helped to increase literacy rates among the general population. As David Cressy (1990) points out, "Not until the sixteenth century did basic reading and writing abilities extend much beyond the clerical and gentle élite, and not before the nineteenth were they found among the majority of the population [of England]" (837–38). By making books cheap and plentiful, the press helped to create more readers and writers. Along the same lines, ASL videos are helping to promote "literacy" in ASL. The recordings of celebrated Deaf performers can only serve to increase viewers' sign fluency. As mentioned above, video has also had a powerful impact on ASL instruction, helping many more hearing people to learn at least the basics of the language. Today it is not uncommon to meet individuals who have some sign fluency. Video has played a subtle but crucial role in spreading knowledge of ASL.

The trend of more hearing people learning to sign has significant implications for Deaf people. On the positive side, it can make society more understanding, unbiased, and "Deaf-friendly," creating more opportunities for Deaf individuals. However, it might also lead to hearing people taking jobs that the Deaf have traditionally held or even affect the purity of ASL itself. As I. King Jordan, the president of Gallaudet University, says: "The more people who are hearing, who are English users who use sign, the more opportunities there are for the influence of English on sign language" (Manning 1996). If more hearing people than Deaf people sign, will Deaf Americans eventually lose control over their language? For these very reasons, at least some Deaf people have expressed reservations about teaching their cherished language to large numbers of others. Once again, we can observe film technology altering the boundaries that have traditionally separated hearing and Deaf people, with both potentially beneficial and detrimental consequences.

PROMOTING NATIONALISM

Finally, the invention of the printing press contributed to forces of nationalism in Europe. Benedict Anderson (1983) argues that print culture brought people together in more homogeneous groups. Readers of printed materials "formed, in their secular, particular, visible invisibility, the embryo for the nationally imagined community," he says (47). By breaking down the Latinate common culture and promoting countries' individual vernaculars, typography reinforced linguistic borders and national affiliations. In the same way, film has helped to shore up Deaf people's cultural identity. Lennard J. Davis (1995) points out that Deaf people, as a linguistic minority, can conceivably qualify as a separate ethnic group or even nationality (77). Through film, Deaf people have made this "nationality" more tangible. They have preserved a body of ASL works that amply demonstrates their shared language, culture, history, and worldview. Historic films by the NAD, Krauel, and others give the Deaf community a stronger sense of their own past. Films enable people to have more access to Deaf role models and eloquent ASL performers. They also connect Deaf people across time and space, allowing them to unite more strongly as a minority group. Above all, they give an increased sense of *legitimacy*. Deaf people can now point anyone with doubts about ASL literature or the Deaf community to a large array of videotapes that demonstrate conclusively the value and distinctiveness of the culture. The twentieth century has seen an increase in Deaf pride and political assertiveness, including the 1988 Deaf President Now protest at Gallaudet University and several important civil rights victories. One cannot say with certainty how much of a difference film has made in this new Deaf activism, but certainly it has had a role. Film technology has helped to transform the way both Deaf and hearing people think about sign language and the Deaf community.

<h2 style="text-align:center">WHITHER ASL LITERATURE?</h2>

The printing press created a demand for books that escalated for centuries after its invention. Now, despite apocalyptic warnings of "the death of the book," print appears to have a permanent place in our society. Will film technology lead to a similar rise in ASL performances? How will such videos relate to traditional manual Deaf culture? Part of the answers will depend on Deaf people themselves. As we have seen, film has paradoxical, two-sided effects on ASL literature. It preserves performances, makes them accessible to many more people, encourages artists to produce more sophisticated works, and gives new cultural authority to Deaf people. Yet video also threatens the same manual culture that is its wellspring. It takes ASL works away from Deaf clubs and schools and commodifies them for mainstream America. It invites solitary viewing rather than collective assembly, makes dynamic performances invariable, and disrupts the all-important tension between performer and audience. By making Deaf images more accessible to hearing people, film has built bridges between the Deaf and hearing, fostering more respect and understanding. Yet as hearing people increasingly make up the audiences for Deaf works, and as film enables more hearing people to learn to sign, Deaf Americans may be losing some control over their language and literature.

Like Native Americans and other minority groups in the United States, Deaf people now find themselves in a curious predicament, where they are simultaneously gaining political power and losing some command over their cultural artifacts. Just as Native Americans and others have turned to festivals and other assemblies to help preserve their cultural traditions in a modern world, so now we have Deaf Awareness Days, ASL Appreciation Days, and Deaf festivals and conferences to nourish cultural identity and pride. Here Deaf people gather to interact in the traditional manual way and often participate in live, exuberant ASL performances. Such events offer a possible antidote to some of the destabilizing effects of film and modern technology on ASL literature. Deaf people are in a very different position today than in 1913, when Veditz made the first grainy black-and-white films of ASL. "As long as we have Deaf people on earth, we will have signs," Veditz said (quoted in Padden and Humphries 1988, 36). "It is my hope that we will all love and guard our beautiful sign language as the noblest gift God has given to Deaf people." If Deaf people continue to heed Veditz's injunction to "love and guard" ASL, it will surely continue to thrive.

NOTES

1. George W. Veditz, "The Preservation of Sign Language," quoted (in translation from the sign language) in Padden and Humphries (1988, 57). For an excerpt of Veditz's original 1913 speech, see the video *The Preservation of American Sign Language* (1997).

2. Despite the development of glosses and other systems for representing ASL through writing, Burnet's observation still holds largely true today. This poses a paradoxical challenge for scholars who want to produce meaningful criticism of ASL storytelling and poetry: we are essentially trying to write about a language that cannot be written.

3. See Bahan, chapter 2 of this volume, for additional discussion of this genre and other forms of ASL folklore.

4. Perhaps this, along with captioned television, computers, and other new technology, helps to explain why some Deaf clubs around the nation are closing due to declining membership.

5. For a helpful overview of this ASL folklore, see Rutherford (1993).

6. One series of videos, *ASL across America,* compares differing regional signs, adding another component to the history of sign on film.

REFERENCES

Anderson, Benedict. 1983. *Imagined Communities: Reflections on the Origin and Spread of Nationalism.* London: Verso.

ASL across America: A Video Series of Conversations in American Sign Language. 1989. Videocassette. Burtonsville, MD: Sign Media.

Bahan, Benjamin, and Samuel Supalla. 1992. *"Bird of a Different Feather" and "For a Decent Living."* American Sign Language Literature Series. Videocassette. San Diego, CA: DawnPictures.

Bloom, Harold. 1973. *The Anxiety of Influence: A Theory of Poetry.* New York: Oxford University Press.

Burnet, John R. 1835. *Tales of the Deaf and Dumb.* Newark, NJ: Benjamin Olds.

Cressy, David. "Literacy." 1990. In *Encyclopedia of Literature and Criticism,* ed. Martin Coyle, 837–47. New York: Gale Research.

Davis, Lennard J. 1995. *Enforcing Normalcy: Disability, Deafness, and the Body.* London: Verso.

Eastman, Gilbert. 1991. *Live at SMI: Gilbert Eastman.* Videocassette. Burtonsville, MD: Sign Media.

Edwards, Viv, and Thomas J. Sienkewicz. 1990. *Oral Cultures Past and Present: Rappin' and Homer.* Oxford: Basil Blackwell.

Eisenstein, Elizabeth. 1979. *The Printing Press as an Agent of Change.* Cambridge: Cambridge University Press.

Feather, John. 1990. "Publishing before 1800." In *Encyclopedia of Literature and Criticism,* ed. Martin Coyle, 848–61. Detroit: Gale Research.

Febvre, Lucien, and Henri-Jean Martin. 1976. *The Coming of the Book: The Impact of Printing, 1450–1800.* Trans. David Gerard. London: NLB. (Original pub. 1958.)

Finnegan, Ruth. 1988. *Orality and Literacy.* Oxford: Basil Blackwell.

Gee, James Paul, and Walter J. Ong. 1983. "An Exchange on American Sign Language and Deaf Culture." *Language and Style: An International Journal* 16:234–37.

Hirsch, E. D., Jr. 1977. *The Philosophy of Composition.* Chicago: University of Chicago Press.

Kouponeti. 1869. [Letter.] *Deaf-Mutes' Friend* 1 (December): 379.

Lentz, Ella Mae. 1995. *The Treasure: Poems by Ella Mae Lentz.* Videocassette. Berkeley, CA: In Motion Press.

Lord, Albert B. 1963. "Homer and Other Epic Poetry." In *A Companion to Homer,* ed. A. J. B. Wace and F. H. Stubbings, 179–241. New York: Macmillan, 1963.

Manning, Anita. 1996. "Signing Catches on as a Foreign Language." *USA Today,* March 6, 4D.

Miller, Mary Beth. 1992. *Live at SMI: Mary Beth Miller.* Videocassette. Burtonsville, MD: Sign Media.

Ong, Walter J. 1982. *Orality and Literacy: The Technologizing of the Word.* New York: Methuen.

Padden, Carol, and Tom Humphries. 1988. *Deaf in America: Voices from a Culture.* Cambridge, MA: Harvard University Press.

The Preservation of American Sign Language: The Complete Historical Collection. 1997. Videocassette. Burtonsville, MD: Sign Media.

Redden, Laura. 1858. "A Few Words about the Deaf and Dumb." *American Annals of the Deaf and Dumb* 10:177–81.

Rutherford, Susan. 1993. *A Study of American Deaf Folklore.* Burtonsville, MD: Linstok Press.

Sacks, Oliver. 1989. *Seeing Voices: A Journey into the World of the Deaf.* New York: Perennial-Harper.

Supalla, Ted. 1994. *Charles Krauel: A Profile of a Deaf Filmmaker.* Videocassette. San Diego, CA: DawnPictures.

———. 1998. "Historical Films: A Window to Deaf America in the Early 20th Century." Lecture, 1998 Annual ASL/Deaf Culture Lecture Series, University of Virginia, Charlottesville, February 6.

Valli, Clayton. 1995. *ASL Poetry: Selected Works of Clayton Valli.* Hosted by Lon Kuntze. Videocassette. San Diego, CA: DawnPictures.

FOUR

Deaf American Theater

CYNTHIA PETERS

In 1993, *Institution Blues* enjoyed full houses during its two-day run at a Deaf community theater in Washington, D.C.[1] The three-hour play about the imminent closing of a state residential school struck very close to home, for at the time increasing numbers of schools for deaf children were shutting down across the nation. Outside the Deaf family, these schools are the primary breeding ground of Deaf culture, and thus their closure is tantamount to gutting the Deaf community. Theatergoers were immediately drawn into this dramatic production; indeed, as the lights dimmed and actors/protesters entered from the back, marched down the aisles waving their placards, and ascended the stage, many viewers joined in the protest. They left their seats and, with arms and hands pumping, signed, "Keep the institution open! Keep the institution open!" They stopped only when one of the protest rally leaders moved to the front of the stage and began speaking passionately and eloquently to the energized house.

Deaf Americans stage numerous productions every year, ranging from mainstream plays, such as Gallaudet University's fall 1997 production of *Dr. Jekyll and Mr. Hyde,* to vaudevillelike productions, such as the National Theatre of the Deaf's *My Third Eye* and *Parade.*[2] In between are both original but conventional plays focusing on Deaf culture, such as *Sign Me Alice, Tales from a Clubroom,* and *A Deaf Family Diary,*[3] and hybrid productions that mix classical and indigenous theater, such as *Institution Blues.* Most are mainstream plays or faithful adaptations; only a handful of original Deaf productions see the light of day. In the 1990s playgoers could see Willy

Conley's *The Water Falls, The Hearing Test,* and *FALLING ON HEARING EYES;* Bob Daniels's *I Didn't Hear That Color* and *Hand in Hand, Foot in Mouth: An Unmusical;* Michele Verhoosky's *Middle of Nowhere* and *I See the Moon;* and Shanny Mow's *Counterfeits, Cat Spanking Machine,* and *Letters from Heaven. Deafywood,* compiled by John Maucere, toured the country for three years in the late 1990s.[4] A few other original productions have been written and produced by theater departments at Gallaudet University, the National Technical Institute for the Deaf, and California State University at Northridge over the past few years. Undoubtedly many unstaged scripts are composed by would-be playwrights working on their own or in creative writing classes or workshops.[5]

Despite their diversity, original scripts by Deaf American playwrights share some general characteristics. Like minority drama in general, these plays draw in varying degrees on both indigenous (i.e., unique to Deaf culture) and conventional (i.e., mainstream) elements. Because of this dual nature, each counters mainstream literary and dramatic conventions in one way or another. In many instances, plays (like *Alice*) are conventional in form but original in subject.

MODERN CONVENTIONAL THEATER AS HIGH ART

Michael Bristol, a drama historian, argues that today's conventional mainstream theater as a whole is a fairly formal affair that helps support the status quo.[6] Most municipalities of any size have at least one separate building—the "theater"—just for dramatic productions. On the infrequent occasions that the building is in use, theatergoers make dinner reservations, dress up, and head out for a night on the town. Once they arrive and get ensconced in their plush seats, the lights dim and the action begins, apart from and above them on a raised stage. Theatergoers stay in their seats, players stay on the stage, and the two groups interact very little. The audience, mostly upper class and college educated, has come to see what the playwright and director have crafted and how the stars interpret what has been given them. The theatergoers have come to be passively entertained, and the privilege rarely comes cheaply.

Manifesting the alienation and differentiation of social structure that Henri Lefebvre finds characteristic of modernity, mainstream theater often has the quality of a high art.[7] Rather than being engaged with everyday life, it usually aims at the transcendent and serious; even its comedy is of a sophisticated sort. As an artistic enterprise, it is carefully crafted and orchestrated for aesthetic ends.[8] Most plays observe the conventional (neo-classical) unities of time, place, and action; in three to five acts, replete with dialogue mouthed by actors all over the stage, they move linearly from start to middle to denouement to end. Typical Broadway dramas and musicals possess scintillating songs or tragic, brooding story lines, marvelous stage scenery, and tightly structured movement. They are high theater that seeks to entertain rather than to accentuate cultural identity (a viewer's sense of self) or to guide an audience through difficult economic and political realities.[9] Rather than addressing critical issues, they usually offer momentary escape: for two to three hours in a darkened hall, the theatergoer is caught up in a completely different, artificial world.

This kind of theater bears little resemblance to the earliest Western drama, which was incorporated into religious festivities and rituals. As part of the general "progress" of Western civilization and art, plays have been made to conform with "classical" conventions derived from Greek drama, whose characteristics have then been "improved on."[10] In contrast, folk or popular manifestations—including vaudeville and its various, sometimes physical, acts—are often perceived to be simple or juvenile forms, worthy of interest only insofar as they have the potential to evolve toward more complex and sophisticated literary or dramatic art.

However, in becoming more "developed," modern theater has traded in its original social and political impulse for an aesthetics of the beautiful. Bristol observes of the older forms, "Because of its capacity to create and sustain a briefly intensified social life, the theater is festive and political as well as literary—a privileged site for the celebration and critique of the needs and concerns of the polis."[11] Theater in this sense is an opportunity for people to gather for a heightened experience that has to do with matters of interest to the community. It may rely on artifice and exaggeration, but not nearly so much as the conventional theater of today. It still partakes of everyday life with an eye to social, civic, religious, and economic conditions.

In the past, dramatics were a more lively and communal affair, as well as an integral part of the social, civic, religious, and economic fabric of local life.[12] People flocked to plays, processions, and various ceremonials and rituals. In classical Greece, the tragedies and comedies viewed in outdoor amphitheaters were an essential part of community life. During festival times in the Middle Ages and Renaissance—such as market days, fairs, and parish feasts—dramatic performances both serious and comic were customary. People gathered to see miracle plays, which depicted the lives of the saints; mystery plays, whose cycles covered history from the fall of Satan to the Resurrection (and which often interpolated comic material); and morality plays, allegorical dramas whose characters were abstract personifications struggling to achieve salvation. Such forms addressed the deep concerns of their audiences, as well as playing an important social role in their lives.

A THEATER OF TWO WORLDS

Like the theatricals of the Middle Ages, indigenous Deaf American theater remains close to the everyday lives of its viewers. When Deaf playwrights create original scripts, they tend to focus on immediate social and political matters. Thus, as it focused on the closing of residential schools for the deaf, *Institution Blues* dramatized related issues in ways that highlighted Deaf culture and strengthened theatergoers in their resolve to take some action. They were caught up during and after the play, lingering on the sidewalk outside the theater and debating the issues that the play had raised.

This socially engaged theater arises in part from Deaf Americans' position as a smaller culture within mainstream culture, part of it and yet simultaneously apart from it. Almost all original scripts, stage productions, and films are concerned in some way with this two-world condition, either explicitly or implicitly. The two-world condition of medieval Europe underlies the serious laughter of carnival and the theatricals interwoven with the people's social and religious life. The experience of living in two worlds is just as important in shaping Deaf American theater. For example:

- *A Deaf Family Diary* depicts a young Deaf couple endeavoring to get their respective Deaf and hearing families to coexist.
- *Sign Me Alice* portrays a young woman's struggle to be herself and not something mainstream society wants her to be.
- *Tales from a Clubroom* takes place entirely and focuses wholly on members' relationships within a Deaf club, but one is always aware that outside this oasis is hearing society.
- *Deafula,* one of the first original Deaf American films, is permeated by

the double and conflicted identity of the protagonist, even though deafness is barely mentioned.[13]

This two-world condition is quite explicitly a subject of the National Theatre of the Deaf's *My Third Eye* (1971–72). Interspersed through its segments of diverse formats are short narratives by individual performers. One performer relates his experience of entering a residential school for the first time: "We walked into the building, and once inside I was immediately struck by a medicinal, institutional smell. This did not look like a hospital, or like any other building I had ever seen before. My mother bent down, turned me toward her, and said: 'This is where you will get all your education. You will live here for a while. Don't worry, I will see you again later.'"[14] This typical story of a deaf child born into a Deaf family is emblematic of the clash between two cultures. In many of these accounts of childhood, hearing people—the other culture—are initially shadowy, background figures. Then, suddenly, they break into the child's world. In *My Third Eye,* a young boy becomes disoriented when he encounters the alien organization of the school with its aural perspective and its hierarchical structure. School is the place where he comes to realize that others—people in mainstream society—have a different view of reality, a different way of thinking, that in fact is authoritative.[15]

For the most part, those within the mainstream are blithely unaware of any world outside their own. They tend toward a uniform and univocal view of deaf people, relying on neat stereotypes to make sense of things. For instance, the popular 1994 TV miniseries *The Stand* presented deaf people as saintly speech readers who integrate amazingly well into mainstream society,[16] while the truth is that most deaf people are not very good speech readers, ground themselves in Deaf communities, and are no more saintly than anyone else.

Bakhtin's festive critique—which does not allow one way of looking at things, one established truth, one established reality—emerges when the official and dominant are mixed with the popular and subordinate. Many indigenous Deaf productions work diligently to demystify pervasive universal and univocal outlooks, relying on a double-voicedness that highlights the relationship between the reality constructed by aural authority and a Deaf reality whose perspectives, needs, and values—frequently ignored or overlooked—are quite different from those of mainstream society. Such double-voicedness sets one point of view against the other, contrasts one evaluation or tone with the other. Thus in the "Side Show" segment of *My Third Eye,* the assertive, self-assured ringmaster—a woman—rebuts the feminization of Deaf culture by mainstream culture and media; in this drama it is the voice readers—those who interpret for the hearing audience—who are inarticulate, limited, and passive (i.e., exhibit the majority culture's view of deaf behavior).[17] In every production, the dominant assumption that sign language is "mere gestures" is countered by the reality that it is a legitimate, vibrant, complex language.

Moreover, the conventional position is often revealed to be rooted in ignorance. In *A Deaf Family Diary,* the Deaf family of the bride find themselves dealing with the groom's hearing parents, who simply do not know how to raise and treat their deaf children and future daughter-in-law. These parents so thoroughly fail to relate to the Deaf family that the play descends into a comedy of errors.

In *Institution Blues,* the state clearly errs in closing the residential state school: the authorities—the blockheads!—simply do not understand. The reporter covering the protest rally is equally lacking in comprehension, and the whole play concerns his learning enough to pass on the true state of affairs to general readers. To show him how a school that segregates Deaf Americans can be beneficial, two alumni take the clueless reporter in hand and back through the years to their own student days. In play-within-a-play flashbacks, they and others act out various scenes that look at the assigning of sign names, the teaching of social conventions such as table manners, the efficacy of peer instruction in the classroom, a Literary Night, a suicide, a prom, and a graduation. As the play's action progresses, it continues to move back and forth in time from the present-day rally aimed at saving the school to the past experiences of the alumni.

A *MUNDUS INVERSUS*

Like many popular rituals of the Middle Ages, these Deaf American plays festively and carnivalesquely turn upside down the usual relations between minority and majority, upending the dominant and focusing on those who are usually marginalized. As we have seen, this is typical of carnival, which, as Carol Simpson Stern and Bruce Henderson explain, "inverts the normal hierarchical order, turning everything upside down and inviting laughter.

The laughter destabilizes authority, not allowing any one view of the world to rule. [Carnival] gives expression to multiple voices and ways of seeing the world, liberating people through the socially acceptable mechanism of laughter."[18]

We see this inversion particularly clearly if we turn once again to the "Side Show" segment of *My Third Eye,* a circus scene with a ringmaster and acrobats. The videotape version shows a red-and-white striped tent in the background and in the foreground a large enclosure—akin to a large, old-fashioned birdcage—with two voice readers inside. Suddenly, the ringmaster appears and strikes the ground with an imaginary whip. In top hat and black leather boots, she promises to tell about "strange things . . . a strange people"—the two voice readers caged as if they were an exhibit. At her behest, various acrobats go through their acts, while the voice readers stand virtually motionless (speaking the performers' words for those in the audience who can only hear). As the acrobats perform onstage, the ringmaster extols the interaction, expressiveness, and freedom of American Sign Language (ASL), which utilizes the face and the whole body. At the same time, she dismisses the poker faces, small mouth movements, and limp body appendages of the voice readers (representing mainstream society). The advantages of the visual language and culture contrast with the stiffness (unnaturalness) and impersonality of the aural-oral language and culture. In effect, Deaf culture is depicted as fluid and free—a little three-ring circus within an aural majority culture shown as sadly limited, inflexible, and authoritarian.

Much of the world today puts a priority on aural communication, whereas Deaf Americans valorize visual/tactile communication and believe they have the best of it. In "Side Show" the distinction between the two modalities is comically drawn. Various acrobats aptly demonstrate how people talk without looking at one another and how one person is hesitant to touch another to get his or her attention. On a train, a woman jumps when another passenger, unable to get her attention aurally, gingerly taps her on the shoulder. A second woman caught up in her own thoughts plays with a pencil in her mouth, moving it with clockwork precision from one side to the other without touching it with her hands. In another vignette, a mother attempts to get her affectionate young son to vocalize "mother," making him touch her throat (and preventing him from signing MOTHER); when he finally does utter an approximation of the word, she beams proudly and shows off the obviously frustrated and miserable little boy. All these portrayals have a slightly parodic quality, and their deft presentation is uplifting for their Deaf viewers.

CULTURAL ENCYCLOPEDIAS

In Deaf American theater, the creation of and delight in a feeling of collectivity take precedence over the more narrow assessment of literary and artistic values.[19] The aim is not to put on a well-made, classical, three- to five-act comedy or tragedy but to bring together and foster cultural pride and identity in a widely scattered people. In its more indigenous form, the Deaf American play is cultural performance, uniting the community (including its marginal members) and facilitating a bonding and defining of the culture's identity and viability. By participating in this production (whether by staging, acting, or simply viewing it), Deaf Americans construct and revel in their identity.[20] In this respect, nativist Deaf American drama resembles the ancient Greek epics, described by the cultural historian Werner Sollars as the "cultural encyclopedias" of their times. As cultural encyclopedias, they attempted to appeal to and bring together a widely dispersed people.[21] In classical times, the Greeks were scattered about in small communities, which sometimes fought among themselves; but they were at greater risk from outside forces and cultural systems. By fostering a cultural identity and thus a shared loyalty, the epics gave the Greek peoples a common history and helped enlarge their sense of a homeland. Drawing on this cultural identity encouraged them to band together to resist foreign expansionist empires.

As cultural encyclopedias, *Institution Blues, My Third Eye,* and other more nativist Deaf dramas make available to a heterogeneous and widely scattered people essential knowledge of both Deaf culture and mainstream culture.[22] Using both vernacular Deaf and mainstream languages and genres, both artistic and extra-artistic, the nativist drama helps Deaf Americans better understand and connect to their own culture and also learn how to deal with hearing society. Indeed, Deaf performances often include too much cultural information. In response to audience feedback at its first staging, *Institution Blues,* which originally ran almost four hours, was whittled down. Even in its shortened form, the play is a big, sprawling production that encompasses a large part of Deaf culture and spans some twenty years, presenting what Peter Stallybrass and Allon White call "a world of topsy-turvy, of heteroglot exuberance, of ceaseless overrunning and excess where all is mixed, hybrid, ritually degraded and defiled."[23]

A COMPREHENSIVE FORM

The inclusiveness of indigenous Deaf American theater represents another break with mainstream dramatic conventions—here, those of unity and linearity. On its surface, *Institution Blues* is a traditional play of three acts and a single theme. But underneath, it is a cultural treasure trove of ASL poetry, ASL art, biography, eulogy, oratory, fairy tales, games, skits, jokes, and satire, framed as a kind of Literary Night. Sollars argues that more popular, festive productions—in contrast with those that adhere to conventions of high literary and dramatic art—characteristically include such miscellanies of genres and forms.[24] In such heterogeneity art and life are intertwined, not constructed as separate realms, and the more indigenous Deaf productions unite the two.[25]

The structure of many of these vaudevillelike productions is decentered and eccentric, for the producers are less concerned with generic distinctions or with creating a homogeneous, "complete," aesthetic product than with reflecting Deaf culture in all its multifacetedness and building a community of laughter. In the process, the producers have fun with the exaggerated, the disproportioned, the abundant, and the diverse. Deaf theater is carnivalesque: an "experience . . . opposed to all that [is] ready-made and completed, to all pretense of immutability, [seeking] a dynamic expression; it demand[s] ever changing, playful, undefined forms."[26] The spirit of carnival plays, experiments, and mixes things up, rather than adhering to dramatic stipulations, classical or otherwise. Such inclusive theatricals are an image-ideal of and for a community as a heterogeneous and boundless totality (Bakhtin's teeming "grotesque body").[27]

Not surprisingly, as Don Bangs documents in his study of practices and principles in Deaf American theater, many original dramatic productions are explicitly vaudevillelike and festive, along the lines of *My Third Eye*.[28] Indeed, many display nonrigid structures and generic diversity. For instance, the theater program at the National Technical Institute for the Deaf (NTID) in Rochester, New York, got its start in 1969, when students under Robert Panara organized a variety show as the first half of "An Experiment in Dramatics." When the NTID Drama Club was established in 1970, its first production was *Footlight Fever*, which contained a number of comedy sketches and routines.[29] In Ohio, not too far away, the first production of the Fairmount Theatre of the Deaf (FTD) was *My Eyes Are My Ears*, a theatrical collage based on popular entertainment forms used by Deaf Americans. FTD's *Story Theatre* (1970), although an adaptation, featured mime, improvisation, visual signplay, and general horsing around. In FTD's *Alice in Deafinity* (1975), Alice traveled in a Deaf world in which each Deaf person signed in his or her own way.[30]

Productions in New York and California in the 1980s and 1990s have also featured a large number of nativist or adapted plays with an inherently heterogeneous quality.[31] *Telling Stories*, Gallaudet University's original offering during the Deaf Way contest, was anything but a conventional dramatic production.[32] In their focus on parts rather than a polished whole, these theatricals connect to carnival; Gustavo Pérez Firmat reminds us that "carnival is partial to parts. Carnival is part time. During carnival every part aspires to the condition of wholeness."[33]

Vaudeville in Deaf culture goes back to the nineteenth century, when it was a vital and popular form of entertainment for deaf and hearing people alike.[34] According to Don Bangs, however, the hearing tradition influenced the Deaf tradition only indirectly and relatively late. Both the acting method and the melodramatic intertitles in the silent films of the 1910s and 1920s drew on vaudeville styles, and these films in turn influenced Deaf American vaudeville by supplying plots and other material. (The silent films were accessible; the talkies that superseded them were not.) When sound was successfully meshed with motion pictures, vaudeville began to die out in mainstream society—but it took on even greater importance in Deaf culture.

With the advent of the talkies, many Deaf Americans turned to vaudevillelike entertainment. Emerson Romero, a famous Deaf star of silent films, organized programs of playlets and skits that combined sign language with pantomime and acting.[35] Wolf Bragg established a New York amateur theater company that put on adaptations of short plays or short stories. The Chicago Silent Dramatic Club did skits and sign language adaptations of one-act plays, all within a vaudeville format. Other similar community groups and indigenous theater companies around the country produced traditional ASL-based entertainment for Deaf Americans: that is, short comedies and variety acts.

Even Gallaudet University, a stronghold of academe, put on vaudeville productions. The vaudeville tradition at Gallaudet in fact began in the 1880s, when college thespians performed shadow and open pantomime and produced spoofs of college life. Men had their Saturday Night Dramatics Club, founded in 1886, with an accent on the amusing; women joined together to form the Jollity Club. Even the Ballard Literary Society, which emphasized the literary, was inclined to present "shorties" such as skits, farce, and sketches. The college's drama department, despite generally favoring conventional theater, at first promoted vaudeville, farce, comedy, melodrama, costume drama, and classical tragedy. It later changed its focus from practical theater to the academic study of drama, leaving various student organizations on campus to carry on the performance tradition.[36]

The National Theatre of the Deaf (NTD), funded by the federal government and geared to mainstream audiences, has also gone in for the medley, although in a modernist (i.e., symbolic, artistic, layered) way. Usually the company presents several short works adapted to sign language in accordance with its philosophy of "See the sign, hear the word."[37] Most NTD productions are simultaneously presented in spoken and sign language, and the company generally avoids Deaf forms and approaches or material specifically related to the deafness of the actors. Aiming at making both the hearing public more aware of deaf people and deaf people more aware of highly artistic and sophisticated theater, it attempts to present "hearing theater" in a visual form and to enhance the theater experience by using material inherently rich in visually dramatic components. Thus it often showcases haiku and other short poems that have strong visual imagery and lend themselves well to the creative use of sign language.[38]

NTD's *Under Milkwood*, for example, is not a conventional three- to five-act play.[39] Based on Dylan Thomas's radio play that offers vignettes of a day in the life of the residents of a Welsh village, the play switches focus from one group of people to another (with some of the players taking on multiple roles). This emphasis on characterization and dialogue makes it possible for the audience to pay attention to a few individuals at a time. As the dialogue is translated into artistic sign language—as much as possible, given that the voice readers are simultaneously reading the original words—the performers concentrate on the ASL/English translation. In doing so, they showcase the visual imagery of sign language and make beautiful pictures in the air.

NTD has staged three indigenous productions: *My Third Eye* (1971–71), *Parade* (1975–76), and *Parzival* (1982–83).[40] *Parzival,* though not vaude-villelike in tone or approach, is a medley. Personal quest stories told by individual performers—several of whom took part in creating those stories—are woven into an epic tale about a questing Arthurian knight. *Parade* has many more characteristics of vaudeville. On its title's framework are hung a number of demonstrations on the part of a group of Deaf protesters who want to establish their own political state, "New Deaf Dominion."[41] It also offers a number of comic vignettes: one features a Deaf American Columbus who discovers a new land, and another provides a glimpse of a Deaf soap opera entitled *As the Hand Turns.* Still another stars a Deaf Superman who does amazing feats and accomplishes daring rescues.[42]

My Third Eye is the most miscellaneous of the three. The videotape version begins by providing a view of the stage through shadowy bars; luminescent globes resembling three balloons hang suspended in the background. This opening segues into a birthing sequence, "Promenade," during which one player after another emerges from under a woman's immense skirt. As the sequence draws to an end, two of the players begin to reminisce about their respective childhoods, either conversing with a fellow performer or speaking directly to the audience. "Side Show," the circus scene discussed above, follows. Later segments, "Manifest" and "Curtain Raiser," include choreographed chorus numbers, "The Quick Brown Fox" and "Three Blind Mice." Other presentations highlight the iconic qualities of ASL. For instance, in "Manifest" several performers showcase ASL's capacity to convey different kinds of light: the breaking of day, fireflies, a flashlight, streetlights, lightning, and so on. In "A Little Dictionary of Slang," the actors depict emotional states, such as the different degrees of love. Frequently, they line up and perform a kind of revue, each doing a brief turn and then going off to the side.

Many nativist Deaf dramatic productions defy classical unity and linearity, as well as ignoring classical decorum. In other words, they disregard the conventional separation of the high genres from the low genres, high behavior from low behavior, tragedy from comedy. To be sure, such generic boundary crossing has a history as long as that of these respective genres; perhaps the playwright best known for nonconformity is Shakespeare, whose tragedies feature rustics and fools and whose "problem plays" and "tragicomedies" famously defy categorization. To this day some object to these liberties; but Shakespeare's refusal to obey the classical canons may also have contributed to his popularity, especially among the common people in his audience, the groundlings.

My Third Eye, like many other vaudevillelike Deaf American productions, is a hodgepodge of the high, serious, and artistic and the low, vulgar, and jokey. Right after the wrenching story of a small boy having to leave home and family to study at a residential school is the rambunctious, bouncy "Side Show." As one critic commented, "The play might best be described as a bittersweet adventure, often depicting incidents that are at once joyous and defeating."[43] *My Third Eye* combines the serious, high "Biography" with the low, comic "Sideshow"; the poignant narratives with the musically visual and amusing group performance of "Three Blind Mice"; and the entertaining ASL signplay with the highly artistic ASL tableau. It is a miscellany structured without regard for classical decorum.

Such mixing comes naturally to Deaf American theater, which exists in two worlds, negotiating two modalities of language and two belief systems. Indeed, some ASL art has no counterpart in any other literature and thus no label. For example, is the ABC story a narrative, a poem, or a performance? Is the ASL tableau a poem, a story, or a performance? Transgression is inevitable when conventional distinctions do not apply.

Graybill's *A Deaf Family Diary* is a more conventional play from the standpoint of classical stipulations. Yet it also depicts more of the vulgarities of life than one would expect in a mainstream comedy. In one scene, the bride's father, who has just undergone an operation, tells the full story to his hearing, soon-to-be relatives. The groom's uptight family is scandalized and set reeling by the gory details—the slicing of the stomach area, the probing to locate the cancerous part, the cutting away of the malignancy, and the sewing up of the incision—but the bride's family relishes the father's artistic use of ASL, including the excellent, if very graphic, visual imagery.

COLLABORATIVE THEATER

The more indigenous Deaf American vaudeville productions also differ from conventional plays in the degree of collaboration involved, both in the work as a whole and in its numerous constitutive elements (the individual acts). The ASL tableau, which is structured by visual images and scenes rather than thematically, is especially dependent on the performers' interaction. In this sequence of images composed of form and movement, which produces an imagic narrative, Deaf Americans relate to the world visually and develop it rhetorically. Rather than presenting oral discourse arranged in a more or less logical progression, the tableau fuses painting, drama (or cinema), and narrative or poetry. The form both exists independently and appears often within dramatic productions, including *Institution Blues* and *My Third Eye*.

The Collective as Creator

Deaf American theater often breaks with the rigid and hierarchical divisions of labor in the Western theater tradition.[44] Despite the large number of participants in a conventional modern play, only a few are seen to be ultimately responsible for the enterprise: the playwright, the director (and sometimes the producer), and the headliners. After a playwright hammers a story into a script, the director stages that script more or less as given, and the leading actors usually work within the constraints set by the director. Every entity and nonentity, from the director and leading lady and man down to the lowliest stagehand, has his or her separate function. Everyone's job is compartmentalized—including that of the theatergoers, who have come to be entertained.

In particular, the mainstream playwright is seen to be a highly creative individual, who receives the bulk of the accolades or condemnation drawn by the play. Even on those occasions when an actor or director draws much attention in a particular production, the play remains the author's—Eugene O'Neill's work, not that of Jason Robards or Jose Quintero. The Deaf dramatist, in contrast, is more of a skilled cultural worker. He or she is not innately more creative or important than the others involved. Don Bangs, for example, was a jack-of-all-trades at SignRise Cultural Arts: he often wrote (that is, guided all the brainstorming and structuring of one or more scripts), directed, acted, and handled public relations. He was also heavily involved in fund-raising, reviewing, and attending to the company's correspondence. Many other Deaf American intellectuals are at once playwrights, public relations agents, producers, fund-raisers, political activists, and teachers.

This de-emphasizing of specialized labor applies to the audience as well. Bakhtin observes that everyone participates during carnival. The distinction between actors and spectators disappears: in the Middle Ages, the clowns and tools of the festivals "remained clowns and fools always," representing "the carnival spirit in everyday life out of carnival season."[45] Productions such as the mystery plays involved large segments of the community; in England, different plays came to be performed by local guilds. Likewise in Deaf American theater, the local populace comes together to create, improvise, and dramatize. So few scripts exist that original text must be created first, a task that is often undertaken collectively.

NTD's *My Third Eye* is a case in point: to come up with the opening sequence, company members were asked to share their individual and collective aspirations in several improvisational planning sessions. J Ranelli,[46] the director, made selections from these and then unified them all by having the actors emerge from under a huge blue cloth in an approximation of a multiple birthing. One company member, Dorothy Miles, encouraged her fellow thespians to discuss their stories about aspects of the two-world condition that they found most disturbing or memorable, and from these reminiscences "Side Show" was born.[47] Thus the director acts more as a facilitator than a taskmaster; and this collective effort extends to producing the play. *My Third Eye,* writes Stephen Baldwin in his history of the National Theatre of the Deaf, "marked the first time that deaf company members had assumed responsibility for directing and designing sets and costumes."[48]

In a typical Deaf American theatrical production, therefore, this process of creating a script is as important as the end product. As those involved in drawing up the script share ideas, buried knowledge and cultural codes come to light. For instance, when company members searched for examples of differences between Deaf and hearing culture, they thought of the famous balcony scene between Romeo and Juliet: such a fervent address to one at a window high above has no place in Deaf culture, where closer proximity and interaction are preferred. Thus this scene was chosen for the "Side Show" segment. Such recollection and discovery of cultural values make theater in Deaf culture both a forum for playmakers' concerns and a cultural encyclopedia for viewers.

Parade also was a collaborative effort; the actors were heavily involved in determining the content and structure of the play, contributing some ideas and suggestions and objecting to and discarding others.[49] Even what might appear at first to be Pat Graybill's one-man show, the collage of vignettes about the residential school experience that constitutes *The World Accord-*

ing to Pat, was created through improvisations and storytelling sessions. The creators of *A Deaf Family Diary* went on the Internet to solicit ideas and suggestions. According to Don Bangs, the guiding spirit of SignRise Cultural Arts, it took a year to develop the play: "Countless hours of interviews, meetings, and rehearsals and 304 pages of writes and rewrites later, *Diary* . . . finally leaped upon the stage." The ongoing creative, collaborative process continued even during rehearsals. Graybill, the director, explains, "When rehearsals began, we had no inkling as to how the play would come together. A brief premise and the preliminary draft of the first four scenes were all we received from the playwright a few days in advance. . . . It is the first time for me to direct a play which is being written and rewritten during rehearsal."[50]

The Collective as Hero

In the hierarchy of mainstream theater, leading men and ladies are near the top. Popular theater and movie stars are often sought to "carry a play," and theatergoers are attracted more by these famous actors than by the play itself or by the idea of being part of a community. In contrast, Deaf American theater has a foundation in ensemble acting, a practice that reflects the communal nature of the culture. Productions are created or selected to showcase the performers as a whole rather than one or two stars. Accordingly, we have not just one hero or heroine but a collective as hero. This pattern is typical of many minority works and performances, in which a whole community is the protagonist and a blurry collective (mainstream society) serves as the antagonist.[51]

When a production does feature a solo performance or spotlight one leading character, that performer is singled out not as an individual but as representative: the spotlight is on *the* Deaf American, the culture, or the language, rather than *a* Deaf American. In comparable memorable mainstream plays, the focus is on one person (usually a man): think of Shakespeare's *Hamlet* or Andrew Lloyd Webber's *Phantom of the Opera.* Vacillating prince and disfigured denizen of the opera house—both are created to be unique individuals. Yet just about the only heroines or heroes in Deaf American theater history are the famous Alice of the two *Sign Me Alice* plays and Sarah of *Children of a Lesser God,* and they are hardly unusual characters; Alices and Sarahs can be found across the United States.[52] Most of the other renowned Deaf American plays examined in this chapter—including *My Third Eye, Institution Blues,* and *A Deaf Family Diary*—are ensemble presentations. Many are vaudevillelike productions with many performers.

Interaction and Viewer Participation

Another aspect of the collective ethos in Deaf culture and theater is the expectation of an intimate connection between actors and spectators. Mainstream theater generally involves carefully orchestrated action and dialogue taking place on a raised stage apart from the audience. In contrast, traditional Deaf American theater is typically interactive, with much less separation between play and viewers. Because they are addressing the playgoers in ASL, an "oral" vernacular that itself is naturally interactive, many Deaf actors and playwrights seek collaboration not only within their productions but also with the viewers.

Patrick Graybill is among those who rely largely on an interactive format in their productions, ensuring that the spectators can relate to the players and even contribute their own material.[53] In this way, Deaf American theater resembles the mainstream theatricals of the past, which were more thoroughly integrated into everyday life. In his *Critique of Everyday Life,* Henri Lefebvre expresses concern about modern passivity: "The discreteness of the elements of the everyday (work-family and 'private' life-leisure activities) implies an alienation. . . . On a higher level, leisure involves passive attitudes, someone sitting in front of a cinema or screen."[54] Leisure in the past was more likely to involve active, communal festivities rather than solitary sitting, listening, and viewing.

In part, such alienation can be addressed by making sure that theatergoers are physically close to the performers and onstage action. Indeed, in any sign language theater such closeness is necessary: actors in a mainstream production can project their voices or even use artificial amplification, but there is no practical way to magnify the face and hands. Therefore, Graybill is in favor of much of the action occurring on an apron extending outward at floor level into a steeply inclined house with only 250 to 300 seats. Also, Deaf viewers are most comfortable when one or two performers or a compact group is onstage; it is visually difficult to follow actors carrying on a conversation as they move around all over the stage.

Customarily, performers in a Deaf American dramatic production face and approach viewers, interacting with them as much as is humanly possible.

Don Bangs and his SignRise Cultural Arts team also worked to facilitate increased intimacy and interaction in their productions. In the 1990s, Sign-Rise Cultural Arts produced *Deaf Theatre Showcase,* three short comedy acts sharing the same bill. Two were original works with Deaf themes, and the other was an adaptation of a Chekhov story. The use of short forms itself made the production feel "small" and more intimate. Bangs also had the players move from one small theater to another in the Washington, D.C., vicinity, rather like medieval players who pulled their sets on wheels to various locations in a town to bring drama to the people. This production was staged at five different sites; in one instance just the upper part of a clubroom floor was set apart for the stage, and ten or so rows of chairs filled the rest.

SignRise Cultural Arts had additional strategies for increasing the immediacy and intimacy of its productions. The protest rally that begins *Institution Blues* started not on the stage but in the aisles—and in fact, as already noted at the start of this chapter, the viewers were made to feel so personally involved that they joined in. Similarly, in *A Deaf Family Diary* the processional wedding march proceeded from the back of the auditorium down through the aisle and up onto the stage. Such techniques, says Graybill, put the viewers "in the thick of a visual feast."[55] Deaf dramatists thus resist the idea of theater as passive spectacle, seeking instead participatory, interactive, embodied communication. They put vision to use in sensuous rather than abstract communication. Deaf performers use their eyes to maintain rapport with the spectators and ensure comprehension. The ringmaster in *My Third Eye* snaps her invisible whip, takes in the assembled viewers with her eyes, and bids them, "Look, and you will see."

THE CARNIVALESQUE EYE

The close interaction, heterogeneity, and engaging physicality of vaudevillelike productions are appropriate for a visually oriented community. The eye enjoys visual stimuli—*variable* visual stimuli—and is inherently restless, in continual motion. The eye revels in color, shape, movement, and gradations of light and dark. The heterogeneity, physicality, and visuality of the vaudevillelike format make it therefore more appropriate for

Deaf viewers, for it holds the attention of the eye and thus of the theater-goer much longer than the typical word-centered, five-act play.

Because the highly verbal quality of modern plays is hard on the eyes, it is not surprising that Deaf Americans go in for the popular and physical over the "high art" of the intellectual, abstract, and serious. Deaf Americans prefer action over verbal/poetic drama, the simple and clear over the abstract, and the humorous (often physical farce) over the serious and heavy.[56] They favor skits, songs, mimicry, melodrama, farce, and thrillers.[57] Thus, as Baldwin points out in his study of Deaf American theater, the two original episodic, physical, and vaudevillelike NTD productions that focused on deafness, *My Third Eye* and *Parade,* were more popular with Deaf viewers than the company's adaptation of Dylan Thomas's *Under Milkwood.* Many bilingual Deaf Americans find that sitting through a college production of *Othello* or *Dr. Jekyll and Mr. Hyde* is more labor than pleasure. Long before intermission comes along they are squirming in their seats, experiencing eyestrain and temporary attention deficit disorder. Not surprisingly, directors putting on mainstream plays for Deaf Americans take their viewers into consideration: they add visual elements, cut down on the talk, and exhort players to sign full body or in profile to the audience—and they remind minor characters not to move an eyebrow when another actor is signing.

Such reminders are not needed in indigenous Deaf American theater, which has an immediacy and relevance for its viewers that go far beyond what plays meeting the classical conventions of Western drama might hope for. As we have seen, such conventions promote the aesthetic, the individual, and the ideal rather than the sociopolitical, communal, and real. In contrast, the dynamic, polyvocal, hybrid, and heterogeneous forms of Deaf American theater provide lively entertainment in the commedia dell'arte style—political, comic, and parodic, consciously or subconsciously, of "high" mainstream genres and conventions. They thereby epitomize the transformation of the spirit of carnival festivities into art. Each production contains a repertoire of festive and popular elements mixing with and countering the serious high languages and forms of mainstream culture.[58]

Most Deaf dramatists are highly educated and very much aware of theatrical conventions; theirs is thus a metadiscourse. They bear in mind that their culture utilizes an "oral" and visual mode of communication very different from that used by hearing playwrights. In selecting suitable elements and rejecting others, they show us something not just about the drama of

Deaf Americans but also about modern conventional drama. Give us a Deaf playwright or actor, and we will give you a jester facilitating the theatric metadiscourse.

NOTES

1. *Institution Blues,* scripted by Don Bangs and Jan DeLap, dir. Don Bangs, prod. Sign-Rise Cultural Arts, Publick Playhouse, Cheverly, MD, October 1 and 2, 1993.

2. *Dr. Jekyll and Mr. Hyde,* prod. Theater Arts Department, Gallaudet University, Washington, DC, fall 1997; *My Third Eye,* dir. J Ranelli, written and prod. National Theatre of the Deaf, 1971–72, videorecording shown on WTTW-TV, Chicago, 58 min., 1973; *Parade,* scripted by Jeff Wanshell, dir. Larry Amick, prod. National Theatre of the Deaf, 1975–76.

3. *Sign Me Alice,* scripted and dir. Gilbert C. Eastman, prod. Theater Arts Department, Gallaudet University, Washington, DC, 1973; Bernard Bragg and Eugene Bergman, *Tales from a Clubroom* (Washington, DC: Gallaudet College Press, 1981); *A Deaf Family Diary,* scripted by Don Bangs, dir. Patrick Graybill, prod. SignRise Cultural Arts, Publick Playhouse, Cheverly, MD, February–March 1991.

4. Willy Conley and Bob Daniels, pers. comm., fall 1998.

5. Stephen C. Baldwin, *Pictures in the Air: The Story of the National Theatre of the Deaf* (Washington, DC: Gallaudet University Press, 1993), 81.

6. Michael Bristol, *Carnival and Theater: Plebian Culture and the Structure of Authority in Renaissance England* (London: Methuen, 1985), 24.

7. Henri Lefebvre, *Critique of Everyday Life,* vol. 1, trans. John Moore (London: Verso, 1991), 32.

8. Bristol, *Carnival and Theater,* 46.

9. Ibid., 3.

10. Ibid., 46.

11. Ibid., 3.

12. Lefebvre, *Critique of Everyday Life,* 23.

13. *Deafula,* written and dir. Peter Wechsberg, prod. Gary Holstrom, Signscope, 1975.

14. Quoted in Carol Padden and Tom Humphries, *Deaf in America: Voices from a Culture* (Cambridge, MA: Harvard University Press, 1988), 18.

15. Padden and Humphries, *Deaf in America,* 18–19.

16. Stephen King's *The Stand,* dir. Mick Garris, ABC-TV, May 1994; based on the novel *The Stand,* by Stephen King (Garden City, NY: Doubleday, 1978).

17. Indeed, in Deaf American drama "Everyman" is often a woman. Like other minority literatures, it often runs counter to conventional expectation by featuring women as leading characters and political activists.

18. Carol Simpson Stern and Bruce Henderson, *Performance: Texts and Contexts* (New York: Longman, 1993), 89.

19. Bristol, *Carnival and Theater,* 5.

20. Ibid., 4.

21. Werner Sollars, *Beyond Ethnicity: Consent and Descent in American Culture* (New York: Oxford University Press, 1986), 239.

22. See John Fiske, "Cultural Studies and the Culture of Everyday Life," in *Cultural Studies,* ed. Lawrence Grossberg, Cary Nelson, and Paula A. Treichler (New York: Routledge, 1992), 157–58.

23. Peter Stallybrass and Allon White, *The Politics and Poetics of Transgression* (London: Methuen, 1986), 8.

24. Sollars, *Beyond Ethnicity,* 239.

25. E.g., see also *The World According to Pat: Reflections of Residential School Days,* scripted and dir. Patrick Graybill, videocassette (Silver Spring, MD, Sign Media and TJ Publishers, 1986), 80 min.

26. Mikhail Bakhtin, *Rabelais and His World,* trans. Helene Iswolsky (Cambridge, MA: MIT Press, 1968), 11–12.

27. Ibid., 19.

28. Donald Richard Bangs, "Deaf Theatre in America: Practices and Principles" (PhD diss., University of California at Berkeley, 1989). Bangs was specifically concerned with how drama as a whole can be promoted for both Deaf Americans and mainstream society.

29. Ibid., 196–98.

30. Ibid., 269, 293, 270.

31. Gleaned from issues of the *Silent News* (New York) from the late 1980s and the 1990s.

32. *Telling Stories,* scripted and dir. William Moses, prod. Theater Arts Department, Gallaudet University, Washington, DC, 1989.

33. Gustavo Pérez Firmat, *Literature and Liminality: Festive Readings in the Hispanic Tradition* (Durham, NC: Duke University Press, 1986), 14.

34. Shanny Mow, "Theater, Community," in *Gallaudet Encyclopedia of Deaf People and Deafness,* vol. 3, ed. John Van Cleve (New York: McGraw-Hill, 1987), 288.

35. The following discussion draws on Bangs, "Deaf Theatre in America," 30–40.

36. Gallaudet's first course in sign language theater in 1940 was primarily aimed at fostering an appreciation for theatrical works from the mainstream stage; the courses in play production were dropped in 1953, when Gallaudet was seeking accreditation. The Gallaudet College Theatre, established in 1963, adapted mainstream plays until 1973, when it put on *Sign Me Alice,* its first full-length original Deaf American play.

37. Bangs, "Deaf Theatre in America," 71, 108.

38. Ibid., 68.

39. *Under Milkwood,* based on the 1954 radio play by Dylan Thomas, prod. National Theatre of the Deaf, 1993–94.

40. *Parzival: From the Horse's Mouth,* scripted by Shanny Mow and David Hays, prod. National Theatre of the Deaf, 1982–83. See Bangs, "Deaf Theatre in America," 153–54.

41. Bangs, "Deaf Theatre in America," 105.

42. Baldwin, *Pictures in the Air,* 51.

43. John M. Heidger, "The History of the Deaf in America: The Silent Stage" (MA thesis, Southern Illinois University, 1979), 35.

44. Honor Ford-Smith, "Notes toward a New Aesthetic," *MELUS* 16, no. 3 (1989–90): 27–34.

45. Bakhtin, *Rabelais and His World,* 7, 8.

46. "J" is not an initial but the director's actual name.

47. Dorothy Miles, "A History of Theatre Activities in the Deaf Community of the United States" (MA thesis, Connecticut College, 1974), 62, quoted in Baldwin, *Pictures in the Air,* 48.

48. Baldwin, *Pictures in the Air,* 48.

49. Bangs, "Deaf Theatre in America," 153.

50. Bangs and Graybill are quoted in the program for *A Deaf Family Diary,* 9.

51. Wolfgang Karrer and Hartmut Lutz, "Minority Literatures in North America: From Cultural Nationalism to Liminality," in *Minority Literatures in North America: Contemporary Perspectives,* ed. Wolfgang Karrer and Hartmut Lutz (New York: Lang, 1990), 11–64. Deaf Americans affirm tradition, culture, and community and thus run contrary to the dominant discourse of this country, which puts individualism before tradition and community.

52. *Sign Me Alice* and *Sign Me Alice II,* written and dir. Gilbert C. Eastman, Gallaudet College TV Studio, Washington, DC, three videocassettes, 60 min. each, 1983; Mark H. Medoff, *Children of a Lesser God: A Play in Two Acts* (Clifton, NJ: J. T. White, 1980).

53. Bangs, "Deaf Theatre in America," 233.

54. Lefebvre, *Critique of Everyday Life,* 32.

55. Graybill is quoted in Bangs, "Deaf Theatre in America," 258–59.

56. George D. McClendon, "The Unique Contribution of the National Theatre of the Deaf to the American Theatre" (PhD diss., Catholic University of America, 1972), 89–90, cited in Bangs, "Deaf Theatre in America," 87. But Bangs (40) observes that despite the developments at Gallaudet University (what I would call the "institutionalization" of drama), Deaf community theaters continue to use traditional entertainment media such as variety acts and short comedies.

57. Dorothy S. Miles and Louie J. Fant, *Sign Language Theatre and Deaf Theatre: New Definitions and Directions* (Northridge: California State University at Northridge, Center on Deafness, 1975). See also Baldwin, *Pictures in the Air,* 48–49.

58. Stuart Hall, "Metaphors of Transformation," introduction to *Carnival, Hysteria, and Writing: Collected Essays and Autobiography,* by Allon White (New York: Oxford University Press, 1993), 1.

PART TWO

The Embodied Text

"Writing" and Vision in ASL Literature

FIVE

Getting out of Line

Toward a Visual and Cinematic Poetics of ASL

H-DIRKSEN L. BAUMAN

Lin (Old English): 1.—Flax. a. The fibre of flax. b. Flax spun or woven; linen thread or cloth.

Oxford English Dictionary, 1971

While this original use of the word *line* more directly relates to the modern-day *linen* and *linseed oil* than to poetry, its spirit is woven deeply into the notion of poetic lines—those metrical threads of words whose length and character lend poems their particular texture and design. As strings of phonemes, syllables, and words, lines form the fiber of verse, often seen as the very ontological stuff of poetic *text*iles. Given the fundamental role of lineation to poetics, questions concerning the line in American Sign Language (ASL) poetry are inevitable and revealing. Is there even such a thing as a signed line? If so, is it every bit the fiber of the ASL text? If not, what is?

Clayton Valli was the first to inquire into the nature of the line in ASL poetry. He begins his essay "The Nature of a Line in ASL Poetry" (1990a) by placing the identification of the ASL line as a centrally important issue: "Since the late 1970s an increasing number of original ASL poems have been recognized, but there has been no definition of the nature of this poetry. A basic difficulty in the effort to interpret ASL poetry and its elements has been the identification of a line" (171). If the ASL line can be identified, Valli reasons, then it may serve as a defining element in ASL poetic discourse.

Valli begins by looking for the signed counterpart to the traditional form of rhymed line breaks, as in this verse couplet by Alexander Pope:

> See, through this air, this ocean, and this earth,
> All matter quick, and bursting into birth.
>
> *"An Essay on Man"*

But what could possibly be the signed counterpart to "earth" and "birth"? Or the alliterative 'bursting into birth"? How do signed languages rhyme? Or rather, *do* they rhyme? Literally speaking, the notion of a signed rhyme is blatantly oxymoronic. Yet decades of sign language linguistic research have demonstrated that sign languages are rich in their own version of phonology. Rather than being constituted through sound patterns, the particular handshape, movement path, palm orientation, and nonmanual signals are all phonemic aspects of a visual, spatial, and kinetic language system. Just as in spoken languages, a rhyme is constituted by the repetition of distinct phonemes. On the basis of the fundamental rhyming of repeated handshapes, movements, facial expressions, and location, Valli proceeds to identify and describe what constitutes a line break in ASL, through the model of end-rhyming patterns. To grasp the basic poetic structure of visual rhymes, see the signed explanation by the ASL poet and humorist E. Lynn Jacobowitz regarding the rhymes in Valli's poem "Snowflake" (**clip 5.1**). Figure 5.1 (using a different transliteration of the poem) shows how the ending of the first line, "TREE—FULL OF LEAVES IN TREETOP—LEAVES FALL," rhymes visually with the ending of the next, "GRASS—SLENDER GRASS WAVE—GRASS WITHER." Moreover, it shows how there may be multiple rhymes simultaneously, something impossible in spoken languages. Both line breaks are signed with a downward motion, downward inflection of the eyebrows, and a "5" handshape that comes to the end of a sign in the same location with parallel palm orientation. Thus these breaks rhyme in multiple ways at the same time.

While Valli's analysis is *linguistically* precise, it may be *perceptually* murky—that is, when one is watching the poem, the poetic lines do not distinguish themselves as such. Only once they are committed to paper and linguistic analysis do they stand out as *lines*. At a national ASL literature conference, I asked a predominantly Deaf-ASL fluent audience to identify the line breaks in "Snowflake" before these were revealed to them. Not a single member correctly identified 'LEAVES FALL' and 'GRASS WITHER'

TREE 'FULL-OF-LEAVES-IN-TREETOP' 'LEAVES-FALL'

GRASS 'SLENDER-GRASS-WAVE' 'GRASS-WITHER'

FIGURE 5.1. Excerpt from "Snowflake," by Clayton Valli, showing visual rhymes. Reprinted by permission of the illustrator, Paul Setzer.

as "line breaks" per se (Bauman 1996). What sort of counterpart to the written line is this? It is unthinkable that a line break could not be identified as a perceptual marker in a poem, whether auditory (*earth/birth*) or visual (literal "breaks" of the lines cantilevered into the blank space of the page).

The model of the verse couplet echoes the conservative tradition that believes that, as Charles Hartman (1980) writes, "[v]erse is language in lines. This distinguishes it from prose. . . . This is not really a satisfying distinction as it stands, but it is the only one that works absolutely" (11). Yet *rhymed verse* and *poetry* are not interchangeable terms. While the line may be the fiber of *verse,* the linear fiber of *poetry* may be cut from a wide variety of different cloths and is capable of creating an array of poetic texts that come in all shapes, sizes, and forms. In the century that has explored such different sorts of lines as found in free verse, concrete poetry, prose poetry, Beat poetry, slam poetry, L = A = N = G = U = A = G = E poetry, performance poetry, Chinese calligraphic poetry, and ethnopoetics, we must be wary of identifying a single model for the line that stands for all.

This is not to say that the line loses its importance in modernist and postmodernist poetics; on the contrary, testing the boundaries, directions, and possibilities of the poetic line becomes a central preoccupation with contemporary poets. In many instances, these forms of experimentation are a reaction against the tradition of the metered line with its rhymed endings. While verse line may have been the form of choice for the elite English literary class, it no longer enjoys dominance in our postmodern, multicultural society.

In attempting to solve the question of the line in ASL poetry, then, Valli's essay actually raises more questions than it answers: What are the ideological implications of the verse model used by Valli? What would a free-verse line in ASL look like? What about an ASL concrete poem or a prose poem? Are there other models of the poetic line more suited for sign than the verse line? What about the lines found in visual arts? In the performing arts? Is the line even worth discussing at all? What is it about the "line" that is so important in the first place? All these questions lead toward an even more basic question: How does one even begin to discuss poetry in a visual, nonphonetic language?

As these questions suggest, inquiring into the element of the line in ASL poetry leads to reflections on the enterprise of ASL poetics as a whole. Much more is at stake here than the description of a single poetic feature in ASL. For once the line is opened up and examined, we find it to be woven with other threads of ideological, literary, and philosophical issues. Inextricably woven into the "line-division rhyme," for example, is a phonocentric ideology, the very form of which has been complicit in the repression of sign as a linguistic and literary medium; also entwined is the wholesale adoption of a formalist poetic tradition—exemplified by Robert Frost's influence on Valli—whose conservative definition of poetry would surely not include ASL as a medium for poetry per se.

Further, as these political threads are teased apart, we find another set of ideological lines: those that inscribe the disciplinary boundaries that maintain a separation between the visual, spatial, performance, and literary arts. The notion of the line is certainly not exclusive to poetry but is a fundamental concept in most art forms: painting, architecture, sculpture, music, dance, and drama are all in*form*ed by their own versions of lines. In each of these arts, the line serves a fundamental structural and aesthetic role, lending distinct shape and texture to the work. Given the ubiquity of the line, why limit our investigation to a single prosodic model that held sway centuries ago? Might the lines in visual poetry and visual arts, for example, bear homological affinities to the lines in ASL poetry? Is there something beyond the poetic line that forms the textual fabric, the poetic *lin* of ASL poetry?

The following inquiry, then, begins by opening up the line, which leads toward the larger lines—those that inscribe the very boundaries of "poetry" itself. To come closer to the poetic *lin,* this essay will have to cross disciplinary boundaries to explore the relations between the visual arts, film, and ASL poetry. In so doing, ASL poetics may be led away from the hegemony of hearing-centered (phonocentric) models of language and literature and guided toward a wider, more inclusive terrain of poetics.

In what follows, this essay moves from the central model of the verse line to an opening up of ASL poetics beyond speech and writing and then toward a wider landscape that includes visual and cinematic art forms. I do not pretend to fully describe this wider landscape but simply to lead toward it. What follows may be read, then, as preliminary notes toward a visually centered poetics and politics of ASL poetry.

PHONOCENTRISM AND THE LINE IN ASL VERSE

Just as poetry is always a specific poetic discourse, so line organization always takes a specific historical form and thus is ideological. In her essay "Lucent and Inescapable Rhythms: Metrical 'Choice' and Historical Formation," Marjorie Perloff (1988) compares the lineation of poets that span three centuries—Goethe (1780), Rimbaud (1873), William Carlos Williams (1916), and Samuel Beckett (1972)—to demonstrate that particular poetic forms emerge from particular historical formations. Perloff concludes, "We must realize that the choice of verse form is not just a matter of individual preference, a personal decision. . . . For the pool of verse and prose alternatives available to the poet at any given time has already been determined, at least in part, by historical and ideological considerations" (39). Rather than writing with a unique voice, the poet is, to a large extent, "ventriloquized by his or her tradition" (Henri Meschonnic, quoted in Perloff 1988, 15). We must ask what sort of ideological ventriloquism takes place when Valli uses the couplet verse as the model for the line in ASL poetry.

Walt Whitman, who was among the first to stretch the limits of the line—literally, to the end of the page—was also among the first to identify the high forms of English prosody with a particular social-cultural elitism. In the work of Alfred Lord Tennyson, for example, Whitman (1892) finds "the verse of inside elegance and high-life. . . . The odor of English social life in its highest range . . . pervading the pages like an invisible scent; the idleness, the traditions, the mannerisms, the stately ennui; . . . Never one democratic page; nay, not a line, not a word; never free and naïve poetry, but involv'd, labor'd, quite sophisticated" (477). The very possibility of this "verse of inside elegance and high-life" depends on an outside language of the not-so-elegant low-life, the unstately voices of pidgins, creoles, oral vernaculars, and sign languages. The metered, poetic line is one such boundary, ensuring that inside the stately house of English verse, poems and their practitioners do not get "out of line," that their prosodic feet march according to the same beat and make their about-faces in pre*scribed* fashion. While the words and images of verse may revel in the beautiful and the sublime, the metered, rhyming couplet line dictates conformity with the high arbiters of literacy and literature.

Such critiques of the high forms of English verse have been rehearsed often and do not need repeating here. However, the wider literary community has yet to see that within this high verse there exists a "hearing-centered" ideology of what is and is not literature. It is perhaps not surprising that this ideological underpinning has been overlooked in the history of languages, for it is often most difficult to see that which is closest to us. As spoken languages have been the overwhelmingly preferred mode, they have attained the status of the "norm"; thus our forms of writing and cultural production have followed suit. As traditional forms of literature reflect the needs of hearing poets and hearing audiences, one can hardly fault poets for making use of the oral and phonetic components of language. Indeed, one does not usually realize that "hearing" could be a part of one's identity and way of being-in-the-world.[1] The implications of this unexamined aspect of human identity extend deep into the core of what it means to be human.

As we have long defined ourselves as "the speaking animal," our modes of language—speech, phonetic writing, and the book—consolidate and deploy this image. As Masten, Stallybrass, and Vickers (1997) recognize, we are beginning to see "how narrow our assumptions of the typicality of a certain kind of book and a certain kind of reading have been" (5). The dominance of left-to-right, linear writing, then, defends the primacy of speech, and is, according to Derrida (1976), "the original and most powerful ethnocentrism" (3). Any modality that runs counter to this version of human identity must be repressed. One need only note the historical suppression of sign as ample evidence of the phonocentric hegemony of the West.[2]

Despite this recent paradigm shift in our understanding of language, the communities and the modes of production that support the old phonocentric paradigm hold sway. So entrenched is the line that it is difficult to perceive language in any other way. But as Derrida (1976) has shown, "The 'line' represents only a particular model whatever might be its privilege," and this privilege is founded on the "repression of pluridimensional symbolic thought" (86). Given that the phonetic line is the structural embodiment of phonocentrism, why should ASL poetics adopt it as the sole model to explore the nature of ASL poetry?

Clearly, for tactical reasons only. While the "line-division rhyme" does describe linguistic properties of sign, it more importantly serves to validate the poetic potential of ASL in the minds of the academic literary establishment. As Kathleen Fraser (1988) writes, "A poem whose line breaks adhere to . . . comfortably established systems can hope for easier access to the literary community, the canon" (152). It makes political sense to first compare ASL poetry with forms that define standard practice rather than with avant-garde forms like concrete poetry, which some scholars do not consider to be "poetry" per se. In this light, the line division that rhyme offers is an important poetic model in the struggle for the recognition of the subaltern literary forms of the Deaf community.

Yet the line-division rhyme is less strategic in guiding ASL poetics toward a deeper understanding of the *nature* of ASL poetry than Valli had hoped, for it is precisely the most normative models that perpetuate the exclusion of manual languages from the domain of literature. When the model of the line-division rhyme is taken as *the* model for the line, it brings with it a whole set of affiliations, like an ideological Trojan horse bearing an elitist, phonocentric literature replete with its traditions, poetics, and genres. Given these ideological implications, we must ask: If the phonetic line is only a model, what other models might be used to explore the line in ASL poetry?

Fortunately, other models abound, models like free verse and visual poetry that have long since superseded the popularity of the line-division rhyme. If, as it has been said, writing poetry without rhymed breaks is like playing tennis without a net, then Valli borrows a phonocentric net and sets out to play the same game as Frost and other traditional lyric poets. Yet once other poets take the net down, the game changes—and so does the field, whose bounds suddenly stretch wider to recognize that poetry, like language, may just as easily be visual as phonetic. Thus it seems quite logical to explore the line in visual poetry for a model for the line in the visual-kinetic form of ASL poetry.

THE VISUAL LINE

The tendency of artists to breach the supposed boundaries between temporal and spatial arts is not a marginal or exceptional practice of the arts, one which is not confined to any particular genre or period.

W. J. T. MITCHELL
Iconology

Since the advent of written poetic texts, poetry has been created for the eye as well as the ear. In fact, poetry's visual qualities are commonly cited as a fundamental distinction between poetry and prose. "The fact that we can tell verse from *prose on sight,* with very few errors," writes Charles Hartman (1980), "indicates that the basic *perceptual difference* must be very simple" (11, emphasis added). Whenever poetry is committed to the page, line breaks are visual, even in the most acoustically rich prosody. And once poetry is written, the poetic impulse comes into contact with the page and seeks what it has to offer. Who says we have to write in straight lines, left to right? Many poets find left-to-right lines constricting and hence compose lines that sprawl, curve, slither, and wind their way over the page. While many examples can be chosen, here consider two poems by the French poet Guillaume Apollinaire (1980), as translated by Anne Hyde Greet (figure 5.2). In "Far from the Dovecote," we see the sinuous curving of the snake from the "sea to the tender hope of the East." And in the "The Little Car" we can see the shape of a car emerging from a complex arrangements of lines—some long and curving, others short, and others circular. The lines are freed to convey a visual image. One cannot, from hearing this poem, grasp its essential visual imagery (figure 5.3).

Within the long history of visual poetry, the twentieth century has witnessed an increased manipulation of the visual nature of poetry. In the various forms of visual poetry, the line is no longer bound to the left-to-right linearity of the phonetic line but is free to explore the open field of the page. Poetry can be every bit a "graphic art," an art of writing.[3] Given that poetry may just as easily be visual as phonetic, it seems only logical to explore the long tradition of visual poetry for alternative models for poetic lines that may serve as starting points for poetic lines in ASL.

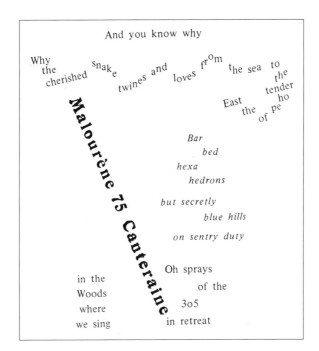

FIGURE 5.2. "Far from the Dovecote," by Guillaume Apollinaire.

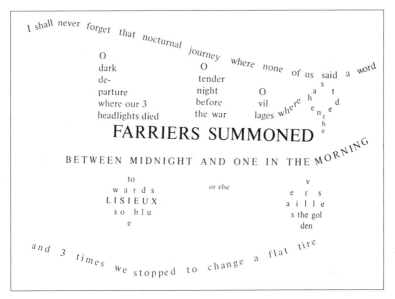

FIGURE 5.3. "The Little Car," by Guillaume Apollinaire.

THE VISUAL LINE AND SPATIAL COMPOSITION
IN ASL POETRY

Line: A direction of course or movement.

Oxford English Dictionary, 1971

The secret of the art of drawing is to discover in each object the particular way in which a certain flexuous line, which is, so to speak, its generating axis, is directed through its whole extent.

LEONARDO DA VINCI
Treatise on Painting

The forms of men must have attitudes appropriate to the activities that they engage in, so that when you see them you will understand what they think or say. This can be done by copying the motions of the dumb, who speak with movements of their hands and eyes and eyebrows and their whole person, in their desire to express that which is in their minds. Do not laugh at me because I propose a teacher without speech to you, who is to teach you an art which he does not know himself, for he will teach you better through facts than will all the other masters through words.

LEONARDO DA VINCI
Treatise on Painting

ASL is at all times composed of lines, invisible and kinetic; they are the paths that etch out a particular "direction of course or movement." In fact, one could say that signed discourse is composed from an assemblage of lines drawn in space through the body's movements. While these lines are woven with other linguistic parameters—a particular handshape, palm orientation, location, movement path, and nonmanual signals—the line is more than the sum of its parts. The line carries a generating capacity, an expressiveness all its own whose speed, tension, length, direction, and duration construct and disperse a particular energy. Consider the simple and confident lines in Bernard Bragg's translation of the beginning of e. e. cummings's "since feeling is first" (figure 5.4). Here the reader, at least, must pay attention to a new "syntax of things": a visual syntax of movement, design, and composition. Like the lines in cummings's poem-pictures, these lines are not bound to a left-to-right order but are free to explore the open space of the text. Even before the repetition of movement paths creates a "line division rhyme," a movement path *is already a line* in a very basic, perceptual sense. These paths, more than an occasional signed couplet, truly weave the visual fabric of the text. They could also be

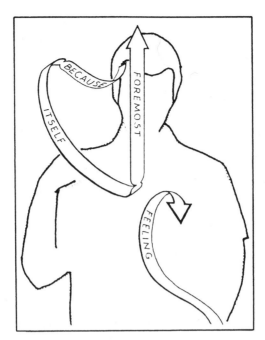

FIGURE 5.4. Bernard Bragg's translation of the
beginning of e. e. cummings's "since feeling is
first." Reprinted by permission of the publisher
from *The Signs of Language* by Edward Klima
and Ursula Bellugi, Figure 14.3 (b). Cambridge,
Mass: Harvard University Press, © 1979 by the
President and Fellows of Harvard College.

thought of as a poem's blueprint or its skeleton, what Edward Klima and
Ursula Bellugi (1979) refer to as the "kinetic superstructure." For the time
being, then, let us consider these "visual lines" in ASL poetry, which may
also be referred to as "movement path lines."

Taken on their own, the individual characters of lines reveal certain
visual properties but do not necessarily shed much new light on a particular poem. Just as in the visual arts, discussion of particular line types is usually not an end in itself. Rather, it is the *lines in relation* that form the fiber
of the visual text. The theory of the visual line, then, must be extended to
understanding how the lines produce an overall *visual composition*. Like the
lines in an Apollinaire calligramme or a Kandinsky canvas, signed lines
forge designs in space for particular aesthetic impact on the viewer.

In Valli's "Snowflake," for example, the lines that are most memorable may be not those created from the verse-based rhyming patterns demonstrated above but rather those created from the strong diagonal lines that are produced through the movement of the two snowflakes and that stand out against the rest of the poem (**clip 5.2**). As you watch the poem, note the overall compositional effect of the zigzagging diagonal lines of the poem's two falling "snowflakes."

Consider how the diagonal line of the first snowflake falling stands out against the dominating parallel vertical and horizontal lines in the beginning section of the poem. The first diagonal is echoed at the very end of the poem when the second snowflake falls from the opposite corner to the center, where it melts on the hand that holds the image of the sun. In this sense, these visual lines lead the viewer's eye toward the center, where the culmination takes place. This is a crucial moment, as the melting of the snowflake—a thing renowned for its unique character—may be seen to convey the melting of the boy's unique Deaf identity in the heat of his father's oppressive presence (Rose 1994; Ormsby 1995). The boy, then, becomes just another trickle in the mainstream of society. This point is made even more central to the poem as it is literally composed in the center, as foregrounded through the meeting point of the two diagonal lines—even though separated in time.

Approaching the line in this way makes the invisible pattern of the poem visible, exposing the threads of the poetic fabric. This allows us to slow down signs to ascertain their design and their creation of a whole poetic architecture. Rather than advocating for a precise quantitative set of terms, the visual model may open up poetic practice and analysis to be mindful of how the visual structure has its own impact on the viewer, a visual dimension interwoven with precise linguistic patterning. While "Snowflake" uses strong diagonal lines, other poems may use other lines, such as the strong circular composition found in Valli's "Hands" and Ella Mae Lentz's "Circle of Life" (1995) or the spiral shape repeated in Debbie Rennie's "Notre Dame" (1990). Not all poems have such an obvious discernible visual structure. If one were to spend time examining the lines of a poem, however, certain visual observations might be made concerning balance, symmetry, perspective, and composition. Moreover, the ASL line is not exclusively a "graphic" line like those committed to the canvas or the page; it is also, in the words of the *Oxford English Dictionary*, a direction and course *of movement* (emphasis added).

THE KINETIC LINE IN ASL POETRY: TRANSFORMATION

Approaching the line in its architectural sense gives insight into its visual design but is an insufficient model in itself. For unlike the lines in buildings, paintings, writing, Chinese calligraphy, and textiles, movement path lines vanish the instant they appear. It is the very *act* of drawing or weaving that creates the poem. In this sense, the actual *movement* of the movement path line conjures relations with dance and performance perhaps more than with painting. Ironically, as ASL poetics crosses into comparisons with dance, it is not drifting away from poetry but actually coming closer to the very origins of the poetic line and its metric feet. As ancient Greek dancers performed to the spoken word, the rhythm of their feet marked what have become known as the metric "feet" of the poem.[4] Although it does not come across in videotapes, performing ASL poets frequently revive this original notion as they keep the beat of their poem with a tapping foot, reconnecting the poetic line with the movements of the body. But the lines in ASL are not necessarily restricted to the tapping of a literal/metaphorical poetic foot; they gesture through time and space, controlling and dispersing energy as a dancer does.

Unlike a dancer, however, the gestures and movements of the body produce precise grammatical and visual images. In fact, often the interweaving of a gestural line with visual images produces lines that startle the viewer and resonate within the poetic text. These lines are the generating axis of the ASL poetic technique known as "transformation." In a *transformation line,* one image or sign transforms into another without a break, threaded together through a single gestural line.

Consider the lines from Ella Mae Lentz's "Eye Music" (1995): strong parallel lines drawn through space, carving the image of passing telephone poles and wires from the moving eyes of a passenger on a train. These waving, parallel lines begin as the bars of written music and then flow off the page in one sinuous line into telephone wires. The *line* here is the continuous movement path used to unite the bars of written music with telephone wires. That is, the lines lift off the page where they represent sound to course through the air, producing a form of Deaf "eye music." The continuous line enables the transformation to surprise and to weave together incongruent images (**clip 5.3**).

While transformation lines occur in the works of most poets, they occur with greater frequency and deliberateness in the works of Flying Words

Project. Of particular interest to this chapter is their *ars poetica,* entitled simply "Poetry." As it explores the relations of ASL poetry and painting, "Poetry" embodies the ideas presented in this essay—the nature of the visual line in ASL poetry—by exploring the analogies between poetry and painting (**clip 5.4**).

The poem begins with a startling transformation line as Cook signs a gun shooting a bullet that transforms through one gestural line into a celestial body orbiting in space. This transformation creates a radical shift in perspective from human to cosmic scale. The shock of two incongruous images becomes the image itself, recalling the nature of the image in the ideogrammic poetics of Ezra Pound, where two juxtaposed images work to produce a "radiant node, or cluster" of ideas. The viewer is left to struggle with competing frames of reference.

As "Poetry" continues, the poem follows the paths of lines through the painting/poetry analogy. Cook alternates between being a painter and the portrait, yet in this portrait the lines become increasingly abstract until the painter finally smashes a plate of paint into the portrait, rips the canvas off the easel, and throws it into space, where it orbits like a planet. In one transformational, kinetic line, the canvas transforms into a celestial orb, and human scale becomes cosmic without forewarning.

When placed in this context, this particular transformation line may be seen as a milestone in the history of the painting/poetry analogy and in ASL poetics. Here it is not any old canvas being destroyed but the entire tradition of comparing sign poetry to two-dimensional art forms. This *ars poetica* points toward the inevitable: that it is time we move out of the flatland of the page and canvas and into the three-dimensional kinetic arts in search of a wider, more comprehensive poetics of ASL. And this is precisely where Flying Words goes. Once released from the limitations of the canvas and page, Cook creates images within a full four-dimensional field that gain a life of their own. First, Cook shows the painter/poet drawing trees into being, but gradually the trees and underbrush grow on their own. The images of the SUN and the FALCON occupy their own realm, not restricted to a canvas or a page. The near-ontological independence of these poetic images is shown most clearly in another transformation line where the falcon swoops down only to become a butterfly landing on the head of the unsuspecting poet/painter. Here, in the words of Ernest Fenollosa (1991) referring to Chinese written poetry, we seem to be "watching things work out their own fate" (9).

Cook and Lerner's moment of transformation from two dimensions to four heralds the necessity of a poetics not bound to the canvas or the page; what is needed is a poetics where lines, handshapes, movement paths, location, palm orientation, and all the other linguistic ingredients are not ends in themselves but, in their various ways, generators of the *moving image.*

This essay, then, will ride along with this deconstructive transformational line that hurls flatland poetics into deep space. We find ourselves now at an opening where a poetics of ASL may more fully embrace its own visual-kinetic nature. In doing so, it finds that there is perhaps a greater, more essential *lin:* the moving image.

FROM LINE TO LENS:
TOWARD A CINEMATIC POETICS OF ASL

> The end of linear writing is indeed the end of the book. . . . That is why beginning to write without the line, one begins also to reread past writing according to a different organization of space.
>
> JACQUES DERRIDA
> *Of Grammatology*

The grammars of sign languages and film are astonishingly similar—so much so that one could claim that ASL bears as much resemblance to film as to spoken languages. The Deaf performer Bernard Bragg originally put forth the idea of the relations between the two media. His insights led William Stokoe, the first linguist to perceive and validate the linguistic status of ASL, to describe the visual grammar of sign in cinematic terms:

> In a signed language . . . narrative is no longer linear and prosaic. Instead, the essence of sign language is to cut from a normal view to a close-up to a distant shot to a close-up again, and so on, even including flashback and flash-forward scenes, exactly as a movie editor works. . . . Not only is signing itself arranged more like edited film than like written narration, but also each signer is placed very much as a camera: the field of vision and angle of view are directed but variable. (Quoted in Sacks 1990, 90)

Given such a close, homologous relation between techniques used in ASL and film, one wonders why the lexicon of film techniques is not a standard part of ASL poetics. This hesitancy may be due, in part, to the need to demonstrate that ASL is not simply a collection of iconic gestures but a linguistic system capable of all the symbolic, abstract content of spoken languages. Not only can ASL poetics rest assured that its status as a valid language has been amply proven over four decades of research, but film has itself been thought to possess its own systematic codes and rules, something akin to a visual grammatical structure (Metz 1974). Drawing connections, then, between film and sign does not lessen the grammatical complexity of signed languages; rather, it enriches our understanding of grammar manifested in a visual modality. Further, we may now look to how language artists explore the cinematic properties of sign to produce a heightened visual-kinetic experience for the viewing audience.

An initial breakthrough in the uses of the cinematic properties of manual languages was made by Bernard Bragg. In his early career as an actor in the National Theater of the Deaf, he devised a performing technique he referred to as "visual vernacular." It is a vernacular in the sense that it appeals to the vernacular codes of the cinematic medium. In **clip 5.5**, Peter Cook describes Bragg's visual vernacular technique.

This technique signifies the beginning of exploration into the visual modality; techniques like the visual vernacular represent a clear use of cinematic techniques, and more subtle cinematic techniques also run throughout ASL literature. In what follows, we will inquire into some basic aspects of cinematic techniques and modes of analysis applied to ASL poetry.

At this point, we have drifted so far from the original notion of the line and its phonetic ideology that we must take leave of the written text and seek "a different organization of space"—in this case, a Deaf space. In **clip 5.6**, Manny Hernandez, an ASL artist, demonstrates the cinematic properties of ASL, offering the beginning of a cinematic lexicon that may be used alongside existing terms from formalist linguistics. The reader is now asked to become more of a viewer, as the following ideas will be presented primarily in ASL.

As Hernandez explains, the modes of analysis developed for spoken and written media do not adequately account for the visual-spatial-kinetic properties of signed languages. However, when one inquires into basic notions of film, there seems to be a greater affinity. In clip 5.6, Hernandez describes three basic cinematic properties that play a role in ASL poetics—camera, shot, and editing. He shows what Stokoe observed decades ago: "[E]ach signer is placed very much as a camera: the field of vision and angle of view are directed but variable" (Sacks 1990, 90). The signer, like a camera, can produce images from any number of angles (high, low, left, right, so on) and movements, from *panning* across a landscape to *tracking* an individual character through a busy street. In ASL, as in film, the *point of view* of the camera plays a crucial role. Take Flying Words Project's "Poetry," for example. When Peter Cook shifts between the painter and the portrait, the position of the camera's shot shifts: when he shows the painter painting, the camera is positioned as if on the canvas; when he shows the portrait being painted, the camera is positioned from the point of view of the painter. This sequence shifts the point of view back and forth, as is common in film. Thus, when looking at an ASL poem, one may begin to discuss its use of camera techniques—its angles, movements, and point of view.

Within its frame, the camera can capture an enormous variety of shots, which are the most basic element of cinematic poetics. Like phonemes, shots are enormously flexible: they are the fundamental and productive components that are woven together to form a visual-spatial-kinetic discourse. The shot is defined as an uninterrupted flow of presentation of the visual field with a distinct beginning and ending. But within a single shot, a variety of perspectives, movements, and compositions may occur, ranging from extreme distant shots (think Hubble telescope) to extreme close-ups (think microscopic flagellating sperm), with the more common distant, medium, and close-up shots in between.

In addition to the varying distances of shots, the length of individual shots provides enormous flexibility. Shots can vary from the split-second visual shards familiar to viewers of MTV to shots that extend over a longer time, such as the excruciating shot in Michael Leigh's *Secrets and Lies* of the first meeting between a white mother and her adult, mixed-race child she gave up for adoption. Leigh leaves the camera on these two women in an empty coffee shop for six minutes and forty seconds, a shot that seems never to end. Further, shots possess great variability in speed, ranging from slow-motion football catches to fast-forward, such as the accelerated images of city life and junk food–producing factories in the film *Koyaanisqatsi*.

While the individual shot is incredibly flexible and offers a nearly infinite number of possibilities, film cannot truly signify without *editing*, or assembling the shots into a stream of shots. Just as in film, there are numerous editing techniques in ASL. Some of the most basic techniques are *dialogue editing*, cutting back and forth between participants in a dialogue (this is known as role-shift in ASL linguistics); *parallel editing*, cutting between two simultaneous events that take place in separate places; *cut-*

away, cutting between two seemingly unrelated shots; and *montage,* editing images together to produce a visual story.

Many of these cinematic elements are foregrounded in Manny Hernandez's "Times Squared," a visual experience of a time-lapsed day in New York City (**clip 5.7**). The poem begins with what is perhaps the most extreme long shot possible: a cosmic perspective in which the earth is a tiny dot in the corner of the sign-space. Then the camera moves the dot to the center of the screen, and the world rapidly comes into focus. In an intersubjective leap made easy through grammatically laden facial expressions, the viewer actually senses the poet's approach to earth. This all appears as an uninterrupted visual flow, or shot, reminiscent of contemporary computer graphic capability. Then we cut to a medium shot of the Statue of Liberty and then find ourselves in the midst of Times Square. This initial sequence—from cosmos to Times Square—serves as a series of *establishing shots* that provide a larger visual context for the ensuing material. We are now clearly situated in a particular place in the cosmos, in a moment not unlike that in James Joyce's *Portrait of the Artist as a Young Man* (1964) when Stephen Dedalus realizes that people were all in "different countries and the countries were in continents and the continents were in the world and the world was in the universe" (15). Hernandez's version of this universal perspective is achieved through an extreme instance of *zoom* technique, in which we can zoom light years into the Northern Hemisphere and to New York and into a particular site within the city. Manny Hernandez also makes use of variability of speed in "Times Squared" as he moves from the *slow motion* of a morning in New York City, with a few pedestrians entering the street, cars starting to fill the streets, and the sun rising between buildings, to *extreme fast-forward,* hordes of pedestrians, cars, and clouds, and then back to slow motion until the sun sets. Taken as a whole, "Times Squared" incorporates a host of cinematic techniques that give viewers the illusion that they are watching film footage. At this point, ASL poetics is poised to explore the phenomenology of the cinematic image to explain how the viewer of an ASL poem registers particular sensations and emotions presented within the text. This is quite easy to do in the work of performers like Bernard Bragg, Flying Words Project, and Manny Hernandez, who consciously exploit the cinematic properties of ASL. But given that ASL has inherent cinematic properties, one should also be able to analyze any ASL poem for its cinematic technique, an analysis that would ultimately lead to a type of viewer-response criticism for ASL poetry.

Take Clayton Valli's "Snowflake" (1990b), discussed earlier in this chapter. It may be viewed very much as a short poetic film, composed through a sophisticated use of camera work, shot composition, and editing. "Snowflake" opens with a montage of images conveying the passage of the seasons from spring into the barrenness of winter. In what follows, each line presents an individual shot. Specific signs appear in capital letters, and comments about the nature of the shot follow.

1. WINDOW OUTLINE OF WINDOW (close-up)
2. PERSON LOOKING THROUGH THE WINDOW (medium)
3. TREE (medium)
4. TREE FULL OF LEAVES IN TREETOP (close-up)
5. LEAVES FALL (close-up)
6. SLENDER GRASS WAVE (close-up)
7. GRASS WITHER (close-up)
8. NO COLOR; NOTHING; GRAY (this shot is less a specific visual representation than an emotional depiction of a landscape)
9. CLOUDS ECLIPSING THE SUN (long shot)
10. DARK SKY   GRAY LAND (again, an emotional landscape shot)
11. SNOWFLAKE (extreme close-up of a snowflake falling in a diagonal path) This image stands out as the first extreme close-up. Previous images of movement involved close-ups of collective movement— leaves falling, grass swaying. Now, for the first time, the camera focuses on a specific element of the landscape. The speed, the energy, and the complementary signs WHITE and BEAUTIFUL foreground the uniqueness of the snowflake amidst a dreary background of gray winter.
12. HEARTBEAT   INSPIRES MEMORY   NEVER FORGET EYES (close-up of a man startled by the sight of the snowflake that triggers a memory of a young boy and his big blue eyes.) In what follows, the dialogue sequence of a father and a young boy is achieved through dialogue editing of close-up shots.
13. Boy looks at the father with WIDE EYES (close-up)
14. Close-up FATHER TALK TALK showing that he is PROUD of his young boy. He turns toward the boy, asking WHAT IS YOUR NAME LITTLE BOY?)
15. BOY SPEAKING: MY NAME IS . . .

16. FATHER; PROUD of his son's speaking accomplishments. He turns to the boy: HOW OLD ARE YOU LITTLE BOY?

17. BOY SPEAKING: I AM FIVE YEARS OLD (emphasis on the S in years)

18. BETTER NOW!   SEE (Father speaking). Now the dialogue editing comes to a close and a single narrator comments:

19. TWO SENTENCES TWO SENTENCES (signifying disbelief that a father would be so proud of such little verbal accomplishment)

20. This shot is a reverse of shot 12, a visual parallel closing the memory flashback. MEMORY to HEARTBEAT

21. SNOW COVERING GROUND DRIFTING AGAINST TREES. (medium shot of the landscape)

22. CLOUD UNCOVERING SUN (long shot; a reverse of shot 9)

23. SUN RAYS FALLING, followed by a single SNOWFLAKE, which melts as it hits the ground.

The symbolism of this ending has been discussed earlier in this chapter and need not be rehearsed now. The point is simply that cinematic description can be applied to ASL poems that are not intentionally cinematic. Valli combines the use of montage of natural images, dialogue editing, and shot composition to make a rich cinematic poem, whether he was conscious of these techniques or not. The techniques are embedded in the visual texture of the language and surface when put to aesthetic use.

Given the inherent cinematic properties of sign poetry, we may begin thinking in new terms to describe the compositional process of the sign poet. What is more, we can begin to muse about the possibilities of the artistic practice of cine-poetics. Who knows what future poetic and cine-matic forms could emerge as Deaf poets try to re-create the special effects of a movie like *The Matrix* while moviemakers re-create the special effects of Flying Words Project's "Poetry."

CONCLUSION

Readers more accustomed to the quantifiable, linguistic nature of ASL poet-ics may find the preceding discussion somewhat unscientific and unsys-tematic. This is admittedly true: I want to open up the notion of line beyond the formal line, measured by its number of feet and its accumulation of rhyming patterns, and set the line free to design its own space, to approach the line in its own visual-spatial-kinetic habitat, to view it as a physical extension of the moving body that generates the poetic energies of a poem— and to realize that the models chosen to articulate poetic features such as the line are themselves implicated in a complex ideological framework. We must begin this new poetics, then, by exposing the ideological context of the line-division rhyme and then realizing that in a wider landscape of artistic practices the line is a fundamental structural and aesthetic device. We may follow the poetic line until we encounter a wider visual, cinematic poetics that recognizes that film creates its own forms of poetic *lin*.

NOTES

1. I, for example, was born with a fully functioning sense of hearing; however, I did not actually become "hearing" until age twenty-one, when I began working as a residential supervisor at the Colorado School for the Deaf and the Blind. Once I came into contact with the Deaf world, I began to comprehend the pervasiveness of our phonocentric heritage.

2. See Doug Baynton's *Forbidden Signs* (1996) for a history of the repression of manual languages in America. Also, see Harlan Lane's *The Mask of Benevolence* (1992).

3. For further inquiry into the history of visual poetics, see Steiner (1982), Mitchell (1987), Drucker (1998), and Frank and Sayre (1988).

4. See J. J. Pollitt (1974).

REFERENCES

Apollinaire, Guillaume. 1980. *Calligrammes: Poems of Peace and War (1913–1916)*. Trans. Anne Hyde Greet. Berkeley: University of California Press.

Bauman, H-Dirksen L. 1996. "From Poetry to Painting: The Line in ASL Poetry." Paper presented at the Second National Conference on American Sign Language Literature, Rochester, NY, March.

Baynton, Douglas. 1996. *Forbidden Signs: American Culture and the Campaign against Sign Language*. Chicago: University of Chicago Press.

Derrida, Jacques. 1976. *Of Grammatology*. Trans. Gayatri Spivak. Baltimore: Johns Hopkins University Press.

Drucker, Johanna. 1998. *Figuring the Word: Essays on Books, Writing, and Visual Poetics*. New York: Granary Books.

Fenollosa, Ernest. 1991. *The Chinese Written Character as a Medium for Poetry*. San Francisco: City Lights Books. (Orig. pub. 1936.)

Flying Words Project. n.d. "Poetry." Personal video.

Frank, Robert, and Henry Sayre, eds. 1988. *The Line in Postmodern Poetry.* Chicago: University of Illinois Press.

Fraser, Kathleen. 1988. "Line on the Line. Lining up. Lined with. Between the Lines. Bottom Line." In *The Line in Postmodern Poetry,* ed. Robert Frank and Henry Sayre. Chicago: University of Illinois Press.

Graybill, Patrick, Debbie Rennie, and Clayton Valli. 1990. *Poetry in Motion: Original Works in ASL.* Burtonsville, MD: Sign Media.

Hartman, Charles O. 1980. *Free Verse: An Essay on Prosody.* Princeton: Princeton University Press.

Joyce, James. 1964. *Portrait of the Artist as a Young Man.* New York: Viking Press.

Klima, Edward, and Ursula Bellugi. 1979. *The Signs of Language.* Cambridge, MA: Harvard University Press.

Lane, Harlan. 1992. *The Mask of Benevolence: Disabling the Deaf Community.* New York: Alfred Knopf.

Lentz, Ella Mae. 1995. *The Treasure.* Videocassette. Berkeley, CA: In Motion Press.

Leonardo da Vinci. 1956. *Treatise on Painting.* Trans. Philip McMahon. Vol. 1. Princeton: Princeton University Press.

Masten, Jeffrey, Peter Stallybrass, and Nancy Vickers. 1997. *Language Machines: Technologies of Literary and Cultural Production.* New York: Routledge.

Metz, Christian. 1974. *Film Language: A Semiotics of the Cinema.* Trans. Michael Taylor. New York: Oxford University Press.

Mirzoeff, Nicholas. 1995. *Silent Poetry: Deafness, Sign, and Visual Culture in Modern France.* Princeton: Princeton University Press.

Mitchell, W. J. T. 1987. *Iconology: Image, Text, Ideology.* Chicago: University of Chicago Press.

Ormsby, Alec. 1995. "Poetic Cohesion in ASL: Valli's 'Snowflake' and Coleridge's 'Frost at Midnight.'" *Sign Language Studies* 88:227–44.

Oxford English Dictionary. Compact ed. 1971. Oxford: Oxford University Press.

Perloff, Marjorie. 1988. "Lucent and Inescapable Rhythms: Metrical 'Choice' and Historical Formation." In *The Line in Postmodern Poetry,* ed. Robert Frank and Henry Sayre. Chicago: University of Illinois Press.

Pollitt, J. J. 1974. *The Ancient Greek View of Art.* New Haven: Yale University Press.

Rennie, Debbie. 1990. *Poetry in Motion, Original Works in ASL: Debbie Rennie.* Videocassette. Burtonsville, MD: Sign Media.

Rose, Heidi. 1994. "Stylistic Features in American Sign Language Literature." *Text and Performance Quarterly* 14:144–57.

Sacks, Oliver. 1990. *Seeing Voices: A Journey into the World of the Deaf.* New York: Harper-Perennial.

Steiner, Wendy. 1982. *The Colors of Rhetoric: Problems in the Relation between Modern Literature and Painting.* Chicago: University of Chicago Press.

Valli, Clayton. 1990a. "The Nature of a Line in ASL Poetry." In *SLR '87 Papers from the Fourth International Symposium on Sign Language Research,* ed. W. H. Edmondson and F. Karlsson. Hamburg: Signum Press.

———. 1990b. *Poetry in Motion, Original Works in ASL: Clayton Valli.* Videocassette. Burtonsville, MD: Sign Media.

Whitman, Walt. 1892. "Poetry To-day in America—Shakspere—The Future." In *Complete Prose Works,* 2:474–90. Philadelphia: D. McKay.

SIX

Textual Bodies, Bodily Texts

JENNIFER L. NELSON

I am a body writing. I am a bodily writing.

ROLAND BARTHES
Empire of Signs

As one who participates in and supports Deaf culture in the face of a dominant hearing culture largely constructed—and also limited—by speech, I present an anecdote that relates to traditional ideas of identity, normality, language, and ultimately, literature. One summer, when I was a college student and a resident assistant in one of the dorms at the George Washington University (to the surprise of many hearing people who thought it impossible for a deaf person to do a job like that), I was checking the IDs of people coming in and out, and I was talking with a few of my hearing friends who were kindly keeping me company. A man, upon hearing my speech, walked up to inquire as to what kind of accent I had. I replied—as one fed up with innumerable questions of this sort—"A deaf accent." He looked confused, and then asked, "What country is that?" I looked him very seriously in the eye as I gave him my answer: "Deafland." He said to himself, "Deafland? Where's that?" and slowly walked off, quite puzzled, trying to figure out where that country was—even as my friends were laughing so hard they cried. I laughed too, but more wryly. Since I talked, albeit with an "accent," and perhaps because of the job I was doing, I couldn't be "deaf" in his scheme of things, even though I had basically told him so. My Deaf identity was nulled and replaced with another belonging to a speech-based model, that of a speaking foreigner. Speech in society sets up expectations and standards of normality, and those who do not fit these standards are reinterpreted in light of the standard of discourse and normality currently in use. I did not see this episode as negative, however; it was an occasion for hilarity, and I saw that it was ultimately more limiting to him and his understanding than it was to me. In a similar way, people often conceive of traditional literature as being a phonetically written, textual form of art only, connected to speech. If graphic writing is seen only as a form of speech—which would seem to rule out many fruitful avenues of literary exploration, such as sign literature—where does this place the signing Deaf person when it comes to "literature"? Under such a limited system, how can manual signs be literature? How can they be a text, or a form of "writing"?

Videotape as "writing," the body as "writing," the Deaf sign (itself) as "writing"—these are ideas suggested by Christopher Krentz's analogy, in chapter 3 of this volume, comparing the effects of the printing press on literature with those of videotape on literature. Philosophers such as Jacques Derrida, Luce Irigaray, Hélène Cixous, Julia Kristeva, and Roland Barthes have proposed a wider definition of "writing" in contexts other than the textual act of print or script on a flat surface such as paper or a wall. The semiotician Roland Barthes has said that the dramatic gestures of puppets and others can be seen as a form of writing (Foster 1995, 1, 19). The French feminist philosophers Cixous and Irigaray talk about "writing the body" in order to produce *écriture féminine,* as well as the concept of the "feminine" or subordinated producer of literature. Concepts such as these apply very well to the "feminized" Deaf person who creates a bodily American Sign Language (ASL) literature in the face of a dominant form of literary discourse.

Here I would like to analyze in particular the historical implications of Jacques Derrida's concept of deconstruction—especially those ideas pertaining to Derrida's thoughts on "writing"—in terms of ASL. Even though Derrida laid out his theoretical framework some decades ago, his discussions of concepts such as phonocentrism, the free play of signifiers, and "writing" in various books such as *Speech and Phenomena* (1973) and *Of Grammatology* (1976) have particular relevance to ASL literature as a bodily writing or textuality in the face of a dominant form of literary discourse; ASL in turn has the potential to affect Derrida's theoretical field—though it has been around for quite some time—as well as literature in general by questioning traditional concepts of literacy and literariness.

Traditionally, at least before Jacques Derrida, with the word *language* the word *speech* also comes without much thought. Modern society has made the frequent assumption that the word *language* means *speech*. Derrida's voluminous writings, in particular *Of Grammatology* (1976), discuss this voice bias in Western civilization, and in *Speech and Phenomena* (1973) he notes the "strange prerogative of the vocal medium" (70). Derrida shows that the reliance on speech as paramount is a matter of arbitrary convenience and not a true given. While this convenience is simpler, it is also limiting in that only one form of discourse is truly legitimate. Such "simplicity" can have far-reaching effects in that it perpetuates a speech bias to the detriment of other communicative media and negates the possible benefits that the interplay of a variety of mediums can provide. Derrida points us in the direction of acknowledging the ideological function of ideas of language and how such ideas establish norms with social consequences. The result of this is "phonocentrism," or voice *as* presence, which means that identities become connected to the voice. Phonocentrism, simply speaking, is a way of life and thought that assumes the voice and hearing to be of primary importance. However, Derrida's philosophy is that anything referential—that is, symbolic—is "writing." Thus manual signs and spoken words occupy equal footing as writings and as signifiers. According to Derrida (1976), "The exteriority of the signifier is the exteriority of writing in general" (14): that is, anything representational is exterior, and anything fitting this category is thus a "writing." Sign language and speech are therefore "writings" in the larger sense of the word.

Sign language as writing? Speech as writing? To justify this, let us look more closely at Derrida, particularly at an essay called "*Différance*" in *Speech and Phenomena* (1973), where he notes that because of *différance* all signs (voice, graphic, and so forth) are simply subsets of a larger "writing." Writing is not just a graphic writing as we know it but a "writing" that has all systems of material signs under it, whether they are speech, written representations of speech, or sign language. What is in speech that is also in all other systems of signs? What constitutes "writing"? For Derrida, everything is "writing" if there is any mediation or spacing present—that is, if there is a signifier and a signified, which implies a distinction between the two, a distance. Writing is *différance*. Derrida uses the term *différance* to enunciate—pun intended—his theory of what is common to all signs. Via a visual pun, he also points out that it is illogical to favor speech over writing, since only in writing is the distinction between the words *difference* and *différance* obvious. Only if we look can we see the difference between the "a" and the "e." We only see the difference between the two words; we do not hear it, since the pronunciation is the same. Derrida is making the point that the temporalizing and spatializing systems of signification and semiosis can be incomplete when one relies entirely on acoustic signals.

As stressed by Derrida's use of "a" and not "e" in *différance*, the word does not simply mean "difference"; rather, it incorporates the idea of difference into its definition, along with the idea of delay or deferral: "The verb 'to differ' [différer] seems to differ from itself. On the one hand, it indicates difference as distinction, inequality, or discernibility; on the other, it expresses the interposition of delay, the interval of a *spacing* and *temporalizing* that puts off until 'later' what is presently denied, the possible that is presently impossible" (Derrida 1973, 129). Being able to see the "a" in *différance* extends the meaning of the word: the written form of the word can show both *differ* and *defer* in tandem, whereas the spoken form of the word cannot. In this way, visual forms of communication can sometimes encompass more than an acoustic form can. The presence of a sign, or signifier, also implies the absence, or delay, of what it refers to; we would not need the sign/signifier if the thing were present or the idea were concrete and observable by all people at all times whenever needed. That is, a sign defers the presence of the thing itself as it stands in for it, which indicates a "spacing." This is *différance*. By extension, if ASL utilizes signs that refer to absences, and these signs derive their meaning in comparison with other signs, then ASL is merely another system of signs, just like speech. Derrida (1973) elaborates:

> Let us begin with the problem of signs and writing—since we are already in the midst of it. We ordinarily say that a sign is put in place of the thing itself, the present thing—"thing" holding here for the sense as well as the referent. Signs represent the present in its absence; they take the place of the present. When we cannot take hold of or show the thing, let us say the present, the being-present, when the present does not present itself, then we signify, we go through the detour of signs. We take up or give signs; we make signs. The sign would thus be a deferred presence. *Whether it is a question of verbal or written signs, monetary signs, electoral delegates, or political representatives,* the movement of the sign defers the moment of encountering the thing itself, the moment at which we could lay hold of it, consume or expend it, touch

it, see it, have a present intuition of it. . . . Following this classical semiology, the substitution of the sign for the thing itself is both secondary and provisional: it is second in order after an original and lost presence, a presence from which the sign would be derived. It is provisional with respect to the final and missing presence, in view of which the sign would serve as a movement of mediation. (138)

So there is something common to spoken words, written words, and signed words that binds them all together: the fact that they signify something and stand in for something else, and mean something because they are sunk within a network of differing signifiers. For Derrida (1973), *différance* is not epitomized in the voice or in the graphic word: "It takes place . . . between speech and writing and beyond the tranquil familiarity that binds us to one and to the other, reassuring us sometimes in the illusion that they are two separate things" (134). Language is then not a function of a speaking subject, and Derrida goes on to say that someone can speak only because of the system of differences that Saussure has called "language *without* speech" (146, emphasis added). As Derrida clarifies further, "He becomes a *signifying* subject (generally by speech *or other signs*) only by entering into the system of differences" such as that provided by a society or culture (146, latter emphasis added). *Différance* is, for Derrida, the meaning of "writing," another name for it, and all systems of signification are "writing." "Writing" is the "institution" of signs and as such represents the probably infinite linguistic domain of signs (Derrida 1976, 44). This infinite linguistic domain of signs includes, of course, the manual signs of the Deaf in that manual signs have meaning by virtue of their representational or symbolic nature. This is almost Chomskian when one considers Noam Chomsky's notion that all human brains are hard-wired for language, regardless of mode (see Chomsky 1988), and recent research by Poizner, Klima, and Bellugi (1987) on speech and sign activity in the brain that shows both languages to stimulate the same areas of the brain, as opposed to the previously held ideas that visual languages must be processed in the visual areas of the brain. Sign languages are actually processed in the same areas of the brain as speech is: ASL is processed in the left hemisphere of the brain, where spoken languages are, not the right hemisphere, where "visual" media are processed.

As noted earlier, a word or sign has meaning only because it is related to other signs around it. A sign "means" because it differs from other signs and therefore carries no inherent meaning. Derrida (1973) says: "The elements of signification function not by virtue of the compact force of their cores but by the network of oppositions that distinguish them and relate them to one another" (139). We "see" black as a color because we have red to compare with, for example, and we can classify people as deaf because we have hearing as a counterpoint or frame of reference. Mairian Corker (1998) notes: "So, to describe oneself as Deaf means that one is not hearing (or deaf), but it also means that being Deaf is defined *in relation* to hearingness, impairment or even vision" (63). *Deaf* thus necessarily carries *hearing* with it as something from which it draws meaning, and the same with *hearing* as well, although in the latter, this process is unconscious; *deaf* calls up *hearing* as its frame of reference, its marker indicating oddity, more than *hearing* calls up *deaf* to derive its meaning from, to "normalize" itself. This perceived matter of degree is due to prioritizing: Derrida notes that many relational terms are hierarchical and that one term in a binary opposition is the normative one.

The hierarchy of the terms can change, however, and what is considered "normal" changes. Harlan Lane (1993) explains: "The late president of Kenya, Jomo Kenyatta, has recounted that when white skin was first seen, it was assumed to be the result of some pitiful disease. Only in that moment did the black man conceive his blackness, as the deaf man becomes deaf only in hearing society" (92–93). Deaf people can also invert this traditional hierarchy of hearing over deaf and see themselves as not disabled, not hearing impaired, but simply normal within a particular language and cultural tradition. That is, after all, what *normal* means—it is always relativized within a particular system. Lane recounts the story of a Deaf child meeting the hearing girl next door:

> Consider first the deaf child of deaf parents; his self is bound up with his likeness to his parents in activities, in language, in the treatment received from other people, notably deaf friends or relatives. *Hearing children are weird to this child;* they apparently have a different self. A deaf friend from a distinguished deaf family recounts how, as a child, he made friends with a little girl next door. He discovered, however, that he could not communicate with her as he could with his family; even the simplest gestures baffled her. So he was reduced to pointing and to bringing her to things, or things to her. He did not know what was wrong with her, but then something happened to confirm his conviction that she was strange indeed. Her mother walked up to them one day while they were playing and started moving her mouth furiously. Suddenly his playmate picked up her toys and left. My friend went to

his mother and asked what this child's affliction was. His mother explained that she was HEARING; she didn't know how to SIGN, so she and her mother communicate with TALK. (92, italics added)

In this situation the hearing girl is "weird," not the Deaf boy. It all depends on perspective—no one term is inherently superior, although in a given society, which defines a norm and then tries to universalize it, one term may conditionally be seen as superior. The validity of this prioritizing of terms, however, is easily troubled by the fact that within the hearing community many hearing children of Deaf adults prefer sign language and the Deaf community and that a number of people in the Deaf community prefer speaking to sign or use both interchangeably—or even simultaneously (a few people can speak English and sign ASL at the same time; in comparison, someone who knows both French and English cannot speak both at the same time). In this sort of free play of languages and attitudes, schematic oppositions and hierarchies can be rendered null.

In this light, then, as Derrida has pointed out, why do so many people have "the illusion that they [speech and writing] are two separate things" and consider speech to be ideal? Why does Derrida call the difference between speech and writing an illusion? For him, they are essentially the same because they both operate from a system of *différance,* they are both writing, and, by extension, sign language is no different from these two or from any other system of signs, despite their varying media. Derrida (1973) discusses the illusion that speech represents the interior self better than any other form of discourse: he asks, "Does uttering or hearing signs reduce the indicating spatiality of mediation?" (72). He thinks not. The "apparent transcendence" of the voice is that words are heard immediately—the "system of hearing-oneself-speak." The divorce between the signifier and signified is not quite as obvious as it is in graphic writing, for example. This is where the "complicity between sound and ideality" (that is, the perception of the voice as ideal) arises (77). Derrida writes:

> The ideality of the object . . . does not have worldly form. *The name of this element is the voice. The voice is heard.* Phonic signs ("acoustical images" in Saussure's sense, or the phenomenological voice) are heard [*entendus* = "heard" plus "understood"] by the subject who proffers them in the absolute proximity of their present. The subject does not have to pass forth beyond himself to be immediately affected by his expressive activity. My words are "alive" because they seem not to leave me: not to fall outside me, outside my

breath, at a visible distance; not to cease to belong to me, to be at my disposition "without further props." (76)

Derrida notes that this illusion is further fostered by the idea that while writing, for example, has a spatial location in the outside world, speech apparently doesn't *seem* to—the sense of the exterior is more marked for written systems of signification than for speech: "In phenomenological interiority, hearing oneself and seeing oneself are two radically different orders of self-relation" (76). It can be inferred from this that the phonocentric tradition that Derrida criticizes would imagine "hearing oneself" via speech as vastly superior to "seeing oneself," as in graphic writing or using sign language. The presence of the self at the moment of speaking enhances the illusion of the signified's closeness: "Such is at least the experience—or consciousness—of the voice: of hearing (understanding)-oneself-speak *[s'entendre-parler]*. That experience lies and proclaims itself as the exclusion of writing, that is to say of the invoking of an 'exterior,' 'sensible,' 'spatial' signifier interrupting self-presence" (Derrida 1976, 98).

Although there might also appear to be an immediacy in sign language that would ally it more with speech than with writing, this does not apply because signs can be seen, whereas spoken words cannot be. Derrida (1973) conflates the manual gesture with graphic writing, as he writes that this illusion of the "absolute proximity" of speech to the signified "is broken when, instead of hearing myself speak, I see myself write or *gesture*" (80, emphasis added). This "absolute proximity" would clearly be broken in the case of "seeing oneself sign." So in the phonocentric tradition, sign language, as it is visible, would be relegated to the socially inferior status of graphic writing below the "transcendence" of speech. As a result, anything other than speech is denigrated, such as the use of signs by the "deaf and dumb":

This self-presence of the animating act in the transparent spirituality of what it animates, this inwardness of life with itself, which has always made us say that speech *[parole]* is alive, supposes, then, that the speaking subject hears himself *[s'entende]* in the present. Such is the essence or norm of speech. It is implied in the very structure of speech that the speaker *hears himself:* both that he perceives the sensible forms of the phonemes and that he understands his own expressive intention. If accidents occur which seem to contradict this teleological necessity, either they will be overcome by some supplementary operation or there will be no speech. *Deaf and dumb go hand in hand.*

He who is deaf can engage in colloquy only by shaping his acts in the form of words, whose telos requires that they be heard by him who utters them. (Derrida 1973, 78, latter italics added)

Even as Derrida notes that to be truly "heard"—not "dumb" or silent—in society, the deaf must speak and hear themselves speak, the pejorative phrase "deaf and dumb" that Derrida quotes from Husserl here is presumably a consequence of the logocentric tradition, one that Derrida critiques. However, as Bauman and others have pointed out, Derrida has conspicuously ignored the deaf in his writings and how they could amplify his thoughts. Bauman (1997) notes: "With its deconstruction of the voice-centered tradition, grammatology, one might say, initiates a 'Deaf philosophy'—if it weren't for the fact that Derrida fails to engage theoretical issues of deafness or signing to any significant degree. The exchange between Sign and deconstruction, then, recognizes the metaphysical implications of Sign while Sign, in turn, extends the project of deconstruction beyond its own limitations drawn by the exclusion of Sign and Deaf history" (317). Bauman further points out that when Derrida does mention deafness, it is always through the writings of others, notably Rousseau in *Of Grammatology,* and that Derrida is clearly aware of deafness as a result. Bauman ascribes this omission to audism: "One may link this critical oversight as being symptomatic of not really *seeing* Deaf people, of tacitly acknowledging their absence from being. If this is so, this audist oversight reinscribes the very phonocentrism Derrida sets out to deconstruct" (318). Derrida tends to "ventriloquize" by writing his thoughts through other people's writings, or "voices," and by using the ultimately voice-biased writings of writers such as Husserl and Rousseau he ends up reinscribing audism in his discussions of deafness and language. But then, since it would be difficult for Derrida to "ventriloquize" in ASL, perhaps it is no wonder Derrida remains silent (pun intended) on the subject. How "audist" is it really to refuse to write about something one really doesn't have firsthand knowledge of?

Even as he avoids direct dealings with deafness, Derrida breaks down this "hearing oneself speak" bias and presumably the issue of "deaf and dumb" as well, since that notion is couched within the tradition of "hearing oneself speak." For Derrida (1973), "hearing oneself speak" is contradicted by "time." Hearing is a sense, and sense is temporal; as such, speech possess the "trace" that contaminates its perception of perfect interiority or ideality. This trace is the relationship of the interior with the outside, and because it breaks the feeling of "hearing oneself speak," there is a spacing there, which means there is no pure interior, unmediated language (85–86). Hearing is also spatial in that sound waves take up space.

I sent out a lot of broken sound waves into space when I tried to learn to talk with the assistance of a speech therapist. In fact, my deafness and its consequent eighteen years of speech therapy—mandated by my school and society—support the idea that there actually is a "spacing" in the process of "hearing oneself speak." Here the supposed perfection of speech really is an illusion, as Derrida says. The extensive work involved in developing my deaf speech with a speech therapist reveals the "trace" structure, the "minimal element of structure that makes any sense of difference possible" or "track . . . in the text" (Payne 1993, 137). I cannot "hear myself speak" and so cannot modify my own voice myself; still, this does not make me "deaf and dumb" just because I cannot hear myself. This speech training requires a speech therapist, which in itself indicates externality and structural coding. Modifying my voice to make it as "perfect," as "hearing," as possible is also the point where the apparent fullness of "hearing oneself speak" breaks down, since it reveals the working of a code imposed by a therapist. This works the same way for the hearing, however, as speech does not arise full-blown on its own either; it arises as the hearing baby first hears others who insist on speaking to it and then comes to speak on its own. To speak is to follow an external code, and this introduces "spacing," "time," and referentiality into the supposed exaltation and purity of "hearing oneself speak."

An interesting consequence of phonocentrism is that even if the deaf are fully educated and assimilated into the production of speech, albeit with an accent, or knowledge of speech writing, they can never approach full societal equality, since even this type of writing is traditionally subsumed under speech. Derrida notes that traditionally speech outranks graphic writing, even as graphic writing is seen to outrank other scriptural events. Speech subordinates graphic writing and everything else under speech, including all that which "has no need, as Leibniz said, 'to refer to the voice' or to the word *(vox)*" (Derrida 1982, 88)—including sign language in its nonreference to the voice or the *vox*. This exaltation of speech, however mistaken, has its implications for the Deaf in writings—"other scriptural events"—other than written speech, as this means that videotapes, which are currently the main "written" form of ASL, and sign language notation systems, such as HamNoSys (Hamburg Notation System, developed at the

Universität Hamburg, Germany) for German Sign Language, Stokoe notation, or the Salk Institute's Sign Font (Sacks 1989, 78–79)—"ideographic"
writing—will never approximate the status of speech, or even speech writing, *unless society widens its perspective.*

Derrida, in his debunking of the voice as primary, has opened a space for
videotapes and other forms of representation as "writing" and therefore
paved the way for ASL to create forms of literature as valid as Shakespeare's
Hamlet. Not only can we borrow the concept of the "literary" from a speaking society and say that ASL is literary, but we can invert this and ask how
ASL literature can influence the tradition of literature and language. The
existence of ASL literature and alternate forms of textuality calls into question what literature means and what it is composed of: it implies a widening of the boundaries of language and literature; it requires a different
mind-set; it requires a different way of looking at people and their creative
expressions. In the words of my hearing colleague Carol Robinson (2001),
after working at Gallaudet University, a university for the deaf:

> I know I learned a lot more than I taught. . . . My two year stint at Gallaudet
> in the early '90s was like being plopped into the midst of a newly renais-
> sanced culture that has been trapped and contained within the sounds of our
> society. . . . I both taught and lived in *Deafland:* I taught during the day and
> at night I went home to a house that I shared with a deaf roommate. Occa-
> sionally, I went for days without speaking a word of English. I was a for-
> eigner, handicapped on two levels: I did not know the native language(s),
> and these sign languages were like no language I had ever struggled to learn
> in my life. I had a lot of "brain muscle" to exercise—not to mention other
> muscles in my fingers, hands, arms and face. . . . I was a legal alien. . . . I was
> at a place where hearing isn't necessary, a place where the dominant culture
> is visually oriented, and it was my job to adapt to this culture, not for this
> culture to adapt to me. . . . In my "natural" world, a deaf person is linguisti-
> cally impaired due to his inability to hear as well as everyone else. In a deaf
> person's "natural" world, I am linguistically impaired due to my inability to
> see as well as everyone else. This experience made me acutely aware of how
> amazing it is that two people, regardless of abilities, are able to communicate
> at all.

For Robinson, as for the hearing girl and Deaf boy who lived next door to
each other, as for any member of one culture being introduced into another
culture, the tables can be turned and a new world opened up. These are the

aims of this book: to turn the tables, to rethink writing, to inscribe the body writing, to become the bodily writing.

REFERENCES

Barthes, Roland. *Empire of Signs.* Trans. Richard Howard. New York: Hill and Wang, 1982.

Bauman, H-Dirksen L. 1997. "Toward a Poetics of Vision, Space, and the Body: Sign Language and Literary Theory." In *The Disability Studies Reader*, ed. Lennard Davis, 315–31. New York: Routledge.

Chomsky, Noam. 1988. *Language and Problems of Knowledge.* Cambridge, MA: MIT Press, 1988.

Corker, Mairian. 1998. *Deaf and Disabled, or Deafness Disabled?* Philadelphia: Open University Press.

Derrida, Jacques. 1973. *Speech and Phenomena.* Ed. John Wild. Evanston, IL: Northwestern University Press.

———. 1976. *Of Grammatology.* Trans. Gayatri Chakravorty Spivak. Baltimore: Johns Hopkins University Press.

———. 1982. *Margins of Philosophy.* Trans. Alan Bass. Chicago: University of Chicago Press.

Foster, Susan Leigh, ed. 1995. *Choreographing History.* Bloomington: Indiana University Press.

Lane, Harlan. 1993. *The Mask of Benevolence: Disabling the Deaf Community.* New York: Vintage Books.

Payne, Michael. 1993. *Reading Theory: An Introduction to Lacan, Derrida, and Kristeva.* Oxford: Blackwell.

Poizner, Howard, Edward S. Klima, and Ursula Bellugi. 1987. *What the Hands Reveal about the Brain.* Cambridge, MA: MIT Press.

Robinson, Carol. 2001. *Kaleidoscope: International Magazine of Literature, Fine Arts, and Disability* 43:56–59.

Sacks, Oliver. 1989. *Seeing Voices: A Journey into the World of the Deaf.* Berkeley: University of California Press.

SEVEN

The Poet in the Poem in the Performance

The Relation of Body, Self, and Text in ASL Literature

HEIDI M. ROSE

Suppose that I put pen to paper and write a poem. In the process of writing, my inner voice speaks the words, and my hand puts those words on paper. What is the relationship between the words on the page and the body who wrote them? The self created in those words does not—cannot—sound or look like me; no matter how implicitly my sense of self may be embedded in the poem, it is necessarily a noncorporeal "me," divorced from my voice and body. When someone reads my poem, whose actual inner voice speaks the words? The reader's, not mine. What then has happened to the "me" of the poem?

Suppose I create a poem in American Sign Language (ASL).[1] The poet's inner "voice" emerges, not in words on paper, but in signs through my body; the body becomes the text. Deaf people possess an inherently physical relationship with text because sign language lives in, and is expressed through, the face, head, hands, torso. To create and give expression to a poem requires the poet to sign it, whether alone or in front of an audience. (Semi)permanence of form is gained through film or videotape.[2] Thus, unlike in writing—in which the word achieves (semi)permanence of form by becoming disembodied, separated from the author—literacy in sign language means preserving the *image* of the author signing; it is a two-dimensional copy (through videotape) of a four-dimensional form.[3] A person viewing (reading) an ASL poem experiences the poem through the poet-performer's body. Sign language literally provides a new *space* for literature to exist.

What are the implications of this new space? The primary question of this chapter is: How does ASL poetry "speak" the self of the poet differently than the poetry of spoken-written language? A written-language poet says, "I wrote a poem. Here, I'd like you to read it," and hands over a piece of paper. A manual-language poet says, "I created a poem. Here, I'd like you to see it," and signs it for the viewer. What can this bodily connection teach us about the nature of identity and poetry? How is the relationship between poet and poem affected when the poet says, "These are my signs in this body" rather than "These are my words on this paper"? And what does this relationship have to do with the overall aesthetics of ASL literary performance?[4]

ASL literature is more than a literature of the body; it is a literature of performance, a literature that moves through time and space, embodied in the author's physical presence. To "read" an ASL text means to view a live or videotaped performance. The literary power of ASL literature is defined by, and coexistent with, its theatrical or performative power; thus the Deaf poet's gift with language is always already a gift of bodily expression and dynamic stage presence. A Deaf poet, it seems, must necessarily be a good performer—a quality not required of hearing poets, whose texts lie dormant on the page, waiting to be awakened by a reader. It is this critical feature of ASL literature *as an art of performance* that drives my analysis.[5]

Of course, not all hearing poetry is limited to the page. In response to what is perceived as absent from the normative written text, many contemporary hearing poets have experimented with ways to create body-texts with spoken-written language in order to make poetry more active, more material, more visual, and more connected with their corporeal selves. There seems to be a need both to challenge the tradition of the page and to project more directly a sense of self to the reader/audience than the page allows. Stanley Corngold (1994) writes that literature "is the discourse of a subject whose saying, by virtue of how it is said, stands for the self in the future" (xvii). For many contemporary poets the literary text should do more than *stand* for the self; the text should directly encompass and reveal the body/self of the poet, allowing the actual body of the poet to live on and allowing the words of the poem to come through the poet's own literal voice.

This trend has not been without a struggle, and many hearing poets have had to turn to other art forms to accomplish their goals. As Marjorie Perloff (1998) points out, "[A]rtists who might, in an earlier time, have become painters or poets, now choose to become video artists or performance poets or makers of bookworks" (xii). It is at times difficult even to label an artist or his or her art as simply poetry, prose, or painting because boundaries have become so blurred; a poem may utilize space and patterns on the page as visually as a painting.[6]

The struggle of Deaf literary artists, on the other hand, has been of a different kind. For generations Deaf people have had to fight the hearing majority to gain control and ownership of their language and acknowledgment of their culture, and this struggle is evident in much of the content of ASL poetry and narrative; in contrast, the individual Deaf artist's literal ownership of his or her literature is unquestionable because the text naturally and necessarily lives in the artist's body. Original ASL poetry and narrative preserved/published on videotape, then, provides a unique example of a literature that encompasses inherently what hearing performance poets and artists have wrestled to create. The literature of sign language solves a problem of contemporary poetics as it demonstrates artists "writing" the body with a literary art based in performance. In ASL performance literature, or literary performance, the performing body matters, space matters, and time matters.

Ella Mae Lentz is one Deaf artist whose work exemplifies the performative power of ASL poetry. I begin with Lentz because in her videotape *The Treasure: Poems by Ella Mae Lentz* (1995), she works with a director, Lynnette Taylor, to "stage" her poems more theatrically than has been seen in other video publications. Lentz clearly recognizes the dramatic elements embedded in any poem—a specific "voice" or persona that translates into character, a specific context or setting, a specific tone—and she physicalizes these elements through costuming, set pieces, lighting, and camera angles. In "Travels with Malz: The Next Generation," a poem that pays tribute to her teacher Eric Malzkuhn, the camera takes an unusual position, focusing on Lentz from above. The poem uses the metaphor of space travel and exploration to describe the students' experiences discovering new worlds of language in Malzkuhn's classroom; the camera angle from above results in Lentz looking up and signing toward the sky, which allows her to open her whole upper body to the possibilities of space. Lentz's upturned face, eyes bright and curious, helps to transform her from middle-aged adult to youthful student, and the viewer's perspective from above reinforces the teacher-student, adult-child relationship. This simple shift in angle helps to bring out the character, attitude, and tone of the poem and, interestingly, creates an effect that would not be possible in a live performance unless the audience were placed high above Lentz as she performed (**clip 7.1**).

In another poem, "Silence Oh Painful," Lentz uses shadowy lighting and costuming to help the poem come to life. This poem reflects the end of a romantic relationship and the ensuing difficulty in communication between the estranged partners. Set during a morning after the breakup, Lentz's bathrobe and the sense of early morning light place the character in a specific context, much the way a play or film creates character and context. The persona, or character, of the poem speaks directly to her ex-partner, focusing on a point slightly off camera. The camera lens observes the scene, allowing the viewer to look in and become a kind of voyeur. The persona does not acknowledge the viewer's presence until the last sign, SILENCE, which she signs to the camera (**clip 7.2**).

The poem could certainly still live in the body of the signer with different costuming, lighting, or set, or with neutral background and clothing, as seen in other videos such as *Poetry in Motion, Selected Works of Clayton Valli* (1995), and the ASL Literature Series. Lentz, however, is a poet-performer who emphasizes the theatricality of her medium. In addition, while not all her poetry is autobiographical, in these two autobiographical poems she uses her body to explore her own sense of self. These two qualities of theatricality and self-body exploration align Lentz's work with that of many contemporary performance artists.

Performance art provides a particularly useful context from which to compare and analyze ASL literature, as opposed to other art forms of the hearing world.[7] A multimedia form that may include any combination of, for example, poetry, monologue, video, dance, music, and painting, performance art is often seen as hard to define; it does, however, possess certain common characteristics. Performance artists

> do not base their work upon characters previously created by other artists, but upon their own bodies, their own autobiographies, their own specific experiences in a culture or in the world, made performative by their consciousness of them and the process of displaying them for audiences. Since the emphasis is on performance, and on *how the body or self is articulated* through performance, the individual body remains at the center of such presentations. Typical performance art is solo art, and the typical performance

artist uses little of the elaborate scenic surroundings of the traditional stage, but at most a few props, a bit of furniture, and whatever costume (sometimes even nudity) is most suitable to the performance situation. (Carlson 1996, 6, emphasis added)

Many, but not all, performance art texts explore autobiographical themes or issues. Whatever topic is explored, however, is necessarily filtered through the body of the artist/performer; the performer is both agent and agency, with no separation between artist and art, poet and poem. The theatricality of performance art reinstates the artist's voice and body as the primary medium of expression (not the page, not video, not canvas, not clay or bronze) and thus transforms the notion of identity in relation to text. The works of performance artists and poets may be seen as attempts to create what Calvin O. Schrag (1986) calls a "new horizon of subjectivity . . . [that] can happen only through exploration of a new space" (120). These performers challenge the traditional space where the subject is positioned "as a container of interior meanings and intentions" and where "works of thought and art become exterior and inert objects, alienated from the creative processes that gave them birth" (120). Performance artists and poets challenge traditional space by creating texts that are more active, more material, more visual, and more directly connected to their corporeal selves. As the performance artist Terry Galloway (1997) describes:

> By the time I finished *Out All Night and Lost My Shoes* I felt I had created what I wanted, a piece about the life of a woman: a woman born deaf and hallucinatory because of a modern medical experiment gone awry; a woman who fought her way through the idiotic folly of the world that surrounded her, fought her own bouts of terror and madness; and if she didn't exactly triumph, she did save herself. I let that woman experience all those things I love about theater: the mystery and hilarity, the inexplicable connections and the sudden changes of emotion, the cathartic clarifying moments and quieter denouements. I let her claim them as her own. And since it was my own life I was writing about I could claim those things as mine, too. Having claimed those things, I could finally imagine myself—within myself—an artist. A great excuse to keep on living. (148)[8]

For Galloway, creating the woman described above in the form of written story or poem could not give her the sense of self that came from creating the woman for the stage, to be performed as a monologue by Galloway herself. The lived, embodied theatricality of performance gives the text a different kind of artist self-understanding and self-knowledge than other art forms, as well as a different kind of audience understanding and knowledge of the artist. In addition, the theatricality of performance art makes the artwork live in both time and space, unlike the printed poem, painting, or sculpture.

Many performance artists have turned to this medium as a means of taking ownership of their art. It gives them autonomy, in contrast to dealing with, for example, publishers, gallery owners, producers, and directors. For example, many feminist performance artists in the 1970s were drawn to the art form because, "[u]nlike traditional actors, they created their own projects—serving as writer, producer, director, designer, cast, and often carpenter and costumer as well" (Carlson 1996, 148). Although she did work with a director, Ella Mae Lentz reflects this independent spirit in her self-produced, solo performance video. But whereas hearing poets and visual artists have needed to turn away from traditional forms to search for performative ways to embody and breathe four-dimensional life into their texts, the body and space are not problematized in sign language literature; the body and space make up the text itself.

The very embodied and performative quality of original ASL texts does, however, problematize the question of textual authority in a way that written texts do not. As ASL poems and narratives become increasingly mass-marketed on video, author-artist recognition increases, comparisons and contrasts are made of different artists' poetic styles, and more people have access to the texts. Does the text belong solely to the author's body? What happens to the text when it is signed—reproduced—by someone else? What are the signer's obligations/responsibilities to the author's original performance? Is there a greater sense of authority in ASL texts than in written texts?

Similar questions have been raised in the study of performance art. Many performance artists would argue that the bodily connection of their texts results in a stronger sense of textual authority than in written poetry. In fact, the autonomy and bodily identification between artist and text make it difficult to conceive of anyone other than the artist performing his or her work. In his foreword to a collection of performance art texts, Mark Russell (1997) asks: "Can or should [performance art texts] be performed by people other than the authors? That is a delicate question. What does it mean to play Spalding Gray playing Spalding Gray in a remembered life of Spalding

Gray? Some of these monologues are more adaptable than others, but all of them would lose something once their original artist was not involved" (xiii–xiv). Russell's comment suggests that the body and voice of the artist are integral to the life of the piece itself. The poem literally lives in the poet, and the poet gives the poem life through performance. This is not to say that people other than the artist do not perform particular performance art pieces. For example, Anna Deavere Smith's solo piece *Fires in the Mirror* is a text published in both book form (the script) and video (the performance) so that it can be—and is—performed by others. Russell asserts that, while the piece possesses its own life on the printed page, it simply cannot live on the page or in another performer's body the same way that it lives in the author's body; the form and structure may cohere with the original, but the actualizing—the interpretation—must be different.

Can an ASL poem live in a new signer's body the same way it lives in the original artist's body? What must a new signer do to retrieve, re-produce the original body/text? And what implications does this present for the relationship between identity (the poet's as well as the new performer's) and the text? All authors must let go of their works once they are created and have an audience, whether that audience is in the form of readers or viewers. One of the remarkable qualities of good literature is its ability to take on a life of its own, becoming open to multiple interpretations and multiple applications. ASL artists are beginning to have the same kind of individual style recognition as hearing authors; the difference, however, lies in the embodied nature of the ASL artists' style. This embodied quality is more akin to the work of performance artists whose very presence makes the text what it is.

Interpreting and performing an ASL text thus presents certain challenges not found in the performance of written texts, and these challenges derive from the body-text relationship—the physical sense of authority found in ASL texts. As a performer analyzes the language, style, and tone of an ASL poem or narrative, that analysis must involve, for example, the author's specific facial expressions—including every nuance of movement of the mouth, eyes, eyebrows—and tilts of the head, tension in shoulders, and so on. These nuances are the inseparable linguistic and performative elements that make the text live. Thus a performer other than the author must be able to create these nuances in his or her own body while reperforming the poem or narrative.

To delve into these issues, let me describe a college student's performance of "Missing Children," created by Debbie Rennie and Kenny Lerner and performed by Debbie Rennie on the Poetry in Motion video series. The student was part of a Deaf and hard-of-hearing performance ensemble at Arizona State University that focused on the study of ASL poetry and narrative. Under the direction of myself and Jaine Richards, an interpreter and director of Deaf/Hard-of-Hearing Services at the university at that time, the group was known as Poetic Images and was active from 1990 to 1995. The group functioned as a literature and performance workshop: activities included performance exercises; viewing ASL works published on videotape; discussing and analyzing the texts according to meaning, form, style, and performative power; performing them; and eventually creating and performing original works by the students themselves.

In 1991 Poetic Images had the opportunity to perform at the Herberger Theater Center in downtown Phoenix. We invited the Deaf artists Sam Supalla and Peter Cook to perform their ASL works, and the students performed various works of Clayton Valli, Ella Mae Lentz, and Debbie Rennie. To my knowledge this was the first public performance involving the *interpretation of ASL literature* by performers other than the authors.

The students came from a variety of performance backgrounds and were all relatively new to the analysis and performance of ASL literature. After analyzing the various texts according to content and meaning, as well as particular styles and poetic features (e.g., Valli's use of three-count rhythm, Rennie's use of metaphor),[9] students selected poems or narratives they wished to perform themselves.[10] The rehearsal process was intensive, combining the prior work in literary analysis with the work of an actor: rehearsal required meticulous study of the subtleties of each moment in the text—the tilt of the head, the expression of the mouth, the pace of the hand's movement—to uncover both meaning and performative power. In addition, the students had to dig deep into themselves to discover what the poem meant to them personally. Finally, their performance of the poem had to reflect simultaneously the integrity of the author's performance and the students' personal, individual response to the poem. These goals were achieved at varying levels based on individual students' experience and maturity; in all the performances, however, the attention to performance detail helped the students fully understand the piece and reflect that understanding in their interpretation of it.

In "Missing Children," Debbie Rennie presents four children, from Nicaragua, South Africa, and Northern Ireland, who all suffer and/or are killed because of civil unrest or war in each country. Framed around the familiar "Have you seen me?" photos of missing children on milk cartons or flyers, the poetic narrative provides snapshotlike glimpses of each child's life and death, with transitions occurring at the moment of death and/or violence. Each child is meticulously created by Rennie through her facial expression, posture, use of stress or emphasis, and use of rhythm and repetition. The narrator's perspective weaves subtly through each child's story, conveying empathy and horror at the children's plight (**clip 7.3**).

"Missing Children" is a kind of narrative poem, focused on social consciousness raising, that indirectly criticizes Americans' tendency to distance themselves from any human suffering that does not affect them firsthand. Much of the power of the text derives from the kinetic, tangible passion that Rennie communicates as a performer; while clearly not an autobiographical text, the poem is stamped with Rennie's personality, particularly in the way she creates characters. For "Missing Children" to come alive in another performer's body, the performer must find his or her own passion to fight injustice. The performer must also be able to convey the deep empathy toward the children that emanates from Rennie, as well as her ability to create multiple, fully realized characters with just a few signs.

For Poetic Images we decided to stage "Missing Children" with four women, one performing the introductory and concluding sections as well as the first child, and the rest performing each of the other three children. This decision was made in part to give more students an opportunity to perform and in part to explore the aesthetic impact of a multiple-performer interpretation of the text. For the purpose of this discussion, I will examine one of the performers.

Missy Keast is a native signer who came to Poetic Images with theater and ASL-English translating experience but with little experience in literary analysis and interpretation. The beauty and skill of her signing, combined with her perceptiveness and sensitivity to language, character, and conflict, resulted in mesmerizing performances. For example, there is powerful double meaning in the way Rennie creates photos of the children falling to the ground. As Rennie uses her closed flat hand, palm facing down, to become the photos gently floating to the ground, her eyes follow her hand. Then in one sharp move she turns her palm over and holds it there, staring at it, creating half the sign meaning "death" or "dead." Keast grasped this metaphor connecting falling and death before any of the other students. In addition, Keast demonstrated the ability to re-create, and make her own, the specific facial expressions, stresses, and rhythms of the text. Through her close attention to the detail and nuance of Rennie's signing, Keast got to the heart of "Missing Children" and made it live the way Rennie does. Keast did not merely "retell" it; she embodied the signs, style, and personality of Rennie and succeeded too in bringing her own self to the text (**clip 7.4**).

A viewer who knew the piece already would clearly see Rennie in Keast's performance. A viewer who was experiencing it for the first time would see a fully realized and engaging text/performance. In the introductory section, note how Keast re-creates the expression of vulnerability and innocence in Rennie's eyes as she becomes the child's face on the photo, looking up at an imagined adult; she captures Rennie's exact smile on the child's face asking, "Have you seen me?"; she reflects the set of Rennie's mouth expressing regret and finality as the viewer of the photo shakes her head "no" in response to the question; she captures the curve and pace of Rennie's arm movement as she moves from a regretful "no" to the photo being tossed away. In the Nicaragua section, Keast embodies the significant changes in pace and rhythm that occur in Rennie's signing: from a slow and gentle pace depicting the peaceful scene of coffee bean planting between father and son—the boy looking at his father shyly and lovingly—to a faster, staccato pace signifying the violence of the soldiers' invasion and attack.[11] Keast's success lies not only in the attention to movement path/visual lines (as discussed by Bauman in chapter 5 of this volume) but in the investment of the physical movement with the feeling tone. The form itself evokes the content.

Much of the power of "Missing Children" derives from the performative qualities, particularly the living images of full, clear characters created through both narrator description and direct portrayal/embodiment, as well as the rapid shifts between the narrator's and children's perspectives. A hallmark of Rennie's style lies in conveying the vulnerability and openness of characters, causing the viewer to become fully engaged in their world and to care about their well-being. Keast finds a way both to match Rennie's style and to add her own interpretation. In the tension and anger of Keast's stance, facial expression, and signing emphasis, the menacing quality of the Nicaraguan soldiers in their initial attack is a bit bolder and more aggressive, with a more heightened quality, than Rennie's original; Rennie's crescendo builds a bit more slowly.

This sense of integrity to the original as well as ability to invest one's own style in the piece was notably absent from other students' performances. While they developed an internal understanding of the poems, their inexperience as performers prevented full expression of that understanding. The other students could reproduce the signs, but they could not invest the aesthetic and emotional aspects of form into their performances, resulting in greater focus on delivery and less focus on the poems themselves.

The act of retelling serves a valuable educational function; it allows young and/or inexperienced signers/performers to refine and improve their skills at whatever level they are able, acknowledging the variability involved in approaching and reaching a text. Keast's rendition of "Missing Children" is of high quality because it demonstrates both understanding of and ability to reproduce the subtle qualities of the text. And these subtleties lie within the body of the original artist. Without in-depth analysis of—and ability to embody—the nuances of the artist's performance qualities, the retelling does not—cannot—capture the poem. The performance nuances do far more than reveal an artist's individual style; they are integrally related to the *meaning* of the poem or narrative. It is these nuances, not the manual signs or nonmanual grammatical markers alone, that give each poem its distinct identity because they are bound up in the *body* of the artist.

By emphasizing the embodied relationship between author and text in sign literature, I am trying to demonstrate the role of the self-body in the realization of the text, not to essentialize ASL texts. A poem will of necessity emerge from one body somewhat differently than from another body. But, since ASL literature is a literature of performance, the performance ability and qualities of the signer will significantly influence the re-creation of the text. An ineffective performance will obscure a good poem, drawing attention to what is lacking in the performer rather than allowing the viewer to focus on the poem. Keast's performance worked because she studied Rennie's original so carefully and had the ability to take "Missing Children" into her body as if it were her own.

Retelling ASL literature has become a useful and popular pedagogical method. In 1995 DawnPictures published *Selected Works of Clayton Valli* (1995), a videotape that features a variety of performers signing Valli's poems, as well as description and literary analysis narrated by Lon Kuntze. Valli himself performs only a few of the poems, but he was integrally involved in the project, selecting the poems to be discussed and directing the video. The viewer does not know how much "coaching" the signers received from Valli, but clearly the range of their experience and skill is vast; at one end is a five-year-old child who stumbles over signs and exhibits little affect, and at the other end is Ella Mae Lentz, who mesmerizes the viewer and makes the poems look like her own. And in between are many other children and adults, some of whom come close to capturing Valli's face and body in their own and others who seem merely to be repeating signs—not living the poem truthfully or spontaneously.

Lentz's performances in *Selected Works* are particularly noteworthy because she is such a well-known poet-performer herself. Deaf audiences are familiar with her poetic style and presence, which in some ways is similar to Valli's. They both began their relationship with poetry through English; they studied written poetry, wrote their own poems in English, occasionally translated the poems into ASL, and only later began creating original poems in ASL. They both create tightly structured poems, working with hand-shape rhyme, pace, and movement to establish specific rhythms and spatial prosody. They both create diverse characters and are versatile in their range of characterizations. Thematically they both explore autobiographical issues, issues relating to the Deaf experience, and other social-political issues as well. Lentz tends to explore human relationships and conflicts explicitly, while Valli often utilizes personification, implicitly asking the viewer to make the connection with human beings.[12] In *Selected Works of Clayton Valli* (1995), Lentz performs "Dew on Spiderweb," a lovely lyric-type poem in which the persona describes a breathtaking view of sunlight sparkling through the dew clinging to a spiderweb. The persona tries to take a photo but realizes too late that he or she has not advanced the film. The persona is at first frustrated and upset that the image is now lost but then comes to the realization that the image will live forever in the mind's eye (**clip 7.5**).

Pace is an important rhythmic feature of this poem. Each time the spiderweb image is presented, the pace changes to reflect what is happening in the persona's mind: the first time is the actual witnessing of the scene; the second time is the quick flash of the image as the persona realizes it is gone; and the third time is the slow, careful replaying of the memory of the image.

Because Lentz is such a well-known poet-performer and because their styles are similar, it is harder to *see* Valli in her performance of his poem than it is to see Rennie in Keast's performance of "Missing Children." What Lentz achieves in her performance, however, is a match or fusion between her body-self and Valli's so that the poem seems to belong effort-lessly in her body.[13] For a performer of written literary texts, the challenge involves matching one's inner and outer self to the implied self of the text, discovered through in-depth analysis of language, tone, and style. For a performer of an ASL text, the challenge involves matching one's body with the body of the poet as an integral part of the analysis of language, tone, and style because in ASL poetry the self of the poem lives in the body of the poet. Thus two signers, or speakers, will necessarily perform a given text somewhat differently because the text is being matched with different bodies-selves, but each performance can still have integrity and can still reveal a truth of the text if the performers have truthfully matched them-selves to it *and* have the performance ability to express it. The viewer who sees Lentz's performance is drawn in to the image of the spiderweb and her response to it; even though the experience may have happened to Valli and not to Lentz, she finds the self of the poem in her self to make it believable.

In contrast, as Keast learned more about ASL poetry and narrative and literally "tried on" different artists' styles through performing their texts, she became not only a knowledgeable student of ASL literature but a bud-ding poet-performer herself. Her embodiment of Rennie's poetic self helped her to uncover her own poetic self. Keast's original narrative "Fate," first performed at Arizona State University, was featured at the 1996 ASL Literature Conference at the National Technical Institute for the Deaf in Rochester, New York, and she has continued to develop her poetic self.[14]

The two performances discussed above do far more than merely retell; they interpret the poems by allowing them to come alive in new bodies. The successful performance of an ASL poem or narrative by someone other than the author is a time-consuming and in-depth search to find the con-sciousness, the persona, the soul of the poem as created through the body of the author. In doing so the performer must understand that the per-formance qualities are literary and the literary qualities are performative. The quality of the performance must be factored into any evaluation or discussion of retelling because it is performance that brings the poem or narrative to life. The key to a successful retrieval of the original body-text is the "matching process," as seen in Keast's and Lentz's performances. If the matching process is not achieved—that is, if the signer is unable to embody the performative nuances of the original—the text-performance will fall flat and the text itself will be obscured. A good performance will allow the text to be reborn in a new body.

What, then, can sign literature teach us about the relationship between the poet and the poem? As I have tried to demonstrate, the body of the poet cannot be ignored or taken for granted in ASL poetry because the body is bound up with the self of the text, even if that self is distinct from the poet's self. Thus, as in the case of performance artists and their texts, the embodied quality of ASL literature results in a heightened sense of textual authority. This becomes particularly salient when a different body re-creates the poem. The interpretation may be different because the poem occurs in a different body, but a successful performance will necessarily encompass some quality of the poet. The poet's physical presence is so bound up in the original poem that he or she cannot/will not completely disappear in a performance by another signer. If the poet does disappear, that may well indicate an ineffective performance. An ASL poem consists of more than specific signs and prosody; the signing style, personality, and physical qualities of the poet are integral to the life of the poem, and the success of a performance by someone other than the author depends upon the performer's ability to integrate the author's style with his or her own. The reborn text exists in the liminal space between the author's and new performer's bodies—the space of the overlap.

Because of this new liminal space, sign language works differ from performance art texts, in which textual authority has clearer limits. Most spoken-written language performance art texts can exist in two permanent forms, printed script and video performance. Anyone can read the script as one would read a play, understanding that it is designed to be performed, but nonetheless can derive some meaning from the words themselves without ever seeing the original artist perform them. The ASL text does not exist separately from the author, and this has fascinating implications when looking at others' performances of the text. The performativity of ASL literature adds depth to our understanding of its nature and impact as a literary art form and clarifies its distinction from both written literature and oral traditional forms. ASL possesses, in a sense, a bodily, performative literacy, in which a whole world may be created in the lift of an eyebrow or shift of a shoulder. ASL literature thus concretizes dramatically the connection between poetry and bodily identity. If the space of the text is the body, not the page, then the body space is the text's prosody. It is thus this body space upon/through which we evaluate ASL poetics; the body becomes the writing.[15]

In ASL works, unlike other forms of literature, *performance quality* is central to the life of the text, whether performed by the author or someone else. I began this chapter with the statement that ASL provides a unique space for literature to exist and that in this space performance is central. A good performer may or may not be able to create good ASL literature, but, at least so far in the development of sign literature, a good ASL "writer" will necessarily be a good performer. As the art form evolves, will ASL "writers" create texts for others to perform rather than themselves, or will these Deaf artists always be, by definition, poet-performers or, utilizing Ben Bahan's term (in chapter 2 of this volume), "smooth signers"? In either case, we know that for an ASL poem to live it must be produced through the body of a skilled performer. Like performance art, the aesthetics of ASL literature are embedded in the performer's body, and new insights may be gained into the aesthetics by studying performances by people other than the original artist.

Sign literature may begin to teach the hearing world more about what language does in performance—how through performance we invest ourselves in language, through rhythm, cadence, tone, inflection, and movement through and in time, connecting to the body in space. Just as performance art has helped to bring the centrality of the body to issues of visual art and poetry, ASL literature highlights the body as the site of a four-dimensional literary text. But unlike performance art, whose early artists responded to a perceived lack in the worlds of poetry and visual arts, sign literature engages the body automatically. And in doing so, it confronts—and does not allow the viewer to forget—the body as a locus of expression. The Deaf poet-performer, however, does not draw specific attention to his or her body as marginalized, in the way that many performance artists do; the Deaf poet-performer's relationship with body, language and self simply *is*. While the mainstream world often looks to the literature, performance art, or performance poetry of marginalized groups as resisting the canonical and as revelatory of cultural insight, sign literature can demonstrate that signing/performing bodies are more than resistant to a perceived "norm." Rather, the performing bodies of sign literature can be seen as a standard from which the hearing world may learn something new about the relation of poetry to time, space, and image; the relation of body, text, and performance; the relation of language, culture, and performance; and the relation of poet to poem. This unique space for literature places the poet in the poem in the performance and thus places an emphasis on the self (or selves) negotiated and emergent through the body-text of the artist/performer.

NOTES

1. This discussion may be applied to all sign languages, though my focus here is on ASL.

2. I include the prefix *semi-* in parentheses here because the notion of permanence of form is debatable. One argument holds that film or video indeed "freezes" the ASL text similarly to writing; another argument claims that the video form is merely one version of the text—that because the texts exist in performance, they are born anew each time they are performed.

3. See Krentz, chapter 3 of this volume, for further discussion of video technology and its impact on literacy.

4. Various attempts have been made, and continue to be made, to develop a system of writing for sign languages. Some arguments suggest that the transformation from speech to writing was no less traumatic and revolutionary than would be the transformation from sign to writing. This view sees literacy as writing, and only writing. Other arguments stress the reconceptualization of literacy necessary when considering sign languages and liken any sign writing systems to dance notation or musical scores—cues to create the art form, but not the art form itself. Written musical notes can convey only part of the reality of the music in the reader's inner ear; the music must be physically played in order for it to live. Likewise, any written system of sign language exists as a code informing the reader of what specifically to sign, but it must be signed in order to live. In this view ASL literacy must still be viewed as embodied, and video provides the place to "read" the ASL text.

5. My previous research on ASL literature has incorporated performance as a primary feature of the texts: "Stylistic Features in American Sign Language Literature" (1994) explores ways in which Deaf artists make ASL aesthetic; "Inventing One's 'Voice': The Interplay of Convention and Self-Expression in ASL Narrative" (1996) looks at college students' creation and performance of personal narratives in ASL as public affirmation of their Deaf cultural membership as well as articulation of artistic "voice"; and "Julianna Fjeld's 'The Journey': Identity Production in an ASL Performance" (1997) explores the construction of self that occurs theatrically through the actual language used in an autobiographical ASL narrative. The present chapter deviates from the previous articles in that it focuses less on analysis of language in performance and more on performance as the pivotal force that drives the text.

6. See Bauman, chapter 5 of this volume, for a detailed look at manifestations of the line in painting and sign language.

7. Film and painting are just two other art forms that are discussed in this volume as approaches to understanding sign literature.

8. Terry Galloway is an oral deaf person in that she uses English as her first language and does not sign.

9. See Rose (1994) for detailed discussion of Valli's, Rennie's, and Sam Supalla's distinct uses of aesthetic ASL.

10. It is worth mentioning that, unintentionally, the student-performers were all the same sex as the poet whose work they performed. Perhaps they identified more with a poet-performer of the same sex; perhaps they felt that the poet's identity was so bound up in the poem that any interpretation had to come from the same gendered perspective. In any case,

it is interesting to see an ASL poem or narrative performed by someone of the opposite sex, as occurs in the video *ASL Poetry: Selected Works of Clayton Valli* (Valli 1995).

11. The video of Keast's performance was taken during a dress rehearsal, and she omitted a few of the signs, such as LITTLE BOY, at the very beginning. What is most important, however, is the tone, attitude, and style of her performance, not the memory lapse.

12. For example, see Lentz's "Travels with Malz," "The Baseball Game," "Silence Oh Painful," "Circle of Life," and "To a Hearing Mother" in *The Treasure* (1995). See Valli's "I'm Sorry," "Mushroom," and "Pawns" in *ASL Poetry: Selected Works of Clayton Valli* (1995) and "Dandelion" in *Poetry in Motion, Original Works in ASL: Clayton Valli* (1990).

13. Wallace Bacon coined the term *matching process* in *The Art of Interpretation* (1979) to explain the journey undertaken by a performer of literature to find a truthful fusion between self and text.

14. See Rose (1996) for a discussion of Keast's "Fate" as well as two other original ASL narratives created by college students.

15. See Jennifer Nelson, chapter 6 of this volume, for discussion of the body as writing in ASL texts.

REFERENCES

Bacon, Wallace A. 1979. *The Art of Interpretation.* 3rd ed. New York: Holt Rinehart Winston.

Carlson, Marvin. 1996. *Performance: A Critical Introduction.* New York: Routledge.

Corngold, Stanley. 1994. *The Fate of the Self.* Durham, NC: Duke University Press.

Galloway, Terry. 1997. "Terry Galloway." In *Out of Character: Rants, Raves, and Monologues from Today's Top Performance Artists,* ed. Mark Russell, 143–53. New York: Bantam Books.

Lentz, Ella Mae. 1995. *The Treasure: Poems by Ella Mae Lentz.* Videocassette. Berkeley, CA: In Motion Press.

Perloff, Marjorie. 1998. *Poetry on and off the Page.* Evanston, IL: Northwestern University Press.

Rose, Heidi M. 1994. "Stylistic Features in American Sign Language Literature." *Text and Performance Quarterly* 14:144–57.

———. 1996. "Inventing One's 'Voice': The Interplay of Convention and Self-Expression in ASL Narrative." *Language in Society* 25:427–44.

———. 1997. "Julianna Fjeld's 'The Journey': Identity Production in an ASL Performance." *Text and Performance Quarterly* 17:331–42.

Russell, Mark. 1997. Foreword to *Out of Character: Rants, Raves, and Monologues from Today's Top Performance Artists,* ed. Mark Russell, vii–xiv. New York: Bantam Books.

Schrag, Calvin O. 1986. *Communicative Praxis and the Space of Subjectivity.* Bloomington: Indiana University Press.

Valli, Clayton. 1990. *Poetry in Motion, Original Works in ASL: Clayton Valli.* Burtonsville, MD: Sign Media.

———. 1995. *ASL Poetry: Selected Works of Clayton Valli.* Videocassette. San Diego: Dawn-Pictures.

EIGHT

ASL Literature Comes of Age

Creative "Writing" in the Classroom

LIZ WOLTER

Philosophies of deaf education vary throughout the United States, but a growing number of programs assert both the validity of American Sign Language (ASL) as the first language of many deaf children and the corresponding value of incorporating ASL in the classroom. While teachers' signing may vary from ASL to PSE to sign-supported speech,[1] the result still permits students to use, and learn about, their first language in the classroom environment. Yet there is a catch: often ASL or various sign systems are employed in the classroom primarily as a means to teach English; the dominant model of language instruction in American deaf education gives priority to the achievement of English literacy. Not that there is anything wrong with that goal. It omits, however, some possibilities for in-depth exploration and understanding of the creative and literary capacities of ASL, as well as the enlightenment that ASL literature can bring to English literacy.

As a high school teacher of English with an extensive background in theater, I have always integrated the study of literature and performance. As I delved deeper into the study of ASL I became fascinated with its capacity as a literary language in its own right, not in comparison to English. When I developed an elective course on the study and creation of ASL literature, "Video Production and ASL Literature," it was groundbreaking in the sense that, although it was part of the English department, the focus of the course was all ASL. Through this course I wanted to find a way to understand more fully the literary nature of ASL and to support and encourage budding ASL literary artists. As a creative "writing" course, creation in ASL is an end in and of itself. In this elective course, Deaf students develop poems and stories in their first language. The models of good literature for the course are the already published videotapes of respected Deaf poets and storytellers. The techniques used by these artists to develop not only characters, setting, plot, and narrative style but also rhyme, rhythm, and symbolism are almost as varied as the techniques of hearing writers. Rather than using ASL as a way to arrive at English, as I sometimes do in my English classes, I encourage the students to create in their first language without having to transfer to a second to be valued. This provides an avenue for empowerment of the students as members of a distinct culture, the Deaf community.

Through the years the students have benefited from workshops led by the ASL poet and storyteller Peter Cook; our collaboration has helped us to map out more fully key steps in ASL literary creativity and to develop better skills in our students.[2] Using extensive interviews with Peter Cook[3] and my many years' experience teaching this elective course in ASL literature, in this chapter I explore the challenge of being a hearing English teacher nurturing Deaf students' literary creativity in their own language, and how this process influences students' personal and cultural identities.

"WRITING" IN ASL: A BEGINNING

During class, much of the discussion of ASL literary form and style occurs through the feedback process, using video playback. The feedback techniques are designed specifically to make students aware of how to increase their ASL fluency as they improve their poems or narratives. As the students begin to give feedback to each other, it is easy for them to distinguish which work is more or less successful, although it is at times more difficult to explain why. The level of reasoning requires an ability to break down and identify elements while simultaneously being able to appreciate them unified. The students develop this ability much as beginning readers move from simple "I like it" or "I don't like it" responses to deeper discussion and literary analysis. With experience and more advanced cognitive development, students become more able to recognize and elaborate on their perspectives. In an interview, Peter Cook and I discuss this process—which is similar to the process used in writing an English paper—in more depth (**clip 8.1**):

LW: The improvement of students' work to reach performance standards, or final-draft quality, relies initially on feedback and revisions, part of the process approach to development. I've learned a lot from observing your work in giving feedback. Could you comment on that?

PC: Many students don't realize the number of drafts required to reach a level of quality. They assume, "Oh, Peter Cook's a professional" or "He's just naturally like that," but it took me many, many years to get here when some of them only work an hour or so. The feedback I tend to give is: (1) facial expression—many lack it, (2) character—shoulder shifts to clarify moving from one to another, and (3) techniques. When it comes to techniques, I encourage them to create interest through variation of speed. I point to the video and tell students where to use slow motion for focus. Their eyes usually show me their degree of understanding or the lack of it. So I ask them to *do* the slow part. We practice again and again. I sign it, and they try again. They always add character but forget the small details. The bigger, more obvious things come first, and, with drafts, they work their way down to the more subtle points.

LW: A similar progression occurs when I read several of my favorite books over and over in teaching them. With each reading, I notice more and more how the author tells the story and I really grow in admiration of the writing itself. Initially it's the story that captures me, later the writing style, how and why the author decided to add certain parts. I appreciate the literature more. The progression from most to least obvious is a parallel process in reading and writing literature in any language.

PC: I agree. Few students naturally pick up feedback right away and are able to revise themselves.

LW: When you are developing a story or poem of your own, do you ever use video the way my students do, like paper, in a process approach?

PC: Often I sign my ideas on video, then look at the tape and edit stuff out, add facial expression, see which signs looked cool from my perspective but not from the audience view. Sometimes I change directionality of signs, playing with them. As I created more material, I began to rely on video. Little movements would disappear, forgotten, without the tape to save them. But the camera is like a mirror, the opposite of reality.

LW: Is that a big difference for you?

PC: Yes, sometimes.

LW: In one of my early assignments to develop settings and characters, I offer old calendar photos and magazine pictures and encourage the students to use classifiers and organize the space so that others can see the picture without looking at the photos. I explain to students that they don't need to reverse their signs for the viewer, just follow what they see. It's the viewer's responsibility to reverse from left to right and front to back. I learned that long ago while interning at NTID [the National Technical Institute for the Deaf].

PC: Right, but video playback is the opposite side of what I see as I sign, so I sometimes have to reverse it.

LW: I see. Only because ASL separates hands from eyes is there a two-sided view; it's three-dimensional, unlike spoken voice, so that's the difference in using video playback compared with audio.

PC: In "The United States of Poetry," I switched the fingerspelling of "Hollywood" from left to right so that the audience would see my signing as they would read the sign on the side of the hill in California.

LW: But you wouldn't do that with the name of a character, which you would rarely use in ASL anyway.

PC: Right . . .

LW: That's interesting. I noticed that a couple of students who worked with you their first year and then extended their development through a second year took more risks. I wondered if they were coming up with material outside of the elective class and then using class time to develop it. I suspect so. They became increasingly more adept, more creative, able to manipulate the language and interchange characters, space, develop duet pieces spontaneously. They still benefited from feedback, an objective eye, but, with video, they were able to mediate their own revisions more and more.

Peter and I realized that the teaching of cinematic techniques to develop literary structure and advance the range of ASL used played a large part in the increasing adeptness of the students. Using cinematic techniques, the signer creates multiple perspectives for the viewer, in much the way that the camera does in film. In ASL one can create the equivalent of, for example, long shots, close-ups, and panorama. We challenged students to tell a story by assuming the perspective of each character and even aspects of the setting, to *become* each part as much as possible. These techniques reflect the use of "visual vernacular," the ability to shift point of view identified by Bernard Bragg as a defining creative feature of ASL. In his example, Peter told a story of a man with an ax chopping down a tree. In the telling, Peter assumed the character of the man and then the tree, shifting back and forth (even the ax could be included). He next challenged the students to tell the same story as an outside narrator in which the perspectives must be portrayed using classifiers to a much greater extent, as if the story were being played out on an invisible stage in the signing space. In this telling, Peter's fingers became the man, the tree, and even the ax. The labels "BIG" (corresponding to close-up or first-person point of view) for the first telling and "SMALL" (corresponding to long-shot or third-person point of view) for the second simplified the contrast. Finally the students were told to combine both stories, to lace them together. In this way the third and finished story gained the benefit of details, expression, point of view, and liveliness inherent in good ASL as well as good storytelling.

LINGUISTIC DISCOVERIES

In addition to a deeper understanding of literary concepts such as character development and point of view, studying ASL literature has enabled us to make discoveries about some of the linguistic properties of ASL. Interestingly, ASL grammar has become more apparent (not in comparison to English) through development of ASL literary technique. One example involves the topic-comment format that is part of ASL's basic linguistic structure. In this format, the topic or subject of the sentence (noun) is signed first, followed by the comment, or description (verbs, adjectives). In one of my early assignments, students create character and setting descriptions using magazine photos, and their work shows consistently that eye contact is important for the gloss sign, or the topic of the photo; then the description, or comment, uses classifiers and indexing, with no eye contact. Without exception, my students made eye contact with the camera/viewer as they signed a topic, such as father and baby, and then broke the eye contact as they described the scene. This is not something any of us has been taught. It is simply the way the language works. Peter and I discussed this finding on one of his more recent visits to the Lexington School for the Deaf.

LW: In class, we discovered how ASL topic-comment structure applies to ASL literature. It seems students must set up the topic of a story first. Recognition or understanding is established first between the signer and the viewer.

PC: It may be a habit, an innate part of language/communication behavior to check with the listener/viewer as we go, then continue when it's clear our message is getting across or adjust it when it isn't.

LW: I agree. That seems a natural part of ASL, perhaps all languages as well, in face-to-face communication. Through our process of working in class on ASL literature, we tend to discover more about the language itself, as part of the process of using it, not intentionally, but through error analysis, i.e., when students' natural use of ASL becomes disrupted in focusing too much to "do it right."

PC: In my experience, there is not nearly as much eye contact involved in ASL poetry as there is in telling ASL stories. In poetry, eye contact occurs only at the beginning and end of a piece.

LW: Perhaps that's because poetry uses few gloss signs, relying instead on classifiers.

PC: When I first started doing school workshops I worked with hearing kids, using facial expressions, gestures (not signs), and body language. I began by doing the same thing with Deaf kids, but signs interrupted them, just as speech interfered with the hearing kids' creations. I realized that recognition of the difference between gestures and signs is not natural.

LW: I've heard you describe gestures as a bridge between Deaf and hearing, how acting replaces ASL classifier use, and how beginners learn to adjust their language to satisfy the need of a formal or informal situation.

PC: Right, I tend to use gesture as a communication bridge. Then I give more signs, create more pictures.

LW: I notice my beginning students act out stories instead of using ASL. It's not their natural way of conversing in the cafeteria, so why do they resort to it in class? Is it the effect of the camcorder? Sitting in the cafeteria with their friends, they must use classifiers because they are not standing or moving around, as they are in ASL literature class. It's hard to get them back to their natural signing behavior. It's a problem for beginners, who substitute movement, acting, in place of signing, using classifiers. Then I show them the basic videotape of your feedback from our initial year with the elective course and they're fascinated but they tend to copy it. It seems to take time to absorb the techniques of an admired "writer" and be able to incorporate their use but with one's own style and material.

PC: That's very natural, the same as beginning writers copying their favorite authors until they find their own voice.

LW: Exactly! It's important to separate the literature from its author, then to analyze, learn, take, play around. Just the same, I warn my students a lot when I see acting with the full body instead of signing classifiers, "C'mon, use your ASL!"

PC: It depends on the audience, on what you want to show. I balance depending on my audience and my goal. Could I use only my body? Then it would become dance instead of sign.

LW: The body is like background support for signs. That seems to be part of the Flying Words Project style [a performance duo created by Peter Cook and Kenny Lerner]. Or perhaps it was because you performed for hearing audiences, not just Deaf people.

PC: Movies, cinematic technique have also influenced me a lot!

LW: A lot more than the literature of the generation before you.

PC: It makes me wonder how, years ago, Deaf people signed "airplane flying"—was it slower? Biplanes, blimps? What about "cars passing through trees on a highway"—it's fast now, but was the signing slow before to represent a different reality at that time? What about riding on horses? Does it influence the form and style of our language, those different perspectives we have (**clip 8.2**)?

As students use the visual language they are attuned to, and play with the qualities inherent in it, their intellectual capacities increase, and they are able to manipulate language to achieve certain effects, which is a hallmark of literacy.

STUDENT GROWTH

With increased understanding and utilization of more complex linguistic and aesthetic qualities of ASL, the students' confidence and creativity soar, particularly if they take the course a second year. For all new "writers," however, the process is lengthy and requires patience.

LW: A similar problem I see in both ASL and English stories is getting a lot of stuff out, brainstorming, but not knowing where exactly the story begins and which details are relevant. I see students in the second (advanced) year of class make big improvements in control of these factors.

PC: True. I call those "walking" or "driving" pieces. The habit comes from a lack of recognition of story form or structure, but it can vary. Murder mysteries, for example, begin at the end and then go back to tell what happened. First-year Lexington students in the workshop lacked editing skills, use of space, outside influence of the arts; they just had knowledge of ABC stories.[4]

LW: And ABC stories are heavily embedded in English, the alphabet.

PC: Yes. I recall working on the transition of everyday signing to literary signing. Stories were initially too long, signed too fast. I advised students not to explain but to let the audience interpret the piece.

LW: "Show, don't tell" is the advice given to writers.

PC: During the second-year workshop together, I worked on refining a long story, say eight minutes, to a tighter piece of literature, more like four minutes, using classifiers. I didn't explain or discuss classifiers at that time because I wasn't sure how. I just focused on handshape techniques and use of the shoulder shift to clarify change of characters. They still had a hard time with editing, figuring out the composition of the piece of literature, how to put all their ideas together, create transitions between parts, eliminate the "walking, driving, riding" aspects. The Fanwood students had a lot of skills in ASL plus exposure to famous ASL artists, in contrast to Lexington students, who had little outside exposure to them.[5]

LW: Yes, that's not surprising in the context of Lexington's strong oral background.

PC: However, Fanwood students also lack technique with ASL. As an example, they understand handshape stories but not poetic schemes such as AABB or ABAB.

LW: This third workshop is the first time I've seen you explore other kinds of rhyme schemes in ASL, following English poetic forms.

PC: True, but it provides a challenge to the use of ASL in poetry. I remember Fanwood students seemed more able to create handshape stories taking turns from one person to the next in a line, while Lexington students needed an example to get started. In that first workshop, I asked them to create group machines, tell handshape stories, and develop transformations of signs. Playing with language was new for all the students. Using a sign, a classifier, and transforming its meaning or referent throughout the piece was new. For example, one Lexington student began by blowing bubbles; the bubbles fell and became a pool ball and cue stick. A Fanwood student transformed braiding her hair to playing the violin. Both pieces used simply the "9" handshape. Wow! Transformations became a great tool for creating poetry, I thought. I looked at other Deaf poets' work and realized no one had discussed it in this way (**clip 8.3**).[6]

LW: Others do employ metaphoric language, though. The technique you mention reminds me of list poems created with spoken language, in which there are connections but the sounds transform throughout the poems, playing with the vocal component of language in much the same way. It's a popular technique.

PC: I think of it as similar to film technique. In many movies, images change to create a change of environment, etc., but I haven't seen that technique discussed anywhere in literature or poetry. I use the same techniques each year but in more complex or challenging ways. One assignment required the use of a few gloss signs woven through a story or poem consisting of classifiers and their transformations. Another asked students to create the same piece from a close-up view (acting out or gesturing, becoming the characters and setting) and a long-shot view (using gloss signs and classifiers only, narrating the characters and setting within the signing space). In teaching perspective, or point of view, I also assigned students to create a piece that changed perspectives, but in which the signer faced the viewer for each of the characters—for example, switching from pitcher to batter to catcher but retaining the body in the same forward direction. I adapted a strong use of film techniques for these assignments. It's the idea of using other art forms to influence the creative process in ASL literature. In one of the workshops, students created group ASL stories based on history. I used the technique of taking turns passing the story's signs and action down a line of performers, expanding the use of space beyond side-to-side to three-dimensional, bending the rules of ASL as students become more confident in their creative use of it. One student involved in an ASL group story of slavery struggled with the idea of sharing his character, passing along his identity through a change in storyteller. I remember him objecting, "But that's *my* character!" and later [being] delighted when he grasped the goal of the process. There was a lot more texture in the third year of the workshop. They had much more control of their work than when they first began the class the previous year.

LW: Fantastic. In the first and second years of the workshop, participants had stories to tell but limited ways to tell them. In contrast, by the third year the group had multiple ways, even the use of symbolism.

Some examples of fascinating, more mature student work include stories from an advanced student group's creation of news stories, all U.S. disasters of recent times. The group piece consisted of individual stories combined through a linking device of their own creation, the concept of a TV viewer watching each disaster reported. This group worked with Peter Cook, and his influence is apparent in their work. The work of two students, Raymond Hawkins and Tamara Costa, is particularly powerful in the use of details, ironies, and range of ASL descriptive techniques.[7] Not only do they use the cinematic techniques that ASL employs, but they also draw the viewers ("readers") in through the perspective of a protagonist that allows viewers to see and feel the disaster personally as it unfolds (**clip 8.4**).

Raymond chose to focus on the burning of African American churches and incorporated the KKK as the responsible party. His main character is the church minister, who has two young children. The most chilling moment of the story occurs as two cars pass in the night, that of the minister on his way home and that of the KKK on their way to do the deed. The eyes of the drivers meet for a slow moment. It is very possible Raymond had seen this clip in film and borrowed it, transforming it into ASL and skillfully re-creating its powerful effect. Tamara, too, includes a minister in her story of the San Francisco earthquake. Her main character rides a crowded subway as the quake strikes. He survives, but many around him do not, including a clergyman. The survivor checks the minister for signs of life and then removes his cross and places it around his own neck as he makes his way out through a hole above and observes helplessly the scene of destruction surrounding him.

In another poem, "War and Peace," Shareen Tyler threads contrasting images of birth and death together through sophisticated use of transformation. Through the course of the poem, we see the sign for WAR transform into a heart beating that becomes a newborn whose mother holds it out only to morph into the sign for DEATH; she then holds the baby to her heart and cries tears that become a river, transforming back into WAR that reaches an explosive climax, ending in PEACE.

In another assignment that works well to combine elements of narrative and imagery, I asked students to create a postcard perspective of New York City in poetic form, selecting just one event, setting, or character as the basis for their creative work. The goal is not necessarily to tell a story but to create a mood, a flavor of the city. Wilson Ng, a student, chose to portray a businessman's morning commute from Staten Island to a Manhattan office building. He managed to include all sorts of obstacles as the man traveled first by ferry, then by subway and taxi to arrive just in time to stop for a bagel and coffee before rushing up to work in the elevator.

Given time, space, and an organized process for development, students in the elective class prove each year how capable they are of creating literature in ASL. For many, their growth here is much more obvious to themselves and others than in any other area of the curriculum.

Peter Cook has, over time, become the main source of fresh examples and provides direction for our work. As the course has progressed, both Peter's and my teaching skills have advanced, and our standards of excellence and ways of getting to the core of our work have become polished and varied. Peter has experimented himself and with us in breaking down the elements of story, poem, and ASL literature techniques in particular, giving us focus for structure and inspiration in the telling once the initial concepts (of story, poem, and ASL) have been mastered.

DEAF ARTISTS: THE NEW GENERATION

What is the impact of classroom exposure to video-published ASL poets and storytellers on the creativity and identity of contemporary high school students? The high school students with whom Peter Cook and I have worked seem to reflect a new generation of people whose needs and interests differ from those of established ASL artists. They seem to wear their Deaf identity in certain ways more comfortably than those of previous generations.

Peter and I discussed our own initial perceptions of Deaf life and various conditions influencing the artists to whom my students have been exposed.

LW: My first experiences with deaf people included a second-grader named Esther, who wore a hearing aid harnessed to her body in my second-grade advanced reading group, and later Ted Supalla and Shanny Mow as visitors to my college ASL class. I held no concept of deafness as disability from the beginning.

PC: Me, too, I had no concept of oppression until I went to NTD [the National Theatre of the Deaf] summer school and heard Martin Sternberg[8] lecture on the history of Deaf culture.

LW: How did you feel?

PC: I knew my experience of oral education with no signing was wrong, but it didn't hit me until much, much later, when I began to read about the history of deaf education.

LW: Of course, I know that written poetry inspired a number of Deaf poets. Clayton [Valli] was influenced by Robert Frost's nature poems. You had Allen Ginsberg. Frost is more formal, Ginsberg more free verse. The different influences really show the way you two developed your own ASL poetry.

PC: True, I enjoy Ginsberg's strong, flashing images. I want my ASL poetry to have the same feeling, the same principle. Bernard Bragg, too, influenced me. He is very visual. I didn't know Bernard Bragg when I first saw him perform, but it was awesome. I really enjoyed it, but I never thought of his technique as part of it, just the experience. Later I learned to see the techniques. In written words, the Beat generation to modern American poetry; in nonwritten work, Bernard Bragg and NTD's compositions—those are my influences.

LW: Let's talk about student perspectives of previous generations' poetry. Patrick [Graybill], for example, passed down ASL stories for a different reason. His main access to ASL was through dorm story-telling, a symbol of Deaf identity. Certain issues are strong for the professionals of that generation, but not as much now. The literature is no longer only about expressing Deafness or identity or history; it's about playing with the language. It's still about self-esteem and pride in ASL, but the students of this generation have communication access, they're not so isolated.

PC: Now there is access through the Internet, interpreting services, relay, pagers, captioning, etc. My wish is that Clayton Valli, Ella Lentz, etc., would be called one school of poetry, while Debbie Rennie and I, etc., would represent another school of poetry. I see no problem with two different schools, but the Deaf community doesn't have a history of ASL poetry yet. We have a tradition of passing stories down about Deaf culture, but in terms of history of ASL literature itself the earlier generation doesn't know in general about art history and literary movements, etc., how techniques are influenced by their time and change with time. If you want to teach folklore, that's valid. It's fascinating, but it's not acceptable to limit the definitions of ASL literature, to say, "You're wrong! That's the way we do it!" That concept is impossible. It's unreasonable to shut out the possibilities for future growth in the field. I think it's important to teach basic techniques, the same as artists have to learn, as do dancers and actors, too. Build a foundation, then create! Experiment! I'm sure what I teach will later become old and outdated, but that's fine! Keep moving on!

LW: So far my students seem to be strongly influenced by your work! Maybe that's because they have a personal connection with you or because of your combination of ASL, gesture, mime, etc. In comparing your work with others' do you think the students' response derives from themes rather than differences in complexity and abstraction—topic relevance rather than form or style? I think at the beginning our expectations were based on form. Now I think they may be based on topic relevance. For example, Ella Lentz's baseball poem, which asserts female equality for girls who want to play baseball with boys: I don't think it was form that attracted my students, but the topic itself.

PC: True, sometimes topics attract regardless of form or style, for example, baseball, sports, humor, scary things—they're fascinating for Deaf culture.

LW: My group one year didn't see the symbolism in Ben Bahan's story "Bird of a Different Feather." They didn't want to see it twice. They laughed but missed the allegory, although other students I've taught have enjoyed it. They don't seem to connect to the topics of Clayton Valli's time, that Deaf generation's experience. Students just don't relate, perhaps due not to the form but to the topic.

PC: And also, Clayton's form has hidden meanings, which makes it harder to grasp.

LW: But it goes beyond direct connection to the experiences portrayed in the literature. People can get hooked on reading because it echoes their experience or it gives them experiences they don't already have.

How to attract readers' interest relies on the development of a poem, story, or song. Either a topic or its telling can be inspiring. Are differences in Deaf culture and Deaf experience a matter of one's age, time period, or something else?

PC: It's true that Deaf experience doesn't have to mean experience with oppression, and maybe that's partly why our students aren't as drawn to the earlier ASL works.

LW: An ASL literature contest required poems and stories to center on Deaf issues, historical figures, and formal poetic devices. Isn't the fact that they're created in ASL "Deaf" enough?

PC: Yes, Deaf culture defines itself by language. I visited several schools that entered that contest. It was hard because everyone's work was on a similar theme, that of oppression overcome, "can't becomes can"!

LW: Or deaf versus hearing issues . . .

PC: Many kids are bored with that.

Deaf students of the current generation have vastly different experiences from the professionals they see on video. They have been exposed to sign communication in the classrooms of residential, day, and mainstream schools. ASL is more frequently studied, often as part of a Deaf studies curriculum. Legislation and the media have made deafness more visible in the hearing world. Accessibility has increased with the growing use of interpreters, relay systems, instant-messaging, and pagers, as well as regular closed captioning. ASL fulfills foreign language requirements in a growing number of high schools, colleges, and universities. In general, the concept of culture in the United States has expanded tremendously, providing Deaf students with a clearer identity as members of a linguistic minority within the United States. To view ASL poetry and stories on video or DVD legitimizes these students' language and culture in a natural and automatic fashion. They do not have to struggle as much to assert a cultural identity as their predecessors did. These students are being encouraged to engage in the study of their language and culture critically and creatively, the way hearing students have always done. And just as is the case for hearing students, they have varied levels of understanding, reactions, and preferences. They are growing and developing in a far different sociocultural environment than the Deaf artists whose work they study.

Contemporary high school students seem to see their deafness as one part of a multitude of identities that include race, ethnicity, gender, and social class. ASL texts that focus solely on the Deaf experience seem limited to them, and this is reflected in the wide range of topics and themes with which they experiment in their own texts.

Perhaps this difference is at least in part age related. Perhaps as they grow older, they will experience a coming of age in the Deaf community, a change that frequently occurs at the college level or soon after graduation. Then again, maturity and cognition skills may account for their lack of identification with the work of older Deaf professionals. My students, especially the young women, embraced Ella Lentz's aforementioned "The Baseball Game." They also selected as a favorite Debbie Rennie's "Missing Children," a piece that explores the plight of children in war-torn countries through the familiar missing child notice on milk cartons. Peter's appeal may lie in both his celebration of playful signing techniques and his perspective, which does not deal with issues of rebellion, victimization, and empowerment—themes that are perhaps more interesting to those who have experienced more oppression or isolation than my students have, at least as it relates to their deafness. All the previous examples of texts created by Lexington students reflect this preference for topics and themes beyond their own personal experience. The current high school generation has sufficient world knowledge through visual observation of life, television, and videos or DVDs—a bank of material from which to draw through rich use of imagination. They create full, lively texts, just as writers do.

Ironically, the Deaf artists whose work my students resisted are in part responsible for paving their path to accessibility and higher self-esteem. Just as the feminists of the last generation have given young women today their expectations of equality, so have the previous generation or two of Deaf artists cleared the road ahead for Deaf pride and equality. Indirectly, these artists have contributed to the increasingly widespread knowledge of Deaf culture through their literary texts and exploration of the power of ASL as a literary language. Directly, they show that deaf adults can be creative, successful, even famous.

These observations may reveal a transition in Deaf culture. For all of the problems that exist (e.g., isolation due to inclusion, controversy over cochlear implants), the general population is more aware and more tolerant of Deaf culture than ever before. Young deaf people are growing up as part of a world that increasingly attempts to accommodate differences and strives to provide equal opportunities.

IMPLICATIONS FOR THE FUTURE

How does the exploration of one elective course in ASL literature in a high school for deaf students forecast its place in the future of deaf education? In some schools, ASL literature is just one facet of a Deaf studies curriculum. For students of ASL, the literature offers a view of ASL's most fascinating linguistic properties raised to a level above that of everyday communication. Peter and I discussed a range of possibilities.

LW: Where does ASL literature fit in the educational process?

PC: English is constantly changing, which allows it to be strong. ASL must be allowed to do the same, too. Let people use it! The English vocabulary base is strong. ASL vocabulary is not, but its ability to modify is strong. ASL literature is perfect for expanding that.

LW: Video and DVD texts may be used as social, cultural, and historical tools for Deaf studies. My course uses ASL literature as a means toward development of styles and performance of ASL literature itself, rather than its relation to Deaf culture. They are just different goals for ASL literature in schools.

PC: I see ASL literature as a medium for performance, not related to Deaf history but performance. I think so far deaf people view it as handed down, not yet as a separate literature in itself. It's still a reflection of Deaf culture because it's in a deaf school. Maybe in the future, ASL literature will surface in film, in dance, and in other interesting applications as an art form, regardless of whether the concepts are used by students immediately. They are stored away and later come up as situations recall them. The foundation is there for connections to be discovered.

LW: Some students have used ASL to tell stories based on historical characters and events. That's another application. How about the effects of exposure to ASL literature? You told me about a little girl at the Indiana School for the Deaf who would go home each day quiet, but started telling her mom animated stories while you were there working, until finally Mom came to school to see what was up, and to tell how her daughter had become so much more expressive—that was impressive! I wonder if, through self-esteem growth in ASL literature, students are more willing to take risks in other academic areas. I'm not saying ASL literature will transfer skills directly to English written stories necessarily, but I think a feeling of pride helps, so that it doesn't matter if a student feels weakness in other classes. Having one thing to hold onto inside makes them willing to try, to take risks in other areas. That's what I'm wondering.

PC: In my experience going to schools annually, to Lexington, Fanwood, and the Pennsylvania School for the Deaf, yes, I've seen students improve confidence, turn from being shy to expressive, but I'm there for such a short period that I can't say it's valid to attribute the change to ASL literature in class. They seem to remember what we've done from one year to the next, making them ready to go ahead to more advanced levels, and I don't have to give them the same feedback again.

LW: So there's no proof of English improvement, just side effects of improved self-esteem.

PC: Personal development. I hope it helps in academic areas, but of course I'm biased.

LW: Similarly, just because teachers and students communicate fluently through ASL doesn't mean they can do so through printed English. There must be someone to mediate, to create a bridge between the two languages; there is not direct improvement or transfer of skills. It's the idea of learning how to think and then applying those cognition strategies.

PC: I believe ASL literature helps a lot with that because it's their language already, a tool for creative skill, but it's true that the students must have cognitive skills and an understanding of literary elements to do the work. They must already know how to express themselves. Whether it helps them improve English or not, I think there hasn't been enough research yet in that area. But I think they'd be more willing to try if their confidence were better, instead of always responding, "I can't! It's hard! Reading is hard!" They may be more accepting. That's what I meant by personal development.

LW: Teachers can become responsible for bridging student gains in ASL literature to their current academic work.

PC: If schools have strong sign language programs, good role models and exposure to the arts, they understand more quickly how to create ASL literature. I wish it could be integrated into classes at a young age.

LW: Sure, it would be great if it were so infused in the elementary program that there would hardly be a need for an elective class at the high school level. Well, actually it would be ideal to use the elective as a time and place for students to create their work. Wow! That could really take off! As a matter of fact, now you're working more with younger students, it seems.

PC: Yes, if I come back to the same schools year after year, that will definitely help their growth.

LW: In summary, then, ASL literature is important for (1) Deaf culture, identity, awareness, and history; and (2) playing with language, skill development, and self-esteem. Here are some questions for you: What does it mean for the current generation to gain access to ASL literature through video/DVD and role models in the school as part of the education system, in contrast to previous generations' residential school experience? What's important about fun, play, the freedom to create, especially in one's own language?

PC: I think Deaf history and self-confidence are part of the answer for the first question. The role of ASL literature, the process of learning, using, and playing with ASL in the role of education today compared with past dorm life involves a big change! The former lack of mobility caused ASL literature to develop in dorms. Now it's a tradition carried on through Deaf teachers and Deaf visitors to the school, who have sign skills and teach kids. I hope that will expand, ASL literature clubs will develop, and possibly even traveling groups. The Flying Words Project grew out of NTID while I was there. Once a month, we started teaching and exposing different groups to ASL literature. That was in 1986, and by 1996, at the third National ASL Literature conference, we saw a variety of students share their work, as well as storytellers and poets with a Spanish theme, African style with dance and literature intertwined, painting the line with ASL poetry—a range of specialized areas. To me, it means the basis for ASL literature has been set. It may lead to the creation of new art forms, as has happened in the visual arts— impressionism, abstract expressionism, and such (**clip 8.5**).

After my students performed at the 1996 ASL Literature Conference, someone in the audience asked, "Where did you learn all that stuff?" Larry, one of the Lexington students, ingenuously replied, "From Peter and from you, Patrick, and you, Clayton." The students watched the professionals on video, then the professionals watched the students on stage, and a special connection was forged. They became colleagues in that moment, all working, thinking, celebrating ASL literature together.

NOTES

1. PSE (Pidgin Sign English) uses ASL signs in loosely structured English word order. Sign-supported speech is a policy at the Lexington School for the Deaf, where I teach, and involves the use of signs to clarify speech.

2. The ASL literature created by our students has been featured on public television and at the 1996 National ASL Literature Conference in Rochester, New York.

3. The interviews were conducted in ASL and videotaped. After I transcribed the interviews in fluent written English, Peter reviewed and approved their accuracy in tone and content.

4. See Ben Bahan, chapter 5 of this volume, for discussion of ABC stories.

5. Some of the most interesting growth and experimentation have stemmed from intensive two-day workshops led by Peter with students from Lexington and Fanwood, the New York School for the Deaf. While the Lexington constituency changed annually during the three-year project, as a natural process of turnover in the elective class, the Fanwood group remained stable, a continuing effort led by two hearing teachers, Maddy Reich and Colleen Logodice.

6. DVD clip 8.3 includes student samples of transformation techniques. These poems were created by Kelly Lenis, Calvin Calandra, Raul Draganac, and Sylvia Ramirez, students at Lexington and Fanwood, during the intensive workshops mentioned.

7. The students' original performances are not available on videotape. In clip 8.4 the students' poems are performed by Peter Cook.

8. Martin L. A. Sternberg, EdD, compiled the first comprehensive dictionary of ASL in 1981.

PART THREE

The Political Text

Performance and Identity in ASL Literature

NINE

"If there are Greek epics, there should be Deaf epics"

How Protest Became Poetry

KRISTEN C. HARMON

For many hearing Americans, March 6–13, 1988, is known as "The Week the World Heard Gallaudet." Prior to that week, three qualified candidates were considered for the presidency of Gallaudet University in Washington, D.C.; two of the three were Deaf and used sign language. Several alumni and student leaders gathered to organize a call for a Deaf president. When Elizabeth Zinser, the hearing, nonsigning candidate, was named the new president, angry and disappointed students and alumni staged a protest and shut down the campus.

The story of the student revolution quickly became an international story, and Ted Koppel invited President-elect Zinser, Greg Hlibok, a student leader, and the Oscar award-winning actress Marlee Matlin to appear on ABC's *Nightline.* On the air, Hlibok responded to Zinser's assertion that one day a Deaf president would preside over Gallaudet by saying, "This statement, 'One day a deaf president,' is very old rhetoric. . . . We've been hearing this for one hundred twenty-four years [the number of years Gallaudet University had been in existence]" (quoted in Shapiro 1993, 82).

After the program, President-elect Zinser resigned, and Irving King Jordan, one of the two Deaf candidates for the presidency, was then named the new president of Gallaudet University. That week in March 1988, the

Deaf community declared its independence, self-governing capabilities, civil rights, and autonomy.

Before the "Deaf President Now" movement, the cultural landscape of the American Sign Language (ASL) community already contained a wealth of what are known in spoken languages as "traditional arts" or "oral traditions." Because this chapter deals with a nonspoken language, I refer to such traditional linguistic and literary forms as "ASL traditional linguistic genres." Such genres include performed jokes, narratives, and poems. Even so, when Gilbert Eastman, a well-known ASL performer and playwright, prepared a new ASL narrative based on the "Deaf President Now" movement, he was not quite sure what to call his creation. From the beginning, Eastman was aware that with this performed narrative poem, "Epic: Gallaudet Protest," he was not working within an established ASL genre tradition. He noted, "To my knowledge, I do not know anyone who performs the same way I do" (pers. comm., Dec. 5, 1994). Shortly after the protest, Eastman told me, he "invited a private audience of about 30 people including the NEW president I. King Jordan to [his] presentation" (emphasis in original). After the performance, "someone in the audience said it was almost like a Greek story . . . [and] thus resulted the title . . . 'Epic: Gallaudet Protest.'" Mr. Eastman accepted the community's description: "If there are Greek epics, there should be Deaf epics! I hope there are [other] people composing Deaf epics." (See **clip 9.1** for the complete performance of this epic with captions and voice-over translation, and see the appendix at the end of this chapter for Eastman's glosses.)

By labeling this performance an "epic," the community recognized that Eastman's performance indexed a new and different genre, but even so it was a genre immediately comprehensible and meaningful for the audience; this community-based recognition was a significant marker of the narrative's grounding within a verbal arts tradition. Whether or not that tradition is more grounded in ASL literature or influenced mostly by knowledge of oral and literary epics in published literature is an open question. While this chapter's analysis is limited by using concepts of oral tradition based on an auditory language, it is worth considering how parameters of genres emerge and are influenced by traditionality and literacy in both English and ASL. Though the composition of "Gallaudet Protest" was original, Eastman built upon existing ASL poetic and narrative forms and performance registers. Yet as an epic "Gallaudet Protest" is a new ASL literary form, which then calls into question the very notion of traditional verbal arts as a process and, by extension, the nature of authorship within such traditions. Why did the story of the Gallaudet protest demand to be told in epic form? What drives a people, singly or collectively, to create an epic tradition?

"We know," states the oral-formulaic theorist John Foley (1990), "that tradition preserves what is of value to it from the past, and we also know that preservation is not a consciously designed undertaking but rather a reflex of the tradition itself" (10). This perspective depends upon a diachronic view of composition and tradition, according to which traditions evolve over long periods of time and incorporate elements from different performers separated by long periods of time. However, in this literate age, when oral traditional performers are also likely to be influenced by the printed media and the widespread dissemination of texts and literatures, it is worth exploring the synchrony of the traditional process itself, the interweaving of historical events and emergent genres. So while using the term *tradition* I also want to emphasize the *process* in cultural memory, the culture-specific and *dynamic* body of meaning that determines the shape and meaning of its linguistic performances. The word *epic* connotes a certain air of grandeur and sweeping drama, and this community consensus in describing Eastman's performance as an epic reveals a synchronic understanding of form and meaning, one that lends insight into the process of evolving languages and traditions, into history and culture.

In a sense, this chapter's argument originated with the "Homeric debate," and discussion on the authorship of the *Odyssey* provided grist for the academic mill for many years; scholars spent decades attempting to reconcile the notion of a single, genius creator with the additive, oral formulaic structure of the epics themselves. However, in contemporary scholarship, the focus has shifted from a text-based, and thus fixed, understanding of epic composition to a dynamic and fluid, yet structured, sense of epic composition. We now understand epic as performed by a poet using culturally determined formulaic structures to aid in composing. In spoken languages, an oral traditional poet composes in and through performance before a knowledgeable audience. In doing so, the poet remains within culturally determined parameters of performance through the use of genre-specific structural formulas and registers. While performing, the poet depends upon the audience to confer meaning upon the genre through cultural memory, and in doing so the audience accepts the performance as a meaningful one.

Yet how does a culturally acceptable genre arise in the first place? Leading scholars in oral-formulaic theory argue that meaning and form arise from the synchronic interaction between "the enabling event—*perfor-mance*—and the enabling referent—*tradition*" (Foley 1995, 1; Foley 1992, 278; emphasis in original). While that assertion has been supported through exegeses of *Beowulf* and the *Odyssey*, as well as through structural and formulaic analyses of midcentury Serbo-Croatian epics (e.g., Lord 1960; Foley 1990), the evolutionary motivation for the genre form has not been adequately addressed. We have spent much time deciding what a genre is, but what determines the *dynamism* of a genre? In other words, I argue that in addition to existing performances and traditions there needs to be a catalytic *agency*, or cultural imperative, driving the evolving form.

With the unique confluence of certain forces of history—the public and private blossoming of Deaf culture, the increased awareness of ASL lin-guistic traditions and multiformity, Eastman's skills as a performer and playwright, and the need for a cultural narrative that answers the question of what happened to the American Deaf community *that* week—we see as the result an emergent narrative and poetic form in Gilbert Eastman's hands: the ASL epic poem. As a genre, the epic poem met the needs of this particular performance situation and historical moment; no other form was grand enough or inclusive enough.

How, then, can one analyze "Gallaudet Protest," a narrative performed in ASL, according to the parameters of a very old oral tradition, based in *auditory* cultural memory and composition? As acknowledged earlier, the term *oral tradition* is a misnomer here, but a comparative approach lends insights into how one might begin to develop a kind of working, yet admit-tedly limited, theoretical vocabulary to describe what is happening in this particular performed narrative, as conceived by Gilbert Eastman. As a very contemporary composition, describing the triumph of a marginalized sub-culture against the dictates of a hegemony, "Gallaudet Protest" may also be categorized as postmodern resistance "literature." Even so, use of many visual techniques found in ASL poetry (discussed elsewhere in this volume) lends a symmetrical rhythm that enacts a formal unity not customarily found in modern and postmodern literatures. This formal unity, along with other stylistic and compositional features, is much like that of oral tra-ditional epic in spoken languages.

The epic is a disputed genre, with many different definitions; an epic is, variously, a long narrative poem that may be composed orally or by pen (Merchant 1971, vii) or "narrative poetry composed in a manner evolved over many generations by singers of tales" (Lord 1960, 4). Traditionalist and formalist critics focused upon structural effects such as an introduction that began *in medias res* (in the middle of the action) and obedience to Aristotelian unities of time and place. They also categorized several epic conventions: a proposition, invocation of the Muse, epic similes, catalogs, prophecies, and intervening deities (McWilliams 1989, 28). In addition, critics such as Johann Wolfgang von Goethe described the epic writer as a "wise rhapsodist 'who recites events which lie completely in the past and surveys them with serene detachment'" (quoted in Mori 1997, 28). According to Goethe, epic characters should be taken from "a cultural period when spontaneous actions are still possible": that is, "when human beings did not act from moral, political or social motives, but from purely personal ones" (quoted in Mori 1997, 28). But as more and more is understood about the theoretical underpinnings of such allegedly "neutral" forms (through the insights of postcolonial, deconstructive, and poststructuralist theories, to name a few), such a claim of purely disinterested and detached characters cannot be accepted uncritically.

Raising questions about the link between genre and sociocultural politics lends insight into the ways the epic form has adapted to contemporary times. For example, what are the implications of the decline of the "war" epic and the now-emerging "peace" or "protest" epic? These "peace epics" are mostly literary and, like Derek Walcott's *Omeros* (Downes 1997, 245), are most often written from the perspective of a member of a marginalized and oppressed subculture. In his discussion of the psychic and social ramifications of the "technologizing of the word," Walter Ong (1982) argues that both "orality and the growth of literacy out of orality are necessary for the evolution of consciousness" (175). The phenomenological assumptions underlying the notion of "consciousness" are another debated topic, but it is my contention here that as a "resistance" or "protest" epic Eastman's work represents an emergent, contemporary epic tradition as well as a new ASL traditional linguistic form. In a literate, democratic society in which subcultures struggle against hegemonic structures, this is what epic now looks like.

Because of its subject—the inherent struggle against an oppressive society—contemporary epic may be possible only as an emergent form in marginalized cultures or subcultures. As such, contemporary "protest" epics often act as a model for fighting oppression through nonviolent means. The key question then becomes: In a literate age, with access to so many information sources, what is particularly compelling about the epic genre? To see the effect of Eastman's performance upon the audience (e.g., in video of a live performance, Eastman 1991) is to recognize the truth of Eric Havelock's commentary upon traditional verbal art poems, that they serve as "'educational encyclopedias' of their time, storing information that an oral culture could not commit to the convenience of the manuscript or printed book but had nonetheless to have ready at hand . . . [as] a 'sort of encyclopedia of ethics, politics, history'" (Foley 1988, 62; Eastman 1991). Yet we have the equivalent of "educational encyclopedias" in the form of cultural narratives and anecdotes describing the protest, in addition to social histories such as Christiansen and Barnartt's *Deaf President Now! The 1988 Revolution at Gallaudet University* (1995). How does history change for its audience when presented aesthetically? Why is this history-based artistic and expressive form so compelling for its audience?

Looking at the epic in psychohistorical terms helps to decipher the unique and powerful impact that "Gallaudet Protest" has upon its viewers as well as the evolutionary impulse for this form. Foley (1987) argues that the epic "is the drama of psychological maturation—the record a culture maintains not about its things, events, and beliefs but about the secrets of the human psyche in its development from birth to adulthood—that is acted out in the story-form of oral epic" (94). "Gallaudet Protest," then, is a dramatic depiction of a cultural assertion of autonomy and rebellion, a declaration of independence from the sensibility that insisted the problem with deaf people was their *lack*. In this pathologizing perspective, deaf people needed to be either corrected, healed, or infantilized. The subject in "Gallaudet Protest" is not only the clash between the students and the board but also the clash between private and public, deaf and hearing, cultural and pathological definitions of the self, and autonomy and oppression. When asked about the protest, Jerry Covell, one of the four student leaders, noted, "It's inside me, part of me, [and] will be for the rest of my life. I think about it every day, constantly—the power, the struggle, the accomplishment, the unity" (pers. comm., Jan. 12, 1995). In viewing "Gallaudet Protest," we are not only viewers, mere spectators; rather, we are all implicated as characters in this epic, day after day.

With this particular contemporary epic comes an increasingly *synchronic* conception of genre, an outgrowth of both literacy/traditional linguistic forms and a mutable, dynamic historical consciousness. In his argument against a reactionary interpretation of history, the literary critic Georg

Lukács (1983) asserts that "according to this interpretation history is a silent, imperceptible, natural, 'organic' growth, that is, a development of society which is basically stagnation. . . . Man's activity in history is ruled out completely" (26). Instead, he argues, "the reasonableness of human progress develops ever increasingly out of the inner conflict of social forces in history itself; according to this interpretation history itself is the bearer and realizer of human progress" (27). What matters with this concept of history as the subject of literary genres "is not the retelling of great historical events, but the poetic reawakening of the people who figured in these events" (Lukács 1983, 42). So life and history provide dynamic and traditional genres with the needed subject matter—collision and conflict—and through this medium demonstrate the capacity for social transformation, both in the moment-by-moment decisions in life and in how we describe—dramatize—it.

In his discussion of the emergent historical novel, also tied to a concrete time and with characters who are connected to a specific context, Georg Lukács (1983) describes the epic as "seek[ing instead] to create the impression of life as it normally is *as a whole*" (46; emphasis in original). The distinction here is key; instead of a focused, individual-oriented "slice of life," we have a cross section (out of several possible) of a society and its values, seen through the lens of a particular conflict. Because "Gallaudet Protest" focuses on the struggle against social forces, it, like other epics, "present[s] the inner life of man only insofar as his feelings and thoughts manifest themselves in deeds and actions, in a visible interaction with objective, outer reality" (Lukács 1983, 90). This community-wide struggle with a hegemonic system may, in part, account for the lack of a central "hero" in the traditional sense.

With the catalytic guidance of the four student leaders and their support systems, the hero of "Gallaudet Protest" is the collective and revolutionary voice of a community in peacetime America; the social transformation enacted is the result of the collision of social forces at an extreme point. And as Georg Lukács (1983) reminds us, epic "lay[s] bare those vast, heroic, human potentialities which are always latently present in the people and which, on each big occasion, with every deep disturbance of the social or even the more personal life, emerge 'suddenly,' with colossal force, to the surface" (52). This sense of grappling with social forces reverberates through older epic and contemporary epic alike, despite all other apparent differences. Genres do not exist in a Platonic or Aristotelian ideal form but are subject to adaptation and must be understood as emergent and tied to history, politics, and social change.

The coexistence of other Gallaudet protest narratives with the appearance of a new ASL narrative and poetic form provides compelling evidence of an emergent variant; epic, then, reveals itself to be a genre that adapts to the changing needs of cultural expression. The "protest" or "resistance epic" retains the epic voice, only this time the "wise rhapsodist"/epic writer is not detached from his or her sociopolitical context; indeed, the emergent epic demands the active portrayal of resistance, presented through the eyes of an omniscient but not uninvolved narrator. Jerry Covell commented to me that Eastman portrays the most important elements of the protest: "I have never seen anyone perform like Eastman. He is the only one who does it and does it very clearly, powerfully, and exactly as to what happened. There were some who have tried to act out or perform about Gallaudet protest, but nothing compared to Eastman" (pers. comm., Jan. 12, 1995). It was not enough to simply describe or to dramatize; there was a need for a wide-ranging, sweeping genre form, one that reawakened a sense of cultural struggle and triumph. In short, there was a need for a genre form of mythic proportions, one large enough to express the magnitude of the protest while retaining the high-register quality of poetic expression; the traditional epic encapsulated the scope and importance of the Gallaudet protest for deaf and hard-of-hearing people around the world. The use of special formulas to signal the beginning, the descent through space to earth to Washington, D.C., and from there to Gallaudet, conveys that the events have universal ramifications, that the campus of Gallaudet is the center of a momentous birth. Indeed, in the performance the stars do shine brightly upon the students as they fight for their civil rights, prefiguring a new age and a new and independent conception of self, in their own eyes and those of the hearing world.

It is with this sense of the mutability of genre that I want to return to a more detailed discussion of "Gallaudet Protest." To recap, while Eastman uses many poetic conventions, his performance clearly distinguishes itself as something that goes beyond the ASL poem or ASL narrative, and his audience recognized and confirmed this new form as a culture-specific epic. Eastman's dramatic rendering of the register of "aesthetic sign" (discussed at length elsewhere in this volume), the extended and episodic narrative, the site-specific setting, the use of stylistic and formulaic structures analogous to those found in traditional oral epic, and other means of achieving unity all outline the parameters of this emergent genre.

When asked about the composition of his work, Eastman said, "Several days after the protest at Gallaudet University, I started thinking of telling a simple story about the BIG EVENT [emphasis in original]. It took me about one week to develop the story. Initially, I signed in my mind and then, jotted down just words" (pers. comm., Dec. 5, 1994). Because Eastman composed this epic in his mind, thinking the story through visually, his composition does present an analogue to spoken languages' conception of "orality," especially if we consider that "a poem is 'oral' if it is composed orally, without reliance on writing" (Finnegan 1992, 17). Significantly, jotting down the key ideas in written English seemed to act more as a mnemonic technique than as composition.

Of course, there are differing interpretations of "orality" and its shading into literacy, just as there are differing definitions of genre and its salient characteristics. If there were no "oral" basis, then when the words were written down the performance would be "fixed." A fixed performance would have very little variation from the listing of ideas and themes in written English; the result would be more accurately described as a text. However, Eastman's epic is not textualized. As he noted, "I have altered some ideas and signs several times without realizing it. I am sure if I did the performance today, it would be a little different in style, but the significant concept remains the same" (pers. comm., Dec. 5, 1994). Such stability of themes is characteristic of the oral epic, and, as Foley (1988) notes, "[S]tability from one performance to the next is likely to lie not at the word-for-word level of the text, but at the levels of theme and story pattern" (43).

A study of "Gallaudet Protest" as a tradition-based, emergent genre requires a detailed discussion of the epic as a communicative medium, with particular keys, or signals, to highlight and intensify its nature as an aesthetic and culturally expressive act. Richard Bauman (1977) argues that "the essential task in the ethnography of performance is to determine the *culture-specific constellations of communicative means that serve to key performance in particular communities*" (22; emphasis in original). Such "keys" include special codes, figurative language, parallelism, paralinguistic features, special formulas, and so on. As one such key, aesthetic sign not only signals the register appropriate for the performance of ASL poetry but also acts as the keying of the performance. From the opening moment when Eastman signs UNIVERSE   EARTH   U.S.A., the viewer knows that

Eastman is not conversing in everyday ASL. In English, this introduction translates as "Within the blackness of space a single planet comes into focus—the earth, in its orbit, rotating on its axis. The face of the earth comes into view—the United States";[1] even in translation, this kind of language use clearly represents a departure from the conventions of conversational or informal written English.

So, to return to the question of genre and catalyst, a closer study of "Gallaudet Protest" helps in delineating the interrelation of performance as enabling event and linguistic tradition as enabling referent. For example, special codes, or incidents of special linguistic usage, are one of the distinctive features of traditional oral poetry in spoken languages. Through the use of such special codes, poetic meaning is amplified in an intensified interaction between connotation and denotation, referentiality and iconicity. The introduction to "Gallaudet Protest" does more than quickly and firmly establish a spatial setting for the events of March 1988. Eastman's introduction acts as a special code, evoking the increasingly localized setting as well as a sense of narrative and kinetic movement; he moves the viewer past the shape of the Capitol dome, the Lincoln Memorial, and the reflecting pool and closer and closer to Gallaudet University. He creates the poetic scene of passing trees and turning on streets to come upon the archways of Gallaudet's campus. Of particular interest is the resonance between denotation and iconicity.

Eastman balances a referential use of language with the figurative to further the narrative and to create the poetic effects. Figurative language, with its semantic density, its foregroundedness, is especially appropriate as a device for performance (Bauman 1977, 17). The signed performance enacts figuration, overlaying denotation with a powerful aesthetic and metonymic evocation. When Eastman shows us the banner carried by students in the march upon the Capitol, with the words "We still have a dream," we see the banner flapping in the breeze, not too hard, not too slow, against the legs of those carrying it. This banner resonates with references to the civil rights movement and places the Deaf President Now struggle within that larger context. Also, as a narrative device, Eastman makes a metaphorical association between the brightness of the stars and the students' spiritual condition, with the stars shining brighter on the scene of increasing independence. In the earlier days of anger and despair, the stars shone dimly.

Another performance key, parallelism, involves the repetition, with systematic variation, of phonic, grammatical, semantic, or prosodic structures.

From a functional point of view, the persistence of these principles underlying the parallel structures may serve largely as a mnemonic aid to the performer (Bauman 1977, 18). While these modes are primarily auditory constructions, best suited not only for spoken languages but also for a performance that can be easily associated with a textual form, Eastman does use diurnal rhythm as an underlying structure and as a mnemonic device. "Gallaudet Protest" runs chronologically, with each day's events framing an episode within the epic. Each transition is signaled by SUNRISE, followed by the sign for what day of the week it is. The signal for the close of each episode varies—DARK INTO NIGHT; CRIES UP IN SKY UP IN DARKNESS SILENCE; STARS FALLING DOWN DISAPPEARING INTO DARKNESS; STARS FAINTLY TWINKLED; CLOUDS CREPT INTO DARKNESS, and so on, with an increasing brightness of stars over time. Eastman said the reason for this parallel structure was largely mnemonic: "To assist my memory, I recalled the daily events of the protest, i.e. Sunrise . . . Monday" (pers. comm., Dec. 5, 1994).

Diurnal rhythm also serves to reference traditional oral epic. In the *Odyssey*, the phrase πηαοσ ε ελιοιο serves as a fulcrum for narrative transition, holding up the "light of the sun" as a diurnal boundary of sorts, not simply as a divider between day and night, but as a belief in the certainty that the present trouble or impasse will soon give way to effective, direct action (Foley 1991, 154). The diurnal boundary serves as a narrative reassurance that "the sun does in fact rise after the night of uncertainty and doom, and the narrative moves forward into a new day of positive action" (154). Such structuring signals transitions and episodes and acts as an interpretive frame, one that implies that the universe is not impartial but participates in, or at the very least witnesses, the unfolding of events.

The use of stars also acts to unify the epic narrative and works on a thematic level. After the first day, students gathered to news of the impending election, and with hope and anticipation, STOOD WALKED AROUND CAMPUS / DARK INTO NIGHT. At the close of the next day, Sunday, March 6, Gallaudet Board Chair Jane Spilman allegedly told the students, "Deaf people are not ready to function in a hearing world." That episode ends with ROW-STUDENTS [row of students] SHOCKED FISTS-UP SCREAMED / CRIES UP IN SKY UP IN DARKNESS / SCREAMS DISAPPEARED INTO NIGHT SILENCE. With anguish, grief, and an all-too-familiar frustration, the students grapple with what to do next.

The next day represents a pivotal moment in the narrative with the introduction of the student leaders and their speeches. Another futile meeting with Spilman ends with a Deaf professor asking students to leave. By Eastman's account,

STUDENTS GOT-UP   LEFT GYM   STOOD OUTSIDE
ANGER   CONFUSED   LOOKED FOR HELP
WALKED TO CAPITOL   RAN-UP STEPS   DOORS CLOSED
CHAOS   LOOKED-UP IN SKY   DARKNESS
STARS FALLING DOWN   DISAPPEARING INTO DARKNESS

The overwhelming sense of futility and despair echoes the continual frustration of dealing with paternalistic institutions that are meant to work "for" deaf people but that all too often end up enforcing a sense of limitations, a ceiling, upon individual and collective potential.

Tuesday brings the first major turning point in the epic narrative, with faculty, administration, Deaf leaders, and students working together. At a press conference, students and interpreters share the story with the world. Here Eastman begins the motif of technologies as tools, not as corrective devices (e.g., hearing aids, FM systems, and the like). Eastman dramatizes the technology at work in this revolution, showing the process of the story becoming news and from there becoming public, becoming history, as the reporters write it down, typing it in their word-processing programs; from there, it is WIRED ALL-OVER USA / CONTINUED THROUGH THE NIGHT   STARS FAINTLY TWINKLED. Hope begins as the news spreads into the public, as the

SATELLITE MOVED   SHOT DOWN [to]
CHINA   [and on the screen there was a] FRAME . . .
INDIA   FRAME   [Gallaudet] GATE
AFRICA   FRAME   PICKETS;
ITALY   FRAME 4 4 4 [demands]
FRANCE   FRAME   SPILMAN OUT
SWEDEN   FRAME   DEAF UNITY
ENGLAND   FRAME   DEAF PRESIDENT NOW
AMERICA   FRAME   BLOND HAIR CREW-CUT [student leader Greg
    Hlibok] SIGNED
. . . .
TED KOPPEL LOOKED AT CLOCK   5 4 3 2 1
CUT   BLACKOUT

Instead of a sense of finality at the close of this episode, the customary calling upon natural diurnal rhythm, there is a sense of an ongoing process. The message is relayed throughout the world, through the night and into the next day. Deaf people are making the news and are not the pathologized subject of news. This time, the world sees us.

The next episode, Thursday, brings a respite for the exhausted students. A virtual feast, another traditional epic theme, is spread before the students, courtesy of a corporate fast food chain. The students tally the public consensus:

ROOM TABLE ROUND   TELEPHONES
INTERPRETERS   HEARING VOLUNTEERS
SAT AROUND TABLE   RINGS   RINGS
ANSWERED   HUNG UP   ANSWERED
DEAF PRESIDENT THUMB-UP MARK THUMB-UP MARK ["yes"
    votes are tallied]
DEAF PRESIDENT THUMB-DOWN MARK THUMB-DOWN MARK
    ["no" votes are tallied]

As a day of taking inventory and energizing, this episode represents the first narrative moment of stasis. At the close of this episode, the students and interpreters continue to express their thoughts and protests to the world; MICROPHONE MOVED, DEAF SIGNED, INTERPRETERS SPOKE / ALL DAY INTO NIGHT / CLOUDS CREPT INTO DARKNESS.

The next episode begins at a liminal moment, between night and day: BEFORE SUNRISE   FRIDAY / DARK   LIGHT FLASHER   GOT-UP / LIGHTS ON   TELEPHONE TDD   ANSWERED / H E L L O G[o] A[head] D R. Z I N S E R R E S I G N E D. Elation at that news gives way to preparation for a march to the Capitol building. At the end of this episode, Eastman signs, FLAG   STAR-SPANGLED BANNER STREAMING / BLUE SKY   BRILLIANT SUN SHINING / SUN-SET   INTO DARKNESS.

In keeping with the action/counteraction/stasis narrative movement, the next episode is a quiet day, full of anticipation, waiting for what happens next. Tables and tables of food are set up for the students and for the volunteers, and at the end of the day, MORE INFORMATION COMING IN / PEOPLE LOOKED AT EACH OTHER / WALKED

AROUND AIMLESSLY ALL DAY INTO NIGHT. The next day, Sunday, brings the final episode of the protest: the board members meet all day, and students are notified at 7:00 p.m. that their demands are met. Spilman has resigned, 51 percent of the board will consist of Deaf individuals, there will be no reprisals, and finally, there is a new, Deaf president:

HURRAH! SCREAMED   JUMPED
DANCED   HUGGED   DRANK   CRIED

The new president, I. King Jordan, is introduced to the world, and before the flashing bulbs and television cameras, PRESIDENT SIGNED "THANK YOU   THANK YOU" / ARMS UP INTO SKY / STARS TWINKLING BRIGHTLY / INTO DARKNESS. The stars not only frame the episodes but indicate the thematic movement from anger and frustration to elation and self-actualization, from despair to hope and opportunity.

The images of lightness and darkness are also strong cultural images, for many anecdotes, speeches, and narratives in the community "are warnings about worlds where one falls into darkness, nonexistence, and despair" (Padden and Humphries 1988, 37). Such awareness of the boundaries between the light of self-realization and the darkness of frustration with, at times, futile efforts at communication with the larger, hearing society, is not surprising. Many deaf persons, signing or nonsigning, know all too well the lifelong struggle not only to understand but *to be understood.*

Deaf and hearing members of the audience for the performance bring in essential information and responses that confer meaning upon Eastman's "Gallaudet Protest." For example, members of the audience know that when Eastman signs BLOND HAIR CREW-CUT he is referring to the student leader Greg Hlibok. Hlibok's name is not finger spelled, though Alison Gibson's script for the voice-over translation on the DVD does provide his name. In effect, the name signs might be seen as analogous to the "noun epithets" of traditional, spoken, oral epic. In the epic tradition, "the semantic value of the epithet—'grey-eyed' or . . . 'of the glancing helm'—would serve as a nominal detail standing metonymically, or *pars pro toto,* for the character in all of his or her traditional complexity" (Foley 1992, 281).

Performance keys aside, Eastman accomplishes narrative unity and coherence through the use of several motifs common to dramatic performances. These motifs are all connected with the image of the collective, the community struggling together. In the first episode, after the sweeping introduction to Gallaudet's campus, Eastman introduces the first character: ONE STUDENT CAME   STUDENTS ONE BY ONE CAME / . . . WALKED   JOINED MORE PEOPLE. That first student, described as a "lone figure" in Gibson's translation, joins a rally of students discussing the upcoming election and the strong likelihood that for the first time, there will be a Deaf president. The students sign, D-D-D-D, the first letter of *Deaf*, as a chant celebrating group solidarity. That "lone figure," as dramatized in Eastman's performance, seems at first surprised, then elated by this celebration, and when it comes time to applaud the speakers, he (as Eastman portrays him) at first claps like a hearing person, is nudged, and, with a look of joy, begins to wave his hands above his head in the Deaf way of clapping. From then on, the individual Deaf person is incorporated into the collective. The "chant," D-D-D-D, with the accompanying sense of interconnection, appears in several episodes when Eastman focuses again upon the people, the collective, struggling together. By intensifying the dramatic, narrative elements, Eastman presents this theme in more comprehensively. Drama "deals with human destinies . . . [and] concentrates . . . upon such as arise from men's antagonistic relations with one another." As such, the "essence of dramatic effect is *immediate,* direct impact upon a *multitude*" (Lukács 1983, 130; emphasis in original).

In addition to the episodic structure, Eastman achieves unity through the introduction and conclusion, through a "panning in" and a "panning out," to borrow a description of a visual framing technique. Beginning with UNIVERSE   EARTH   U.S.A.   WASHINGTON, D.C. / LINCOLN MEMORIAL and so on, Eastman concludes with that same movement in reverse, once again enhancing the sense of biblical and universal sweep. The last episode is a quiet, reflective day, a week later after the conclusion of the protest. Students are back in school, thinking of their success, and a plane flies over the university, trailing a banner that reads "Gallaudet: The Whole World Salutes You." In response, students LOOKED UP   TAP-SHOULDERS [to draw attention to the plane]   TAP / . . . / WAVED   SMILED   CRIED   WAVED. From there, Eastman lifts the narrative up to the point of view of the pilot, looking down at

CROWD   CAMPUS   BUILDINGS
CAPITOL DOME   WASHINGTON MONUMENT
LINCOLN MEMORIAL   ALL-OVER-CITY

WASHINGTON, D.C.   FADE IN
U.S.A.   WORLD   EARTH ROTATING
MOVING INTO UNIVERSE.

As is the case with many other traditional poets, "It is sometimes tacitly assumed that the productions of [oral] poets in some sense stand for the whole society; reflecting the views and aspirations of the people at large and being essentially 'their culture'; so that even if one individual poet can be recognized as the composer or performer, he is really speaking not as himself, an individual, but as the 'voice' of the community" (Finnegan 1992, 205). Like other ASL narratives, "Gallaudet Protest" asserts social attitudes and values that the Deaf culture holds dear: the linguistic use of ASL for cultural communication, the common experience of frustration with and rejection by hearing individuals and institutions, the pride in autonomous action apart from the frequent oppressiveness of mainstream hearing society, the aesthetic enjoyment of ASL in performance, and the love of a good story.

Eastman recognizes that his role as an individual is somehow subordinate to the value and importance of his creation and its expression of cultural mores. As a professional in the theater, he knows that the submersion of self is necessary to create a fully realized dramatic character, and in his narrative he removes himself, the consummate comedian and character actor, from the foreground. Eastman's role evolved over time, and as he said, "I saw myself as a performer in the beginning and eventually, I became a participant" (pers. comm., Dec. 5, 1994). The subordination of his role as creator and omniscient narrator is so complete that Eastman's use of ASL facial grammar implies that he becomes a representative participant and is emotionally moved by the dramatized sight of students marching on the Capitol, holding the Martin Luther King Jr. banner in front:

STUDENTS   PROFESSORS   STAFF   ADMINISTRATORS
ALUMNI   MOTHERS, FATHERS   BROTHERS, SISTERS
BABIES   STROLLERS
DEAF-BLIND HOLDING HANDS
WHEELCHAIRS
FRIENDS   STRANGERS   DOGS   TV CAMERAS
MARCH[2]

Interestingly enough, Eastman is so successful in submerging himself within the performance that the display of emotion does not seem to "break character" but instead seems to indicate his own deep response to the events and people as they "pass by" before him. In effect, Eastman the creator joins with the audience at that moment, and the creation—the epic—takes over. This submersion into a visual narrative is so complete that audience members approached Eastman afterwards and said that "they thought they were watching a movie" (pers. comm., Dec. 5, 1994). For persons who participated in the movement, Eastman's performance is no less moving. Jerry Covell, one of the four student leaders, felt the epic was "very powerful and moving . . . makes me have goose bumps when he finished the performance" (pers. comm., Jan. 12, 1995).

Looking at the traditionality of both a specific performance and the register and keys used assumes continuity, or the continued performance, by others, of similar epics using that register. Eastman's performative register may prove to be more traditional for future generations of poets and performers, but as a prototype for an ASL epic genre "Gallaudet Protest" demonstrates that the relationship between history and the traditional oral epic is perhaps more synchronic than originally thought. John Foley (1988) suggests "epic's roots in myth" (or a genre that acts as a similar charter of belief) and agrees with Albert Lord that "history *enters into* or is in its general characteristics reflected in oral epic and ballad tradition rather than originating it" (47). While Foley is arguing for a diachronic conception of genre, working as he does from traditions that exist in fragmented textual form or are documented within declining pools of performers (such as the *guslar* and the Yugoslav epic), I wonder if the ever-increasing levels of literacy and the increasing use of technology to record these performances may short-circuit the long process of oral traditional composition in former times, particularly in those *emergent* forms that begin as a personal response to oppression. Even so, that personal response depends upon accepted traditions, and as a result, in very specific, and in some ways delimited, settings, particularly ones that share common sociopolitical struggles, it becomes a community-sanctioned aesthetic response.

In Gilbert Eastman's work, we have a synchronic example of history provoking the form; a cultural and psychological need for assimilation of these events is fulfilled in a form that is clearly self-contained, with an interpretive frame that does not rest on the pronouncements of any one person but is rather the universal, even elemental, praise of the events of March 1988. Eastman's "Gallaudet Protest" bears many striking similarities with traditional spoken oral epic, and though it is an original composition, it was made possible only through a unique confluence of forces. What we have in this work is history *becoming* culture, growing in stature until it is truly mythic—and deeply meaningful—in the minds of its viewers.

APPENDIX

Epic: Gallaudet Protest

Gilbert C. Eastman's Transliteration

UNIVERSE   EARTH   U.S.A.   WASHINGTON, D.C.
LINCOLN MEMORIAL   STATUE   HANDS: A & L
LOOKED BACK   124 YEARS AGO
CHARTER   SIGNED   ANNOUNCING
COLLEGE FOR THE DEAF
FACE-PROFILE   COLUMNS   LOOKED AT REFLECTION POOL
WASHINGTON MONUMENT   STREETS   CARS
CAPITOL DOME   U.S. FLAG
TURNED STREETS   TREES   BUILDINGS
STOP. FENCE   GATE: "GALLAUDET UNIVERSITY"
ENTERED   ROAD-CURVE
CHAPEL HALL   TOWER CLOCK
ARCHES   TERRACE   STEPS   STREETS
STATUE BASE   GALLAUDET AND ALICE
ONE STUDENT CAME   STUDENTS ONE BY ONE CAME
LOOKED AT STATUE   WALKED   JOINED MORE PEOPLE
LONG LINE OF PEOPLE   FOOTBALL FIELD   BLEACHERS
GOT BUTTON   FADE-OUT "DEAF PRESIDENT NOW"
FADE-IN   LOOKED AT CROWD   PICKETS
SPEAKER WITH BEARD CAME   SPOKE   CLAPPED
ANOTHER SPEAKER   SPOKE   SCREAMED
ANOTHER SPEAKER   SPOKE   WAVING-HANDS
DEAF DEAF DEAF "D" UNITY ALL-OVER
STOOD   WALKED AROUND CAMPUS
DARK   INTO   NIGHT
****
WEEK-LATER   SUNDAY   MARCH 6   TIME 7:00 P.M.
ONE BY ONE CAME CROWD WAITED AND WAITED   BECAME NERVOUS

LOOKED AT COP WALKING TOWARD CROWD
PAPERS STACKED   PASSED OUT
PAPER ANNOUNCING NEW PRESIDENT:
ZINSER WOMAN HEARING HAIR-CURL, SCARF
PAPER CRUSHED, SET AFIRE
BURN Z   ANGER
"GO!" CROWD RAN   STOPPED HOTEL
DOORMAN STOPPED   COPS STOOD IN ROW
STUDENTS STOOD IN ROWS AND ROWS
LEADER CALLED   SPILMAN
HAIR-UP, RUFFLES, CAME-DOWN   STOPPED
FACED STUDENTS   WITH INTERPRETER   SPOKE
"DEAF PEOPLE ARE NOT READY TO FUNCTION IN A HEARING WORLD."
ROW-STUDENTS SHOCKED   FISTS-UP   SCREAMED
CRIES UP IN SKY   UP IN DARKNESS
SCREAMS DISAPPEARED INTO NIGHT   SILENCE
****
SUNRISE   MONDAY
GROUP   POINTED AT GATE   CHAIN LOCK
POINT GATE   CHAIN LOCK   POINT GATE   CHAIN LOCK
RAN TO MAIN ENTRANCE   STOOD ONE BY ONE
ROWS AND ROWS   CLOSED GATE
CARS TRIED ENTERING   COULDN'T   LEFT
ROWS   GUARD
GROUP DISCUSSED   CALLED STUDENTS   FLOCKED
LEADER MAN BLOND, CREW-CUT CAME WITH RED BAND   STOOD
FOLLOWED THREE PERSONS, BLUE BANDS
ONE TALL, THIN, GLASSES, JACKET, BUTTONS
ONE MEDIUM, THIN FACE, SMOKING
ONE WOMAN, SMALL, STRONG, HAIR SHORT, GLASSES
THREE JOINED LEADER, FOUR FACED
FIRST ROWS   YELLOW BANDS
MORE ROWS   MORE ROWS   LOOKED AT LEADER
EXPLAINED   "NO VIOLENCE!"
"UNDERSTAND!"   "GIVE UP NO"
ROWS HANDS-RISING, WAVING. STOPPED
4 DEMANDS: 1) DEAF PRESIDENT
        2) SPILMAN (HAIR-UP, RUFFLES) OUT

3) BOARD 51% DEAF

4) NO REPRISAL

ROWS CLAPPED   RETURNED TO GATE, GUARDED

SPILMAN ARRIVED WITH GROUP, MEETING DOORS CLOSED

CALLED STUDENTS   FLOCKED TO BUILDING   GYM

LARGE ROOM   SAT   HANDS-WAVING

VIPS ENTERED   STOOD-IN-LINE   SAT

SPILMAN ENTERED WITH INTERPRETER

SPILMAN SPOKE, INTERPRETER SIGNED

SUDDENLY DEAF PROFESSOR INTERRUPTED   SIGNED "PLEASE LEAVE."

SPILMAN TRIED TO STOP THEM BUT COULDN'T

STUDENTS GOT-UP   LEFT GYM   STOOD OUTSIDE

ANGER   CONFUSED   LOOKED FOR HELP

WALKED TO CAPITOL   RAN-UP STEPS   DOORS CLOSED

CHAOS   LOOKED-UP IN SKY   DARKNESS

STARS FALLING DOWN   DISAPPEARING INTO DARKNESS

****

SUNRISE   TUESDAY

GUARDS   LET SOME PEOPLE COMING IN

FACULTY   STAFF   STUDENTS   SUPPORTERS

UPPERS (ADMINISTRATIVES) OUT

PROFESSORS ASKED WHAT? STUDENTS ASKED HELP US! FOUR

DEMANDS!

PEOPLE FLOCKED, SAT ROWS. EACH EXPRESSED PROBLEMS

THEY LISTENED   FORMED COMMITTEES   MEETINGS

FUND-RAISING   HOW? THERMOMETER WITH ROUND-LINE RED

MONEY-GIVING   RED-RISING

PRESS CONFERENCE   NEWSPAPER REPORTERS PLUS

TV REPORTERS CAME   ASKED QUESTIONS

DEAF FELT HELPLESS   LOOKED AT GROUP COMING

"INTERPRETERS!" THEY HELPED US!

DEAF SIGNED, INTERPRETERS SPOKE TO REPORTERS

LOOKED AT FIVE DEAF LEADERS COMING

NATIONAL ORGANIZATIONS DIFFERENT

LEADER BY LEADER SPOKE   CLAPPED   WAVED HANDS

REPORTERS WROTE DOWN   RAN TO CARS   DROVE AWAY

STOPPED AT NEWSPAPER BUILDING   ENTERED   RAN INTO OFFICE

TYPED   COMPUTER   LINE BY LINE

PUSHED KEY   CAME-OUT PAPER   TOOK IT AND RAN
TO HUGE ROOM   PUT ON MACHINE   TURNED ON
ROLLED   PRESSED   FOLDED   STACKED
PUT-IN TRUCKS   DOORS OPENED   TRUCKS HURRIED OUT
SAME TIME   PRESSED   WIRED ALL-OVER USA
CONTINUED THROUGH THE NIGHT   STARS FAINTLY TWINKLED
****
SUNRISE   WEDNESDAY
GUARDS   ROWS   ROWS   TIRED
BLOCKADE   LOOKED AT TRUCK   LET IT IN
OPENED DOORS   PACKS OF NEWSPAPERS   CAME OUT
HEADLINE: "GALLAUDET PROTEST"
HURRAH   RETURNED TO GATE, GUARDED
PROFESSORS   WORKERS MET TOGETHER
DISCUSSED   VOTED.. APPROVED FOUR DEMANDS
HELPED STUDENTS   HURRAH   BUT
ONE RAN IN, STOOD, BREATHED, ANNOUNCED
Z HAIR-CURLED, SCARF FAVORABLE
LOOKED UP, DISAPPOINTED   HEART BROKEN
ONE BY ONE GRAB FLAG   ROSE HIGH
INSPIRING   HANDS WAVING
OVER THERE   BUILDING   ROOM   TV CAMERA LENS
TED KOPPEL HAIR, APART, SAT, TABLE CURVE
POINT BLOND CREW-CUT, POINT Z HAIR-CURLED, SCARF
POINT CALIFORNIA, MM HAIR-LONG-CURL, GLASSES
TED LOOKED AT WATCH   LENS TO CAMERA
FRAME, DOWN WIRE TO NEXT ROOM
MAN EARPHONES, MICROPHONE, TV SETS
1) FIX TIE   2) FIX SCARF   3) FIX HAIR
COUNT 5 4 3 2 1 0   PUSH BUTTON
LINE RAN DOWN   WENT THROUGH TO DISK
THEN, SHOT UP INTO SPACE   REACHING SATELLITE
SATELLITE MOVED   SHOT DOWN
CHINA   FRAME   BURN Z
INDIA   FRAME   GATE
AFRICA   FRAME   PICKETS
ITALY   FRAME   4 4 4
FRANCE   FRAME   SPILMAN OUT

SWEDEN   FRAME   DEAF UNITY
ENGLAND   FRAME   DEAF PRESIDENT NOW
AMERICA   FRAME   BLOND HAIR CREW-CUT SIGNED
ZINSER SPOKE, CAPTIONED
MM EMOTED
TED KOPPEL LOOKED AT CLOCK   5 4 3 2 1
CUT   BLACKOUT
****
SUNRISE   THURSDAY
GATE   GUARDED   TENTS   SLEPT
WOKE UP   CLOTHES DIRTY   HUNGRY
GOT UP   JOINED GROUP
ANOTHER TRUCK CAME IN   LET IT IN
OPENED DOORS   BOXES BOXES OUT OF TRUCK
LOOKED AT BOXES   PUZZLED   OPENED
FOOD! FOOD! FOOD! GRABBED   GAVE OUT   SHARED
TRUCK LEFT   GUARDED ALL DAY
MAIL TRUCKS ENTERED   DOORS OPENED   BAGS
LETTERS PILE
BUILDING (OLE GYM) RAILS   DOORS OPENED
PEOPLE STOOD   BUSY RUNNING AROUND
ROOM TABLE ROUND   TELEPHONES
INTERPRETERS   HEARING VOLUNTEERS
SAT AROUND TABLE. RINGS   RINGS
ANSWERED   HUNG UP   ANSWERED
DEAF PRESIDENT THUMB-UP MARK THUMB-UP MARK
DEAF PRESIDENT THUMB-DOWN MARK THUMB-DOWN MARK
THERMOMETER RED-LINE UP   UP
BOX   COINS   BILLS   CHECKS   UP   UP
TAP SHOULDER, LOOKED AROUND   PUZZLED   NOTICED
GIRL LITTLE HOLDING DIME   PUT IT IN BOX
INSPIRED   TEARS IN EYES
GATE GUARDED   TV TRUCKS   ANTENNAS
TV REPORTERS   NEWSPAPERS REPORTERS
MICROPHONE MOVED, DEAF SIGNED, INTERPRETERS SPOKE
ALL DAY INTO NIGHT
CLOUDS CREPT INTO DARKNESS
****

BEFORE SUNRISE   FRIDAY
DARK   LIGHT FLASHER   GOT-UP
LIGHTS ON   TELEPHONE TDD   ANSWERED
H E L L O   G[O] A[HEAD] D R. Z I N S E R R E S I G N E D
HURRAH   WOKE-UP   WOKE-UP   STUDENTS GOT UP
WHAT?   WHAT? Z HAIR-UP SCARF RESIGNED!
HURRAH! WAIT! CHANGED CLOTHES   WENT BACK TO GATE
FLOCKED   STOPPED   WATCHED   GUARDED
BUSES ARRIVED   DOORS OPENED   PEOPLE CAME OUT
WHO? NTID HURRAH   ANOTHER BUS
FROM WHERE? PHILADELPHIA! HURRAH! NEW YORK
MORE PEOPLE CAME IN   FLEW IN
ROWS AND ROWS OF PEOPLE HOLDING PICKETS
SOME HOLDING BANNERS
MORNING   NOON   STRUCK 12   GATE OPENED
POLICE CARS MOVED   SIRENS ON
MARCH BEGAN   ROW BY ROW
LEADING ROW   LONG SIGN "WE STILL HAVE A DREAM"
MARCH   HOLDING PICKETS   MARCH
MARCH   HOLDING BANNERS   MARCH
STUDENTS   PROFESSORS   STAFF   ADMINISTRATORS
ALUMNI   MOTHERS, FATHERS   BROTHERS, SISTERS
BABIES   STROLLERS
DEAF-BLIND HOLDING HANDS
WHEELCHAIRS
FRIENDS   STRANGERS   DOGS   TV CAMERAS
MARCH   MARCH LONG   LONG LINE
ONWARD TO CAPITOL   STOPPED
ROWS   ROWS   ROWS   WATCHED
UP STEPS   TWO PERSONS CAME ONE-STOOD, ONE-ABOVE-PERSON
BLACK HAIR, CURLED, WHITE SHIRT, YELLOW BAND
HANDS-WAVING   "DEAF PRESIDENT NOW"   HANDS-WAVING
SPEAKER ONE BY ONE CAME   SPOKE   SUPPORTED
CLAPPED   SCREAMED   HANDS-WAVING
DEAF POWER SUPPORT   HANDS-WAVING
FOUR DEMANDS SUPPORT   HANDS-WAVING
SCREAMS FLEW UP   SKY   CAPITOL DOME
FLAG   STAR-SPANGLED BANNER STREAMING

BLUE SKY   BRILLIANT SUN SHINING

SUNSET   INTO DARKNESS

****

SUNRISE   SATURDAY

QUIET ALL-MORNING

GATE   GUARDED   QUIET

TABLES FULL OF FOOD ON SALE

PEOPLE CAME-IN   READ BULLETIN NEWS

MORE INFORMATION COMING IN

PEOPLE LOOKED AT EACH OTHER

WALKED AROUND AIMLESSLY ALL DAY INTO NIGHT

****

SUNRISE   SUNDAY

HOTEL   CALLED BOARD   SAT AROUND TABLE   DOORS CLOSED

DISCUSSED HOURS, HOURS   ALL-DAY

EVENING   OLE GYM RAILS, DOORS OPENED

PEOPLE MOVED AROUND, LOOKED NERVOUS

LIGHT FLASHER   TDD!   ONE ANSWERED

BLOND CREW-CUT "FOR YOU" HE CAME   SAT

PEOPLE LOOKED AT HIM

BLOND HAIR CREW-CUT TYPED   ONE BEHIND READ, SIGNED

  1) SPILMAN (HAIR-UP, RUFFLED) RESIGNED

   HURRAH. SCREAMED. STOPPED

  2) BOARD 51% DEAF ACCEPTED. HURRAH. SCREAMED. STOPPED

PLUS CHAIRMAN DEAF! HURRAH!

  3) NO REPRISAL

   HURRAH. SCREAMED. STOPPED

   QUIET   4TH?

  4) P R E S I D E N T   D E A F

   DEAF PRESIDENT?

   YES! DEAF PRESIDENT

   HURRAH! SCREAMED   JUMPED

    DANCED   HUGGED   DRANK   CRIED

   TURNED TV ON   WATCHED

HOTEL   BOARD ROOM   DOORS OPENED   CAME OUT

PRESS CONFERENCE   ROWS   ROWS

INTRODUCTION IRVING JORDAN KING

CAME-IN WITH WIFE   FACED AUDIENCE

LIGHT FLASHERS   TV CAMERAS   MICROPHONES
PRESIDENT SIGNED "THANK YOU   THANK YOU"
ARMS UP INTO SKY
STARS TWINKLING BRIGHTLY
INTO DARKNESS
****
WEEK   MONDAY   MARCH 20
GATES OPENED   CLASSES   STUDENTS WALKED IN
ROOM   SAT   LISTENED   PROFESSOR   LECTURE
WROTE-DOWN NOTES   WATCHED   THOUGHT OF THE BIG EVENT
NOON   STRUCK 12   CLOSED BOOKS   ROSE   WALKED OUT
MOVED AROUND   STOPPED   FROZEN
LOOKED UP   TAP-SHOULDERS   TAP
AIRPLANE FLEW AROUND WITH LONG SIGN
"GALLAUDET: THE WHOLE WORLD SALUTES YOU."
WAVED   SMILED   CRIED-WAVED
CROWD   CAMPUS   BUILDINGS
CAPITOL DOME   WASHINGTON MONUMENT
LINCOLN MEMORIAL   ALL-OVER-CITY
WASHINGTON, D.C.   FADE IN
U.S.A.   WORLD   EARTH ROTATING
MOVING INTO UNIVERSE   DISAPPEARING

NOTES

1. Alison Gibson's English translation of "Gallaudet Protest," the voice-over on DVD clip 9.1.

2. Throughout the rest of this chapter, the use of all capital letters indicates a quotation from Gilbert Eastman's English transliteration or glosses on the ASL concepts used in the poem.

REFERENCES

Bauman, Richard. 1977. *Verbal Art as Performance.* Prospect Heights, IL: Waveland Press.

Christiansen, John B., and Sharon N. Barnartt. 1995. *Deaf President Now! The 1988 Revolution at Gallaudet University.* Washington, DC: Gallaudet University Press.

Downes, Jeremy M. 1997. *Recursive Desire: Rereading Epic Tradition.* Tuscaloosa: University of Alabama Press.

Eastman, Gilbert C. 1991. *Live at SMI: Gilbert Eastman.* Videocassette. Burtonsville, MD: Sign Media.

Finnegan, Ruth. 1992. *Oral Poetry: Its Nature, Significance, and Social Context.* Bloomington: Indiana University Press.

Foley, John Miles. 1987. "Man, Muse, and Story: Psychohistorical Patterns in Oral Epic Poetry." *Oral Tradition* 2, no. 1:91–107.

———. 1988. *The Theory of Oral Composition: History and Methodology.* Bloomington: Indiana University Press.

———. 1990. *Traditional Oral Epic: The Odyssey, Beowulf, and the Serbo-Croatian Return Song.* Berkeley: University of California Press.

———. 1991. *Immanent Art: From Structure to Meaning in Traditional Oral Epic.* Bloomington: Indiana University Press.

———. 1992. "Word-Power, Performance, and Tradition." *Journal of American Folklore* 105:275–301.

———. 1995. *The Singer of Tales in Performance.* Bloomington: Indiana University Press.

Lord, Albert. 1960. *The Singer of Tales.* Cambridge, MA: Harvard University Press.

Lukács, Georg. 1983. *The Historical Novel.* Preface by Fredric Jameson. Trans. Hannah and Stanley Mitchell. Lincoln: University of Nebraska Press. (Original pub. 1963.)

McWilliams, John P. 1989. *The American Epic: Transforming a Genre, 1770–1860.* Cambridge: Cambridge University Press.

Merchant, Paul. 1971. *The Epic.* London: Methuen.

Mori, Masaki. 1997. *Epic Grandeur: Toward a Comparative Poetics of the Epic.* Albany: State University of New York Press.

Ong, Walter. 1982. *Orality and Literacy: The Technologizing of the Word.* London: Methuen.

Padden, Carol, and Tom Humphries. 1988. *Deaf in America: Voices from a Culture.* Cambridge, MA: Harvard University Press.

Shapiro, Joseph P. 1993. *No Pity: People with Disabilities Forging a New Civil Rights Movement.* New York: Times Books.

TEN

Visual Screaming

Willy Conley's Deaf Theater and Charlie Chaplin's Silent Cinema

CAROL L. ROBINSON

A *visual scream* is the visible gesture of a person, an animal, or a thing (such as a combination of images) making a loud screeching sound, without the sound accompaniment. A visual scream is an extreme form of silent shouting, an alarm given by the sender that is usually intended to jolt the receiver into attention toward something fearful, anxious, desperate, erotic, or hilarious.

CAN YOUR EYES HEAR THIS OKAY?

A study of visual screaming in two different media demonstrates how a gesture can be transformed through time, culture, and matter. It also demonstrates the semiotic relationships between speech culture, sign culture, and cinematic culture. Willy Conley's Deaf play *FALLING ON HEARING EYES—a museum of sign /anguish for people with communication disorders*[1] (1998) and Charlie Chaplin's silent film *A Dog's Life* (1918) use visual screaming to expose both the frustrations and the humor of miscommunication, as well as to protest the oppression of one group by another.

Willy Conley, an award-winning and published Deaf playwright currently associated with Baltimore's Center Stage Theater, the American Sign

Language Shakespeare Project, and Gallaudet University, often illustrates the bonds and tensions between Deaf and hearing cultures through his theater. However, his Deaf theater also illustrates how motion pictures are a sort of mediation for and between Deaf and hearing cultures. Indeed, when asked if film inspired him, Conley responded, "Yes, I'm very inspired by film. . . . It's so readily available, anytime," and he described it as outperforming the theater in terms of accessibility to those who cannot hear: "This is why I'm in awe of film so much" (pers. comm., Feb. 27, 1999). For Conley, it seems, the theater stage is similar to the film screen.

Cinema culture—particularly silent film—also fosters relations between Deaf and hearing cultures. Charlie Chaplin's apparently close association with Deaf painter and actor Granville Redmond is perhaps the most noteworthy. According to John S. Schuchman (1988), Redmond appears in at least five of Chaplin's films (25). David Robinson (1994) observes that Redmond and Chaplin "established a perfect pantomime communication, as his performances in *A Dog's Life* and *The Kid* testify" (232). According to Nicholas Mirzoeff (1995), "In 1929, the *California News,* a deaf periodical, reported that 'Chaplin is fond of Redmond because no oral conversation is possible between them. Instead, they talk in signs which is soothing to Chaplin, who tries to avoid people who talk too much'" (252).

To study a gesture of communication—the visual scream—shared between the hearing world's silent film era of the early 1900s and the Deaf world's theater era of the latter half of this century is fascinating. Both Conley's Deaf theater and Chaplin's silent cinema make a lot of "noise" against prejudice and social injustices toward those who differ from the so-called "norm" of the dominant hearing society. However, while Charlie Chaplin's pieces tend to focus upon conflicts between and among the rich and the poor (regardless of creed, race, gender, or handicap) and are full of hope for social change, Willy Conley's pieces tend to focus upon language conflicts between and among the hearing and the deaf (regardless of creed, race, gender, or class status) and are often full of cynical laughter and the knowledge that significant social change takes a lot of time. Though their politics vary, both express these political points via the visual scream.

That the visual scream is being used politically, according to the philosophy of Gilles Deleuze and Félix Guattari (1987), is obvious, since all signs of communication (including language) are political. "There is no mother tongue," they write, "only a power takeover by a dominant language that at times advances along a broad front, and at times swoops down on diverse centers simultaneously" (101). Regardless of how one communicates—through sign language, through spoken language, through theater, through film—the expression and the content will be ultimately political. Deleuze and Guattari are not describing traditional semiotics; rather, they are challenging it. Ronald Bogue (1989) understands Deleuze and Guattari to "reject any universal semiotics which seeks to explain all of reality in terms of signs" (125).[2] Deleuze and Guattari draw upon the nonlinguistic semiotics of C. S. Peirce and the metaphysics of Henri Bergson, rejecting any semiology that limits itself to language biases, such as Saussurian linguistics. Because the original biases of Saussurian linguistics and related semiotics disappear under this more objective approach, application of this semiotic philosophy to the study of visual screaming allows one to more fully appreciate this gesture's visual volume.

Deleuze (1989) argues that "talking cinema had nothing in common with the theatre and . . . the two could only be confused at the level of bad films" (228). He does not make the same observation about silent cinema and theater, and he does not seem aware of the existence of Deaf theater. So it is possible that Deaf theater and silent cinema have at least some gestures in common, and one such gesture might be the visual scream. For example, the possible expressions of a visual scream within the parameters of silent film and Deaf theater might be the shape of the mouth and face, the movement of the body, the arrangement of printed words, the shape of the text (such as using ALL CAPS to SCREAM at someone through the printed words of an e-mail), or the shape of an image either on stage or on screen. According to Deleuze and Guattari (1987), a visual scream contains "segments of expression" that are complicated even further in how they are tied to "segments of content" (67). Not only are those shapes affected by their medium of expression, but they are even more varied by the mode of the expression: tone, emphasis, voice, point of view, lighting, color, mise-en-scène, acting, movement, and editing arrangement. The possible contents are also numerous. With or without sound, we do not know the nature of that scream unless there is a context. For example, the scream could be expressed out of anguish or eroticism, from physical pain or physical pleasure, at the injustice of a wrong thing done or the excitement of a right thing happening.

Furthermore, the environment directly affects the shape of both expression and content. According to the philosophy of Deleuze and Guattari, a sign is by no means cut off from the other senses, including sound, or from surrounding contexts. In both *A Dog's Life* and *FALLING ON HEARING EYES,* visual screaming is complicated by the surrounding politics and aesthetics of theater, cinema, Deaf culture, and hearing culture. So before we examine visual screaming in either Chaplin's silent film or Conley's Deaf play some background of historical and philosophical context must be projected.

A LITTLE BACKGROUND NOISE

The aesthetic and political relationship between cinema and Deaf culture is historically strange, not completely what would be expected. Schuchman (1988) illustrates a long history between the Deaf and Hollywood: it includes the silent screen Deaf actors Granville Redmond, Emerson Romero (a.k.a. Tommy Albert), Albert Ballin (who wrote *The Deaf Mute Howls),* Louis Weinberg (a.k.a. David Marvel), and Carmen de Arcos (23), as well as the silent screen actor Lon Chaney, who was a child of deaf parents (32). However, while silent film was one of the few aspects of hearing culture in which the deaf could participate as both creators and appreciators on equal ground with the hearing, it did not ever totally belong to the deaf; it belonged to hearing culture. Likewise, in what is known as Deaf culture,[3] film has never become a major artistic medium, as, for example, painting, sculpture, and photography were in nineteenth-century France. Mirzoeff (1995) observes that the process of reproducing the "moving image was marked from the beginning by its association with speech and with the cure of physiological trauma," such as the collaboration between the Institute for the Deaf and Pathé Films "to produce a series of short films for use in oralist education" (252–53). The Hollywood Classical Style film, for example, was so set upon creating realistic fantasies with happy endings that there was no room for realistic "tragedies" with so-called sad endings. Chaplin's films exemplify this: the "happy" Tramp's adventures always leave the audience smiling or even laughing at the end of each film—never mind that he lacks the basics to quality living (food and shelter). Such purposeful misrepresentations have kept audiences (from moviegoers to video renters) content for over a century. Moreover, many members of these audiences seem to have believed in the projected ideals: that some people happily choose poverty (an intended sarcasm of Chaplin's) and that the hearing "impaired" (including the Deaf) need/choose to be cured. Such fantasies are truly misguided, since one person's tragedy may be another person's fortune.

The semiotic association between Deaf and cinema communication began to weaken when Thomas Edison and others conceived of silent film as a mere technical fluke in cinema history. When Edison, who became physically deaf in his youth, employed William Dicksen to create the kinetograph, he had not envisioned the motion picture industry, much less silent movies. Edison wanted a machine that would accompany his phonograph with images. David Cook (1990) explains that "he envisioned a coin-operated entertainment machine" (5). The idea of having motion pictures apart from sound was never intended by Edison. Cook concludes that "in some sense the silent cinema represents a 30-year aberration from the medium's natural tendency toward a total representation of reality" (5). Whose reality? A hearing reality. For Mirzoeff (1995), the talkies ended an age—which had begun in the Renaissance—in which Deaf artists stood on equal ground with the hearing and were even at times "close to the center of artistic practice" (254). The breakdown of communication and collaboration between the Deaf and hearing was completed in what Mirzoeff points out as "a strange irony for the deaf," when Al Jolson declared in the first talkie, *The Jazz Singer* (1927), "You ain't heard nothing yet!" (254).

The Deaf were not the only ones to suffer this loss. William K. Everson (1998) observes: "There was a glorious kind of fatalism in the last days of the silent films. The films were being produced purely for the moment; in a year or two, they would be dead for all time. Producers, directors, stars, and studio heads all seemed united in an unofficial and unspoken mass conspiracy to create one great last stand of the silent film, to show what it could do before the ultimate death at the coming of the microphones and sound tracks" (335).Gilles Deleuze (1989) points out several semiotic differences between silent film and the new talkies—apart from the obvious factor of speech—that further tie silent film culture to Deaf culture. In the new talkies, speech was no longer a primary function of the eye; it was no longer read (from the actors' lips or from title cards). Instead, it became a function primarily of the ear. "What the talkies seemed to lose," Deleuze writes, "was the universal language, and the omnipotence of montage" (225).

Of course, there is no such thing as complete silence in silent movies. Deleuze also argues that silent film is anything but silent in communication. Images of moving lips, galloping horses, trains chugging along a track, screaming maidens in distress are all muted, made inaudible by the lack of a sound track, but all function as obvious signifiers of sounds (225–27). Imitation of speaking without sound is one example of a visual signifier of sound in some plots of Deaf theater. According to Deleuze, the visual emphasis of silent cinema "shows the structure of a society, its situation, its place and functions, the attitudes and roles, the actions and reactions of the individuals, in short the form and the contents" (225–26). This is also true of Deaf theater—while the emphasis is placed upon the visual, the existence of sound is not denied. Music, sound effects, and sometimes even live (behind the screen) voice-over and/or dubbing often accompany silent films, and the same is true for Deaf theater. Most Deaf theater also uses sound effects and music, most shows provide voice-over interpretation for the signing actors, and sometimes actors alternate between voicing and signing within the play, such as when a deaf character is supposed to be speaking to a hearing character who doesn't know sign language.

Nor is there complete silence in Deaf theater. It is a myth that the Deaf world is a world of silence. Many deaf can hear at least the sound of a 747 roaring next their ears, just perhaps not very well. Some deaf teenagers can hear a blasting heavy metal song, just perhaps not very well. If a car is playing music so loudly that it is rocking while moving, more than likely the people inside are deaf and have the volume turned up so they can hear the music. There are even sounds that accompany American Sign Language (ASL) signs—heard or not: "Pah!" *(Finally!)* or the piercing yelp that many deaf people make to get each others' attention.[4]

The silent film era at the beginning of the twentieth century is thus audiologically and visually parallel to the Deaf theater era at the latter turn of the century. Both *A Dog's Life* and *FALLING ON HEARING EYES* reflect this unique and limited parallel dimension of the early 1900s silent cinema hearing culture and later twentieth-century Deaf theater culture. Both works use the visual scream as a substitute for the audiological scream. However, there is a difference in the way Conley and Chaplin contain their visual screams, a difference in the environment. It is a difference not only of media environment (theater vs. film) but of cultural environment (Deaf World vs. Tramp World). Chaplin invites the audience to merely look into the world of the Tramp; the film screen serves as a safety barrier between the Tramp's troubled life and the comfort of their moviehouse seats. In the intimacy of the theater, however, Conley breaks down the barriers completely, forcing the audience to become a part of the Deaf world—comfortably or not (**clip 10.1**).

FALLING ON HEARING EYES is just what the subtitle says it is: *a museum of sign /anguish for people with communication disorders,* including those who can't sign. The play attempts to immerse the audience into the realm of the Deaf world right from before the beginning of the play. "As the audience waits in the lobby to enter the theatre," instructs the script: "lights flash off and on. An usher announces in ASL (with no voice interpretation) that the Deaf and those who know sign language may sit anywhere they please. Those who don't know sign need to sit in the seats marked for the SIGNING-IMPAIRED. The usher answers any questions that the signers may have. If signing-impaired people ask questions, the usher should play 'deaf' (or just be deaf), feign ignorance, exasperation, and gesture for them to go on in" (1). Clearly, Conley's portrayal of the Deaf world is a polarization of the hearing world—a reversal of circumstances—where it is the Deaf who are the norm and the "signing-impaired" who are handicapped.

This play's utopian Deaf world, where the Deaf are dominant and the primary language is ASL, makes direct ties to the days of the silent film era in several ways. For one thing, the play is full of sign-mimes. A sign-mime is a series of pantomimed images combined with ASL commentary that is performed in imitation of the structure of film, illustrating narrative action through shots, angles, slow and fast motion, freeze-frame, and point of view—and according to Conley (2001a) is "a dying form of storytelling performance in Deaf culture" (57) (**clip 10.2**). Another tie to silent film in Conley's play is the "Shoo Fly Soup" scenario, which the script says should be "Chaplinesque" and scored by "a tune that typically accompanies silent films." In making the preparations for this scene, Techie gets confused in showing the three-part label for this music, arranging and rearranging the cards so that they read "Silent Music Films," "Film Silent Music," "Music Silent Film," and "Music Film Silent." The play features two characters, Techie and Guide, who somewhat resemble Laurel and Hardy (in both their silent film and talkie eras). Techie is a kind of Laurel-esque hearing fool whose job is to provide technical support for Guide. Guide is somewhat like a "deaf Hardy," making a grandiose presentation on aspects of Deaf culture that is both lecture and demonstration. The mishaps in communication (technical and human) between Deaf and hearing people that constitute its overlying narrative are reminiscent of the mishaps in communication that are so prominent in the sketches of Laurel and Hardy. Each represents, scorns, and even laughs at the nightmares of both miscommunication and misunderstanding.

Conley's personal passion for cinema and the way he says he constructs his writing suggest that he purposely creates a cinematic art on the stage (a "cinematic theater"). In an e-mail interview I held with him, Conley explained: "Many of my poems and short stories are composed from still photo or cinematic images in my head. Much of the dialogue is mobile, since it involves sign languages in some form. Being a dramatist, my stories tend to involve action or movement. I like to use the macro, telephoto and zoom lenses a lot for the images in my head. These lenses bring details in up close. It's hard for me to imagine that other writers don't do this, because isn't this the essence of fiction or poetry writing? To previsualize?" (pers. comm., Nov. 2, 2001). What Conley doesn't point out is that no writer thought of this sort of "previsualization" in cinematic terms until film was invented. In fact, in the early part of cinema's history, writers such as Virginia Woolf and James Joyce were already beginning to consciously draw film technique back into the construction of literature.[5] Indeed, some have argued that film and literature can now share not only cinematic qualities but literary qualities as well. "Print biases," Charles Eidsvik (1974) once wrote, "are so built into literary criticism that it is difficult to think fairly of literature in any other medium" (18). However, before the twentieth century, when film didn't exist and photography was still considered to be more a phenomenon than an art form, cinematic and photographic qualities were not as extensive in literature, and certainly cinematic conceptions were non-existent in the writing process! So Conley's modest observation is not necessarily universally applicable, and when we take into consideration other pieces of the puzzle of Conley—such as the fact that he is also a professional photographer and has several years' experience teaching film aesthetics at Gallaudet University—it becomes clear that his visual world has been shaped by both Deaf and cinema (and photographic) cultures.

In turn, Chaplin's works suggest a direct rapport between silent film and Deaf cultures. *A Dog's Life* (1918) is the first of three short films spliced together under the title *The Chaplin Revue* (1959). Chaplin provides a brief voice-over narrative as introduction to all three films and at the end of the narrative says: "And now let me take you back to the good old silent days. There will be no talk, no realistic sound. I think it would spoil the mood. I have composed two hours of music which I hope will be more agreeable than the sound of footsteps on the gravel path, as it were, or a lot of yakity-yak talking, as I'm doing now. It will be music and action, a sort of comic ballet." To fully appreciate the pantomimic art of Charlie Chaplin, one must again acknowledge that, while he fluently heard and spoke the Queen's English, he often preferred to communicate in gestures, mimes, and signs with his good friend Granville Redmond (Mirzoeff 1995, 252). (Granville Redmond, by the way, plays the supporting role of the dance hall manager in *A Dog's Life*.)

Schuchman (1988) points out that "there is no direct evidence that Chaplin acquired any nonverbal communication skills or techniques from Redmond" (25). However, he also points out that the affinity Chaplin held with the Deaf in preferring silent communication over the "yakity-yak" of speech was genuine. For example, Chaplin uses Redmond to make an ironic statement in the opening of *City Lights:* the microphone is provided for the dignitaries, but the speeches are literally represented by "Blah, blah, blah" sounds, and one of the speakers is played by Redmond. Schuchman (1988) observes: "Although there is no direct evidence that Chaplin chose a deaf actor who would be oblivious to the noise of the dedication, the fact remains that Redmond is there. Unfortunately, even if the symbolism were deliberate, it ends as a private joke since the audience was not privy to the fact that the actor was deaf" (25). However, Conley not only saw this symbolism but taught it to his film and literature classes at Gallaudet University. Furthermore, it was known that Chaplin was making this film in protest against the talkies, and everyone was aware that he was one of the last great silent filmmakers to make the transition into talkies. (*City Lights* was released in 1931.) Clearly, Chaplin's silent cinema was and is at least empathetic to Deaf culture (figure 10.1 and **clip 10.3**).

The realization that Chaplin's A Dog's Life and Conley's *FALLING ON HEARING EYES* are related to each other through the more general connections between cinema and Deaf culture can better frame the study of visual screaming in both works and how it changes from the first work to the second. However, it is important to remember that observation of the visual scream is partial. This gesture is highly elusive (as are all gestures in any form of communication). What we see is difficult to fix our focus on because the nature of the expression(s) and the nature of the content(s) are multiple (there is more than one possible sign to an image). In looking at these elements of expression and content, we must keep in mind that such observation is incomplete. It is perhaps possible to hold a "freeze-frame" upon a variable sign of an image that can be identified as a visual scream.

FIGURE 10.1. Granville Redmond and Charlie Chaplin signing the letter "D." Reprinted by permission of Gallaudet University Archives.

However, each example of a visual scream below has been taken out of its context and medium; each has been taken out of the fluidity of its narrative, imagistic form as presented on the stage or on the screen.[6]

TURNING UP THE VOLUME

Both *FALLING ON HEARING EYES* and *A Dog's Life* scream in laughter and tears over the apparent madness of interactions between and among people (whatever their physical and social strengths and weaknesses) on the battleground of miscommunication. While Chaplin seems to romantically appeal to the universal possibilities of silent cinema communication and comprehension, Conley goes a level deeper and focuses his plays' screams upon the inane and insane nature of society's current pit of political, aesthetic, emotional, and intellectual babble. While Chaplin's works suggest the power of silent film as a universal language, Conley's works demonstrate that the powerful idea of universal communication (such as that of a universal language) is impossible. We all understand the same expression in different ways, and thus we associate different meanings (even if only slightly different) with those expressions. Conley's play points to the inevitable greater chaos born out of the oversimplification of an already chaotic problem of communication between members of more than one culture. Conley is visually screaming not only about the amusements and evils of society but also about the naïveté of Chaplin's films.

Conley is not the first to scream in this manner. In fact, he is not even the first to scream over the absurd "help" offered to the deaf and hard of hearing by mainstream society. Several years prior to the instatement of the Americans with Disabilities Act (1992), the deaf and hard of hearing had extremely little access to either television or film. Closed captioning or an image of someone signing at the lower corner of the screen was provided voluntarily by television corporations and film studios. There is a wonderful parody of this dilemma, a direct message intended for those of us with "good" hearing ability, in a skit by the original cast of *Saturday Night Live* in the 1970s. (The skit was used often enough so that a variation of it was included in the Twenty-fifth Anniversary show [Morris 1999].) In the skit, someone announces that special services are being provided for those television viewers at home who are hearing impaired. Usually, in a lower corner of the screen, Garrett Morris is half-shouting/half-screaming every word spoken by the other actors out toward the television audience. This repeated skit humorously points to the difficulties deaf and hard-of-hearing audiences suffer (even today) from either the poor quality or the lack of interpreting and closed-captioning services. Each variant of the skit contains at least two examples of the gesture of screaming. Audiologically, Morris is screaming at the top of his lungs. But even if there were no sound, the viewer could see that Morris was blasting his lungs out because his hands are cupped around his mouth (for projection) and because he visibly takes deep breaths before he mouths words with a face that is contorted enough to suggest great physical effort to project. This physical effort to make sounds further emphasizes the unimportance of the image, as the hands cupped around his mouth greatly interfere with any efforts to read Morris's lips (if one happens to have such a talent to do so). These skits as a whole are also a visual scream in that they point to the outrageousness and absurdity of the television industry's efforts to make itself "user friendly" for the deaf and hard of hearing back in the 1970s.

FALLING ON HEARING EYES makes visual screams over the very same point that the *Saturday Night Live* skit makes: the play puts hearing audiences (who typically do not know sign language) in the uncomfortable situation of communication impairment. The programs for at least one presentation of the play had written on them: "INTERPRETED FOR THE SIGNING IMPAIRED" (May 1998, Towson University Studio Theatre). In the play, as with the above-described Garrett Morris interpretation for the hearing impaired, an inadequate system of interpretation is provided for "the signing-impaired" (the visually "deaf") members of the audience: a slide projector that constantly gets jammed or else has missing or improperly installed (upside down and/or backwards) slides. Early on, a series of slide projections puts forth a list of statements (the play's directions suggest that the first slide gets stuck and repeats itself):

> A person with no ears?
> A person with no ears?
> A person with no ears?
> Deaf as a post.
> Falling on deaf ears.
> Turning a deaf ear.
> Deaf and dumb.
> Deaf mute.
> What's the matter, you deaf?
> Read my lips.
> Can you drive?
> Deafening sound!
> You're lucky you can't hear that.
> You speak well for a deaf person.
> I'm not deaf, I'm ignoring you.
> Are you death?
> Can you speak sign language?
> How do you wake up in the morning?
> Can you read Braille?
> (Conley 1998, 8–9)

Those dependent upon sound are mocked by the written words projected on the screen, which visually scream ignorance and a babble of incoherent nonsense. Conley bombards the audience with mostly clichés upon clichés—and those that aren't clichés are idiotic and/or insensitive statements ("A person with no ears?" "Can you read Braille?"). The constant mismatching of slide titles is a persistent deconstruction of one level of narration to make an abstract point. In this case, the point seems to be addressing the communicative, political, and cultural struggles between Deaf and hearing cultures.

A Dog's Life also bombards the viewer with text, though Chaplin's humor is absurdist in a less cynical way than Conley's. For example, after the viewer meets Scraps the dog on screen, a title card comments, "Scraps, Thoroughbred Mongrel." The juxtaposition of the words *thoroughbred* and *mongrel* generates a scream over the absurdity of race distinction and elitism. Another example can be found on one of the chalkboards outside the employment building: "Wanted! Strong Men for Sewer Work. Bring Recommendations." First, the interjection at the beginning is a scream to draw attention to the job description. Second, the request for recommendations to perform sewer work is a scream at the absurdity of requirements for a job—why would one need recommendations for such a lowly and undesirable job? Thus the request also screams over the economic desperation of the times: employment is so scarce that limitations must be placed upon who can and cannot have even the simplest and sometimes most degrading of jobs. On the other chalkboard, there is a notice for a very desirable job at a brewery. The screaming of these printed words is emphasized by the Tramp's reaction to them, as if the words were trying to jump out and grab him, and he runs inside to catch them before they fall into the unemployed hands of another eager worker.

FALLING ON HEARING EYES also uses text in ways other than for subtitling/interpretation in order to visually scream at an even higher decibel level than *A Dog's Life*. One way it does this is through the various exhibits set up in the mise-en-scène of this "museum of sign /anguish"—such as the traditional diamond-shaped yellow road sign SLOW! DEAF CHILD AT PLAY. Instead of leaving the sign as it is, Conley instructs that a slash be drawn through the word "AT" and that a little arrow be inserted that points to words written by hand above the word "AT" reading "IN A"—thus setting up a binary opposition: SLOW! DEAF CHILD AT PLAY versus SLOW! DEAF CHILD IN A PLAY. Here is a sign intended to benefit deaf individuals, originally created by the hearing. By rewriting the sign and changing the signifier's meaning, Conley is commenting on the invasion of the dominant hearing culture into the cultural territory of the subordinated Deaf, thus marking the boundaries between the two cultures. Another example is the earlier quoted compilation of slides, which (according to the text of the written play) does not have to end with the final naive question, "Can you read Braille?" The last slide shown is supposed to be "Silence is golden," and after a bit of audiological silence while the audience reads this slide, the phone on stage is expected to ring/flash. This juxtaposition of gestures—the printed texts on the screen and the phone disrupting the golden silence as we read the text—is akin to Chaplin's style of humor.

Deleuze (1986) argues, "Chaplin knew how to select gestures which were close to each other and corresponding situations which were far apart, so as to make their relationship produce a particularly intense emotion at the same time as laughter, and to redouble the laughter through this emotion" (170). Deleuze also argues that, in cinema, "there are several signs—two at least for each type of image" (69). In other words, a visual scream is only one possible sign for an image. If this is true, then it must also be true that a visual scream can be expressed simultaneously with other expressions in the same image. The Tramp's whole body visually screams in reaction to the chalkboard that is visually screaming of jobs at a brewery: he stops, jumps back in alarm, and falls over himself scrambling to get into line first. Chaplin also juxtaposes the gestures of separate actors that include visual screaming, as when Scraps the dog is snuck into a dance hall, the Green Lantern. Here we see a dog's tail happily wagging out of a hole in the Tramp's pants; the reaction of the drunks in the dance hall is visual screaming in bodily reactions, such as fainting or jolting to a frozen state of shock. (One might imagine as well that the audience was screaming in laughter at the image.) However, Chaplin also combines acting gestures with printed text to create collective (a regime of) signs of visual screaming. For example, he relies upon the Deaf actor Granville Redmond to select gestures that clearly express lewdness and exploitativeness, and he juxtaposes these gestures (directed toward the female protagonist—the singer at the dance hall) with the singsong title card, "If you smile and wink, they'll buy a drink." It is very evident that Redmond is not saying a single word, and it is also very clear that his gestures are suggesting much more than a smile, a wink, and a drink. This combination of gestures and words collectively make the sarcastic visual scream: "Prostitution!"

Conley also combines acting gestures with various modes of language to generate visual screaming. One way is through gibberish. The entire performance is plagued by miscommunication and misunderstanding between this hearing man and that Deaf man, including many signing mistakes that are common among careless signers (regardless of hearing ability). One example appears toward the beginning of the performance. According to the play's text, when Guide tries to inspire him to help get the show going, Techie both speaks and signs gibberish (an attempt to combine spoken English with ASL) rapidly:

vnmoijwlkmromcv**DEAFCULTURE.**
fmoimoijrlmwlmmlr**DEAFPEOPLE.**
melxgioourtx**DEAFPRESIDENTNOW.**
sroutrecglpoolwer**DEAFSCHOOL.** xciwhidybcciu**MARLEEMATLIN.**
skguvbeobloiuyew**ASLFOREVER.**
xomelbhtwoiyubw**ASLNOW.**
srubiwlnblkuty**ASL, ASL, ASL DEAFPOWER!**

These words and nonwords are a *visual scream* at the incompetence and shame of anyone who speaks or signs (Deaf or hearing) so recklessly: it is madness. But it is also a political scream against the practice of SIM-COM, the practice of trying to speak grammatically correct English while simultaneously mangling ASL into an English word order. One or both languages tend to suffer when combined.[7] Even on the page of the script, the above babble is a visual scream, a lot of noise meaning ultimately nothing, yet sounding as if it should mean something. It is also a protest against the emptiness that expressed words can have—talking the talk without walking the walk, speaking/signing in support of Deaf rights and yet doing nothing about them.

Another type of gestural communication combined with language is to be found in Conley's use of puppet paws. Puppet paws are the use of bare hands as puppets, as if they were inside a sock or hand puppet's head: the tips of the four fingers come down to the tip of the thumb of each hand, and these touching tips signify lips or the front of a mouth. Thus the hand signifies a head, and the wrist and arm signifies a neck. The mimetic motions of these puppets are incorporated with ASL signs. To make sure that the signing-impaired members of the audience understand his explanation of the differences between the signs for "I love you" and for "bullshit," the character Guide does a bare-bones puppet paws skit. The skit is a courtship dance that begins with one puppet paw signing "I love you" (a single hand sign with the thumb, pointer, and pinky pointing upward and the two middle fingers closed against the palm) and the other puppet paw responding with "bullshit" (which is almost identical to "I love you" except the thumb is closed up against the palm with the other two middle fingers). At some point during the skit, the communication switches so that the second puppet paw is suddenly signing "I love you" and the first puppet paw is responding with "bullshit." The conversation happens very quickly, back and forth between each puppet paw, emphasizing the similarities between these two single-hand signs. The skit ultimately illustrates how easily miscommunication can occur (the slight change of a finger in this case) and can lead to conversation that is meaningless and insanely frantic. The mania in the hand puppet show is one of love, as the hands crazily sign back and forth "I love you" and "bullshit" until the madness ends with the two both accidentally saying "I love you." At this point, in the actor Adrian Blue's performance of the skit, they fall to the floor and start "making love" until he becomes aware that he has gotten lost in his expressive art and, embarrassed, stops the sign-mime. Clearly, this is a visual scream over the madness of miscommunication as well as the madness of love.

Madness is ultimately what both Chaplin and Conley visually scream about. The madness of hunger and starvation permeates *A Dog's Life* as a theme, whose incidents add up to a gesture of visual screaming that almost seems to mean: *Can't you see that this man is honest and trying to work but just can't get a break? Can't you see he needs a home and food? Feed him! Clothe him! Give him shelter!* But the screaming is not just indignation, frustration, and anger. It is also humorous, as illustrated by the last image of the "baby" in the happy couple's cradle (the Tramp and the Singer/Prostitute get the money and move to live happily ever after): the image visually screams the hilarity of two proud parents adoring the newborn pups suckling at Scraps the dog (who seemed to be very male up until this scene).

While Chaplin visually screams over the madness of society's treatment of the economically challenged, Conley visually screams over the madness of the linguistically challenged—those who can't sign, that is. *FALLING ON HEARING EYES* is all about the madness of miscommunication. But the final scene of the play emphasizes what Conley seems to be screaming at the audiences: *Can't you see that it takes at least TWO to successfully communicate? Can't you see that it is a hell of a lot easier for a hearing person to learn sign language than it is for a deaf person to pretend to hear? Can't you see that deaf people are human beings, not guinea pigs?* Conley also illustrates madness by portraying an outrageous mock cochlear ear implant surgery that uses a melon for a head, while commenting that such surgery is "as popular as breast implants" and pointing to the price of suffering deaf individuals have had to endure in order to appear "normal" in the hearing world (clip 10.1). Choosing the controversial subject of breast implants allows Conley to take issue on another more subtle, yet equally sarcastic level. The comparison is stating that, while women also feel pressured to have invasive surgery to become more acceptable within our society, breast implants are not nearly as dangerous or invasive as cochlear implants, and cochlear implants are hardly done for cosmetic purposes.

The rejection of the importance of sound over all else permeates *FALLING ON HEARING EYES* right through to the end. For example, there is a bust on the stage, upon which GUIDE keeps his hearing aids—playing upon the imagistic pun of one being "stone deaf" as well as upon the bitterness of just how useful these aids really are both to the technically deaf (who are turned into "imperfect" hearing people) and to the Deaf (who do not need them at all to communicate, since their primary language is a sign language). For another example, there is a telephone on the stage. Throughout the play, the phone has rung, sometimes for use with an old TTY, sometimes not, pointing to the frustrations that the deaf and hard of hearing encounter with the telephone. Indeed, at one point, Guide becomes so frustrated with his failed efforts to communicate on the phone with his hearing aids that he throws the hearing aids away. In the final scene, the telephone rings one last time:

TECHIE: Hello? Uh-huh, yes he is. [Gestures that it's for GUIDE. He also gestures it's not a TTY call but a voice one.]

GUIDE: [He impulsively goes to the bust but remembers that he threw the hearing aid away. He goes to the receiver, which TECHIE holds out to him. GUIDE signs obscenities to it—no voicing. Shocked, TECHIE hold his hands over the mouthpiece. At the blackboard, he writes: "Alexander Graham Bell tried to invent a device that would help his deaf wife visualize speech." He does the following scenario, experiencing the whole gamut of emotions from anger to indifference to pleasure: snatches the receiver from TECHIE, looks at it from all angles, waves his hand in front of the receiver, peers closely into the holes of both ends of the receiver, unscrews one end to look inside. . .]

(Conley 1998, 26)

At the end of this scene, Guide has fully "dissected" the phone's "anatomy" right down to the wall jack into which the cord is plugged, unplugged it, plugged the wall jack up "with a wad of bubble gum from his mouth," and then gone back to the blackboard to add a comment about Bell's attempts to help his deaf wife: ". . . and he failed miserably!" This is a visual scream over the efforts of the hearing world to make deaf people's lives better and their claims to have made the world of the deaf better when they actually have not done so.

CONCLUSION: I THINK I BROKE AN EYE-DRUM

Madness is ultimately what both Conley and Chaplin visually scream about. While neither the play nor the film portrays the most obvious (literal) visual gesture of screaming, both FALLING ON HEARING EYES and A Dog's Life scream in laughter and tears over the apparent madness of battles to communicate between and among people (whatever their physical and economic strengths and weaknesses). Chaplin's film and Conley's play share at least four gestures of visual screaming: screaming with humor and frustration over miscommunication, screaming about the power and impotency of languages and other forms of communication, screaming about the oppression of social injustice, and screaming about the suffering of enduring social injustice. These gestures of visual screaming are expressed in printed text, through the setting up of objects on screen or stage (the mise-en-scène), through the juxtapositions of performances, and through the juxtaposition of images.

Ultimately, A Dog's Life and FALLING ON HEARING EYES are narrative attacks upon the audience as communicatively dysfunctional members of society. The heroes of each piece—the Tramp and the Guide—appeal to the hearts of audience members through humor. The visual screaming concerns the prejudices of those who have toward those who have not. However, while Chaplin's film screams that it is the poor who are the have-nots, Conley's play twists the audience assumption around: it is those who cannot sign (regardless of hearing ability) who are the have-nots—they are visually deaf. Thus, while Chaplin is screaming at the haves to give to the poor (the have-nots), Conley is screaming at those who are unable to comprehend ASL (the have-nots) to stop helping those who can sign (the haves) and to start helping themselves. This twist in argument, this transformation of the visual scream from hearing silent film culture to Deaf theater culture, might have been successful because of Chaplin's association with Deaf culture in making *A Dog's Life,* but it is also successful because of Conley's familiarity with Chaplin's version of silent film culture. The visual scream does not demonstrate either the "cinematic" nature of Conley's play or the "literariness" or "cultural deafness" of Chaplin's films. What it does demonstrate is how a simple gesture can be transformed from a hearing culture's silent movie into a Deaf culture play with only a little twist of meaning.

NOTES

1. *Sign /anguish* is also a pun, an inside joke that deaf people would get right away because it alludes to the extreme anguish most deaf people suffer in attempting to understand someone's speech through lipreading techniques. But Conley intends much more than this pun. He explains: "There's a space between *sign* and */anguish.* The backslash doubles as a droopy lower case 'L.' There [. . . is a] triple-entendre involved with the word */anguish* which is supposed to give a sense of (1) all of the anguish involved with the sign language and language of 'Signs' (as in poster-type of signs, which is rampant throughout the play), (2) the play on misspelling of 'language' as 'languish,' (3) the actual definition of *languish* which means to lose vigor; fail in health; to live under distressing conditions; continue in a state of suffering" (pers. comm., Nov. 2, 2001).

2. Deleuze (1989) complicates this concept by freely interchanging definitions of *signs* and *images*—possibly intending all applicable meanings at once. He also writes, for example, that a sign is "a particular image that refers to a type of image, whether from the point of view of its bipolar composition, or from the point of view of its genesis" (32).

3. The rift between hearing and Deaf cultures is founded in language, but the alienation between the dominating hearing world and Deaf culture is further expounded within Deaf culture. The *hard of hearing* are those who have difficulty in sound-based communication; the *deaf* are those who cannot hear words and can at best hear only lower-pitched sounds; and the *Deaf* are those for whom hearing loss is not the issue and for whom identity is based not so much upon the identity of a so-called "handicap" as upon membership in a culture that communicates primarily through a sign language. Those who are deaf or hard of hearing and who communicate primarily through voice and lipreading are Oral, not *Deaf.* Owen Wrigley writes in *The Politics of Deafness* (1996): "The degree of hearing loss matters relatively little. What is important, and what is deemed primary evidence for membership within the broader community, is the use of sign language" (15).

4. One might argue, then, that the hearing and deaf audiences of silent cinema were much more akin, and the shock of sound in the talkie for those with hearing ability might be considered slightly analogous to the shock of the sound in life when one first hears sound through hearing aids.

5. See, for example, the numerous groundbreaking articles that analyze the relationships between film and literature in the anthology edited by John Harrington, *Film and/as Literature* (1977).

6. In the case of Conley's play, isolating "freeze-frames" particularly belies the work's fluidity because theater is by nature always changing from one performance to the next. Its being a Deaf play makes it even harder to grasp because translation from performance into the printed text of a script is difficult. As Conley (2001b) explains, "Unlike hearing playwrights of the English language who may occasionally incorporate dialect or second languages, deaf playwrights must work with the Deaf community's signed language, ASL, and its many dialects, as well as a range of signed English systems. They have the added task of considering the most accurate and efficient way of expressing this polyglot dialogue in written English, because ASL itself has no written form that is in general use among Deaf signers" (147).

7. Indeed, a pidgin language is growing out of this madness, known as Pidgin Signed English (PSE), a combination of ASL and Signed Exact English.

REFERENCES

Bogue, Ronald. 1989. *Deleuze and Guattari.* New York: Routledge.

Chaplin, Charles, dir. 1918. *A Dog's Life.* In *A Chaplin Revue* (1959).

Conley, Willy. 1998. *FALLING ON HEARING EYES—a museum of sign /anguish for people with communication disorders.* "Interpreted for the signing impaired." Laurel, MD: Deaf Writes Studio.

———. 2001a. "Away from Invisibility, towards Invincibility: Issues with Deaf Theatre Artists in America." In *Deaf World: A Historical Reader and Primary Sourcebook,* ed. Lois Bragg, 51–67. New York: New York University Press.

———. 2001b. "In Search of the Perfect Sign-Language Script: Insights into the Diverse Writing Styles of Deaf Playwrights." In *Deaf World: A Historical Reader and Primary Sourcebook,* ed. Lois Bragg, 147–61. New York: New York University Press.

Cook, David A. 1990. *A History of Narrative Film.* 3rd ed. New York: W. W. Norton.

Deleuze, Gilles. 1986. *Cinema.* Vol. 1. *The Movement Image.* Trans. Hugh Tomlinson and Barbara Habberjam. Minneapolis: University of Minnesota Press. Originally published as *L'image-mouvement* (Paris: Editions de Minuit, 1983).

———. 1989. *Cinema.* Vol. 2. *The Time Image.* Trans. Hugh Tomlinson and Barbara Habberjam. Minneapolis: University of Minnesota Press. Originally published as *L'image-temps* (Paris: Editions de Minuit, 1985).

Deleuze, Gilles, and Félix Guattari. 1987. *A Thousand Plateaus.* Vol. 2. *Capitalism and Schizophrenia.* Trans. Brian Massumi. Minneapolis: University of Minnesota Press. Originally published as *Mille plateaux,* vol. 2, *Capitalisme et schizophrénie* (Paris: Editions de Minuit, 1980).

Eidsvik, Charles. 1974. "Soft Edges: The Art of Literature, the Medium of Film." *Literature/Film Quarterly* 2, no. 1:16–21.

Everson, William K. 1998. *American Silent Film.* New York: Da Capo Press.

Harrington, John, ed. 1977. *Film and/as Literature.* Englewood Cliffs, NJ: Prentice Hall.

Mirzoeff, Nicholas. 1995. *Silent Poetry: Deafness, Sign, and Visual Culture in Modern France.* Princeton: Princeton University Press.

Morris, Garrett. 1999. "Special Services for the Hearing Impaired." In *Saturday Night Live 25; 25 Years of Laughs,* dir. Beth McCarthy-Miller and James Signorelli (Los Angeles: NBC Home Video).

Robinson, David. 1994. *Chaplin: His Life and Art.* New York: Da Capo Press.

Schuchman, John S. 1988. *Hollywood Speaks: Deafness and the Film Entertainment Industry.* Urbana: University of Illinois Press.

Wrigley, Owen. 1996. *The Politics of Deafness.* Washington, DC: Gallaudet University Press.

ELEVEN

Hearing Things

The Scandal of Speech in Deaf Performance

MICHAEL DAVIDSON

In the film version (1986) of Mark Medoff's play *Children of a Lesser God* (1980), James (William Hurt) is a speech instructor at a school for the deaf who believes that his students must be educated into oral culture by being taught to lip-read and speak. He falls in love with Sarah (Marlee Matlin), who is Deaf but who refuses to participate in his pedagogical project. She signs throughout the film, insisting on her right to remain silent, until one climactic scene when, under James's badgering, she suddenly screeches out a stream of speech. It is a powerful scene because it is the first time the hearing audience has experienced her voice and realized that she *can* speak but prefers not to. It is also powerful because, instead of achieving the desired result, Sarah's vocalizing illustrates the coercive force of an educational system based on speech rather than manual signing. What James witnesses is a kind of deaf performative—a form of speech that enacts or performs rather than describes—its meaning contained not in the content of Sarah's words (most of which are unrecognizable) but in the results it achieves in shaking his oralist bias. In Henry Louis Gates's terms, it signifies "on" speech as much as "by means of" it. For the hearing educator, speech is the key to normalization in hearing-based culture; for the Deaf signer, speech is the sign of an alienating process that merely performing can make evident.

I want to extend the concept of a deaf performative to describe the work of Deaf language-artists for whom the use of speech and vocalization is a kind of scandal and who utilize that scandal to critical ends. By *scandal*, I mean that the eruption of speech (or, as we shall see, text) in Deaf performance challenges the conventional opposition of signing and speech and allows for more complex, hybrid combinations. In the wake of the Gallaudet "Deaf President Now" protests of 1988 and the launching of a powerful political movement for the empowering of Deaf persons, the use of speech-based pedagogies represents the continuing authority of hearing culture.[1] The attempt by audiologists, psychologists, educators, and legislators to reinforce oralist values has been combated by an increasingly politicized social movement of the Deaf who regard themselves not as a handicapped population but as a linguistic minority with distinct cultural and historical traditions. As Bauman (1997), Lane (1995), Baynton (1996), Padden and Humphries (1988), and others have observed, audism—the ideological replication of humans as hearing subjects—has influenced treatment of Deaf persons from the outset. The incarceration of the deaf in institutions, the denial of ASL as a language, the imposition of medical aids (cochlear implants, hearing aids), mainstreaming in education, punishment of children for manual signing—all constitute what Harlan Lane (1995) has called a "colonial" subjugation of deaf individuals (31–38). A postcolonial regime is very much underway, and performance is one of its key venues.

Padden and Humphries (1988) refer to the portmanteau ASL sign for "think-hearing," which transfers the sign for "hearing" (a finger rotating near the mouth) to the region of the head in order to describe someone who "thinks and acts like a hearing person" or who uncritically embraces the ideology of others (53). ASL poets like Clayton Valli, Ella Mae Lentz, Debbie Rennie, and others have made "think-hearing" a subject of aesthetic critique while using ASL as a powerful counterdiscourse to phonocentric models of literature. In their work, "performing the text" means utilizing ASL signing to establish community (the Deaf audience understands a sign's multiple meanings) and politicize the occasion (the hearing audience cannot rely on acoustic prosodic models). Thus a key meaning in every Deaf performance is a set of shared cultural values implicit in the use of ASL. One might say that in addition to the four categories foregrounded in Deaf performance—space, body, time, language—a fifth must be added: that of Deaf culture itself.

But to speak of "Deaf culture" as a single entity is to generalize a rather broad continuum of persons variously positioned with respect to deafness.

The phrase would include children who are deaf but whose family is hearing or hearing children of deaf parents as well as persons who have become deaf later in life or who still retain some hearing.[2] And in descriptions of Deaf performance such differences often become obscured in a more general celebration of an authentic (e.g., soundless, textless, ASL-based) poetry. The decision by Ella Mae Lentz and others not to have their ASL works voice-interpreted is an understandable refusal of hearing culture, but it has limited the venues in which they may participate and the audiences they might reach. I would like to look at three Deaf artists, Peter Cook, Aaron Williamson, and Joseph Grigely, who violate such authenticity and in doing so comment suggestively on issues of language and communication in general, insofar as they are based on a phonocentric model. In my conclusion I will suggest some of the implications that such performers pose for the intersections between performance, disabilities, and multiculturalism.

Peter Cook is the deaf half of Flying Words, a collaborative performance group, the other half of which is Kenny Lerner, who hears but also signs. The two create performances that draw on several vernacular Deaf traditions, including mime, deaf ventriloquism, and storytelling. Where Flying Words differs from Deaf poets like Clayton Valli and Ella Mae Lentz is in its use of sound and collaboration. Not only does Lerner occasionally vocalize (speak over) Cook's signs, but Cook sometimes vocalizes while he signs. For Deaf nationalists such collaboration with the hearing world is problematic, to say the least, but for the two of them it is a way of extending the gestural potentiality of ASL into what we might call an "immanent critique" of audist ideology. Furthermore, Lerner's vocalization is seldom used to translate or interpret Cook's signing. Often the former is silent, while the latter punctuates his signing with words or parts of words.

Such is the case in "I Am Ordered Now to Talk," a performance that dramatizes pedagogical tensions between oralist and manualist learning. The two performers, standing on either side of a stage, render a poem recounting Cook's oralist education at the Clarke School. Cook speaks the poem while Lerner signs, thus reversing the usual interpreter/interpreted role.[3] Cook's voice is, as Brenda Brueggemann (1999) points out, "loud, monotone, wooden, 'unnatural,' nearly unintelligible," while Lerner's signs are "a bit stiff and exaggerated as well" (205). The unsettling nature of oral delivery is reinforced by the poem's violent denunciation of oral education, compared at one point to a kind of lobotomy, "for the sake of ma bell." Cook's repeated version of the speech instructor's refrain, "you/must/

now/talk," becomes increasingly agitated as the poem moves to its conclusion. At one point, the two performers come together, Lerner standing behind Cook, posing as the "speech freako" who, in demanding vocal articulation from his deaf student, imitates a brain surgeon. Cook, as patient, warns,

> don't stare at me
> I was on that cold metal table
> that speech freako wants me
> as example for the society
> rip my brains with
> peanuts buttered spoon
> scream with blackboard trick:

B IS NOT P
D IS NOT T
S IS NOT Z

(Brueggemann 1999, 206)
(figure 11.1 and clip 11.1)

Like James in *Children of a Lesser God,* the oral instructor wants to make an "example" of the deaf student by asking him to pronounce phrases like "peanuts buttered spoon." Such phrases are replete with phonemes that, for a lip-reader, are difficult to distinguish. The oralist teacher's corrections, "B IS NOT P / D IS NOT T / S IS NOT Z," are counterposed to Lerner's signing, in which the verbal distinctions among phonemes become spatial and readable distinctions among manual signs. Cook's unintelligible speech suggests the limits of oralist education, while Lerner's signing, however tentative, provides a corrective. Both performers utilize a language "foreign" to their usual cultural milieu and as such embody the very alienation thematized in the poem. The deaf student is forced to signify under orders; the hearing person "translates" into readable signs a speech that is all but incomprehensible.

Before beginning their performance, Lerner announces that Cook will sign briefly—without vocal interpretation—to the Deaf audience. Lerner points out that Cook "will be focusing on hearing people. So, please, feel paranoid" (Brueggemann 1999, 205). Such framing of multiple constituencies creates a certain edginess that reverberates throughout the performance. It also foregrounds the "audio" in "audience," the latter of which, for most

FIGURE 11.1. Peter Cook and Kenny Lerner in a Flying Words performance of "I Am Ordered Now to Talk" (flyingwordsproject@yahoo.com). Reprinted by permission of the photographer, Roy Sowers.

performers, implies an homogeneous (hearing) entity. For Peter Cook to "speak" the poem is to show the ideology of "think-hearing" at its most flagrant. But by collaborating with Lerner, who remains silent, he does something more. He illustrates a fruitful mixture of sound and sign contributing to a critical as well as aesthetic performance.

The links between hearing and Deaf culture are established in the collaborative nature of performance, yet by occasionally placing the hearing Lerner behind him wearing a mask, Cook stresses the ghostly presence of hearing culture—assisting but invisible. In this sense, Flying Words redirects the paternalist hierarchy of hearing to nonhearing persons by placing the deaf performer in front, reversing the spatial (and audiological) proximity. The spatial positioning of hearing and deaf, English and ASL, interpreter and interpreted within Flying Words performances maps an indeterminate space between and within audist culture. Lerner and Cook utilize their bodies and their bicultural experiences to define and critique a world that must be spoken to be known.

What would a world look like in which sound followed, rather than preceded, signs created by the body? A contrasting view might, in Owen Wrigley's (1996) terms, "see a world built around the valence of visual rather than aural channels" (3). This is the subject of work by Aaron Williamson, a British performance artist who began to lose his hearing at a young age and who was profoundly deaf by his mid-twenties. Although he has been deaf for most of his adult life, he retains a strong connection to hearing culture and makes his bicultural condition a major theme in his performances. Like Peter Cook, he often collaborates with other performers, including musicians and drummers (he has appeared in punk bands since the mid-1970s).[4] But unlike many Deaf performers—including Flying Words—he does not make signing a prominent feature of his work. Rather, it is among the arsenal of gestures that he uses to confront the liminal situation of the late deafened: those with one foot in Deaf and the other in hearing communities.

A good introduction to Williamson's work is his 1999 performance *Phantom Shifts,* a series of lyrical reflections on the authority of the ear. In one sequence the ear, in the form of a large plaster sculpture, is carried on the performer's back.[5] The title of this segment, "Breath," refers to the sound track, which features Williamson's labored breathing as he bears his physical (the plaster ear is, in fact, quite heavy) and ideological burdens. But the sound track often cuts out, leaving silences that impose their own acoustic burden on the hearing viewer, who expects some continuity between image and sound.

The second segment, "Wave," takes the metaphor of breathing another step by introducing vocalization in the form of a single syllable. Thus *Phantom Shifts* shifts from breath to the beginnings of significant sound. The performer stands facing us at the end of a long room, wearing a white shift. Before him and extending toward the camera position is a long piece of translucent white material. In the foreground the plaster ear is faintly outlined beneath the material. It is, in British slang, covered by cloth or "cloth-eared," meaning mute or stupid. Williamson takes a series of deep breaths, approaches the white sheet, raises it and suddenly lowers it, creating a wave that rolls from him to the ear. The material is flexible enough to create a continuous unfolding wave or ripple the full length of the room until it reaches the ear. On one level, the wave seems to emanate from Williamson's breath, exhaled at the moment the material is lowered. On another level, the wave is a dramatization of sound waves traveling through space to strike the tympanum. For the Deaf performer, however, Williamson's gesture is about the separation of breath from sound, of sound from sense. The ear is less an extension of the body than a prosthesis toward which the body aspires. Williamson's breathing exercises resemble a kind of ritual gesture made toward the fetish at the opposite end of the room, but instead of animating the fetish with significant speech, Williamson's breath simply creates a wave (figure 11.2 and **clip 11.2**).

In the final seconds of the brief performance, Williamson comes to speech, uttering a loud "ha" before lowering the sheet. This time, the ensuing wave uncovers the ear, permitting the performer to leave the space. In a discussion of *Phantom Shifts* Williamson has said that he uses this open-throated "ha" because it is the most expressive and primal of sounds, deployed equally in laughter and crying.[6] Thus the sound that lays bare the device of the ear is one that defies the purely semantic features of speech and calls attention to the body's expressive functions. If he cannot hear his own voice, Williamson can represent the scene of its emergence, the agon of its production. Moreover, by cutting the sound track off and on, he may embody for the viewer the discontinuity of images detached from their animating sounds.

What animates this and other performances by Aaron Williamson is a recognition of the constitutive force of speech and hearing in the production of knowledge. In Western theology and philosophy, the Logos or reason

FIGURE 11.2. Aaron Williamson performing "Wave," from *Phantom Shifts*.
Reprinted by permission of the photographer, Tertia Longmire.

is represented as a voice, the spirit as breath. Such metaphors have been active in constructing much postwar poetics, from Charles Olson's projective verse and Beat testimony to the anthropological oralism of Gary Snyder or Jerome Rothenberg, to sound poetry and spoken-word performance. For Williamson, the Logos is figured not as a voice but as an ear, the agent of reception in a Saussurean communicational diagram. The poet short-circuits the Judeo-Christian model of the Logos-as-Voice by treating the ear as a fetish, a stony recipient of cryptic messages that wash up on its shore.

This same deconstruction of a logo- and phonocentric tradition can be seen in Williamson's recent work *Hearing Things* (1999). This performance is a kind of cybernetic meditation on the Oracle at Delphi. According to the story, the Oracle purportedly delivered cryptic messages that were then decoded by her acolytes. Williamson's Artaudian version uses a technological interface to turn himself into a cyborg creature, half oracle, half scribe, part technology, part human. To effect this synthesis, Williamson uses voice recognition software to generate a text that becomes the focal point for the performance. In its most recent manifestation, *Hearing Things* uses software that picks up the sounds of audience members, who are encouraged to speak into a microphone placed in the gallery space. In an earlier version, upon which I will focus here, the sounds are produced by Williamson himself, converted by the software into a text of recognizable English words. That text is then projected from the ceiling onto the floor and reflected in two transparent auto-cuing glasses behind the performer. Williamson moves around the text, gazing at the words and making a variety of whoops, cries, chatters, and moans—the indecipherable words of the Oracle. Although he cannot hear his own voice, he may see its representation in words generated by it, the computer acting as an interpreter of the deaf speaker's sounds. Thus, by a curious inversion of agency, Williamson may encounter his own words as alien—which for the deaf person living in an audist world is precisely the case. Moreover, he performs "on" and "within" the text, with the words occasionally projected onto his white shift, making him both the reflector and the creator of the text to which he gives birth, and his status as "poet" is confirmed by the laurel wreath he wears on his head. And since he is wearing a dress, gender confusion reinforces the mixed nature of this originary word, half female oracle, half male amanuensis. Against the Judeo-Christian model of a male Jehovah, speaking from the whirlwind, we have a female oracle whose signs have yet to be learned by a patriarchal scribe (figure 11.3 and **clip 11.3**).

FIGURE 11.3. Aaron Williamson performing *Hearing Things.* Reprinted by permission of the photographer, Tertia Longmire.

The title, *Hearing Things,* is elaborately unpacked in this performance. On one level it refers to language as unreality—"I must be hearing things"— a phrase that refers to the phantasmal quality of words when encountered as alien forms. For a late-deafened person, words have become wraiths of their former semiotic bodies. Williamson literalizes this aspect by seeing them projected on his body from some outside source. But at an epistemological level, "hearing things" refers to the binary opposition by which humans are measured in hearing culture—in which an originary Logos (the Oracle) must be heard in order to be incarnated. As Derrida has pointed out, via Rousseau, hearing subjects are granted human status by their ability to hear, but as such they become merely "things" that hear, objects whose only claim to identity is their possession of an intact auditory nerve.[7] The title fuses persons and/as things, made palpable by Williamson's use of a series of objects—a large plaster of paris ear, a navel stone, and a metal tripod (as used by the Delphian Pythia)—that he attempts to animate. At three points in his performance he goes offstage to bring these objects into view, moving them around, attempting to animate them much as Beckett's characters interrogate stones, bicycles, and biscuits. The objects become similar to the projected words themselves, inert, contextless, and foreign. Yet in Williamson's interrogation they gain new life and function.

Williamson poses a number of problems for any consideration of Deaf literature, beyond the fact that he uses voice in his performances. The recursive manner by which text and body, computer and script, interact frustrates the idea of creativity as something that gives "voice" to some prior meaning. As an allegory of deafness, such recursiveness embodies the ways that deafness is inscribed in what Foucault (1988), in another context, has called "technologies of the self." For Williamson (1999), speaking of his use of technology, "[T]he biological becomes fused with the digital as normal relations between cause and effect—between human and computer—are broken down. . . . As the digital and biological circulate with each other the boundaries of linguistic agency and textual authority erode as both components—computer and performer—desperately try to interpret, respond to and prompt each other's cracked, inauspicious stimulation" (18).

This "cracked" or fractured relation between human and machine suggests a fissure in the edifice of postmodern performance based, as it often is, on the authenticity of the body and gesture in an increasingly technologized world. One dream of modernism was to return the text to its materiality, to make the text speak authentically by removing it from the instrumental purposes to which speech is linked. For postmodern d/Deaf performers, this materiality can no longer sustain its purely aesthetic focus. In this sense, Flying Words and Aaron Williamson could be aligned with Chicana/o interlingualists such as Gloria Anzaldua or Lorna Dee Cervantes, or feminist performance artists such as Laurie Anderson or Eleanor Antin, for whom performing or materializing the text always implicates the word as a problem, not a conduit, and in which cultural identity is hybrid, not unitary.

Thus far I have treated "speech" as the presumed antithesis of manual signing, "scandalous" within Deaf culture because complicit with audist or oral theories of communication. But as Derrida has made abundantly clear, speech defines less a phenomenon than an ideology of presence, a reification of signification within a phonocentric model. As such, the intrusion of textuality into Deaf performance would pose the same threat, not unlike the use of vocalization to "translate" or interpret the Deaf poet's signing. The use of printed English text to "interpret" the Deaf person's intentions would once again co-opt manual signs by linking them to English syntax and grammar. Since there is no written representation of signs, communication among the Deaf must be performed, as it were, *in situ*. For this reason, philosophers of language since Rousseau have seen manual signing as primitive or narrowly iconic.

The intervention of textual communication into deafness is central to the work of Joseph Grigely, a literary scholar and visual artist who has written extensively on textual matters.[8] He has been deaf since childhood and is fluent in ASL, although in his art installations his focus is written English. Grigely diverges rather sharply from Peter Cook and Aaron Williamson by stressing writing over sign or gesture, yet like both performers he is interested in the "foreignness" of writing when encountered through a deaf optic. My oxymoron—a deaf optic—describes a bicultural approach to communication in which the hearing viewer must communicate with the deaf interlocutor by nonacoustic means. Since 1994, Grigely has created installations out of the written notes passed back and forth between himself and hearing others. These bits of discursive flotsam—Post-its, bar napkins, gallery programs, sheets of notebook paper—contain partial communications between deaf and hearing worlds. As such, they are metonymies of whole conversations rendered telegraphically through a few words: "Although it was no whiskey in it"; "Squid? oh my"; "What's your second best ideal." Not unlike most oral conversations, the content of such remarks is less important than their furtherance of communicational intentions. But since they are written, they gain a materiality that spoken words do not. By displaying them on the walls of a gallery, Grigely refers to a lost site of communication, one that the viewer must complete by conjecture. And because the slips are placed next to each other, they create their own internal dialogues (figure 11.4).

Unlike artists from the Dadaists to Cy Twombly or Robert Indiana, for whom writing and calligraphic elements are design features, Grigely's words are drawn from actual conversations. His scribbled messages are not *invented* but rather *collected* by him, displayed like archeological finds whose genetic origins are obscure. Occasionally he adds descriptive plaques to explain circumstances of various meetings, giving a mock-docent quality to his survey of ephemeral pieces of paper. As a collector he is interested in the materiality of ephemerality, the textures and color of paper, pen, and

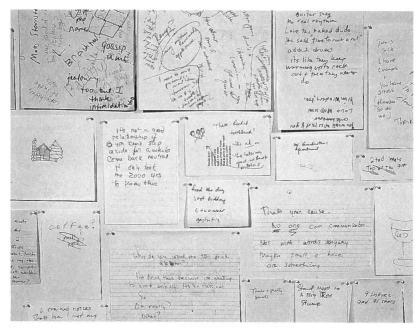

FIGURE 11.4. *White Noise,* by Joseph Grigely, 2000, ink and pencil on paper, 26.5′ × 19.5′ × 13.5′, installation view (detail), Musée d'Art Moderne de la Ville de Paris and Whitney Museum of American Art. Reprinted by permission of the artist.

handwriting, as they instantiate a moment of sociality. That such moments are often about Grigely's deafness is never far from their materiality: "Do you read lips?" one slip says, followed in the same hand by "Do you prefer written words?" Another reads, "I guess it's an *Economy of Words* that I'd like." Such metatextual remarks remind us that however immediate the exchange of conversation slips might be, the fact of one interlocutor's "difference" from the other can never be severed from the conversation.

Grigely titles his earlier exhibitions "Conversations with the Hearing," reversing the ethnographic stereotype of the medical scientist who studies the deaf native. As an ethnologist Grigely collects the "rescued" written slips from various conversations and makes them the subject of his archive. His occasional descriptive plates provide a deadpan narration of a given meeting: "I met Tamara G quite by chance in New York, where she was spending a few months working on a project. She's from Frankfurt. During the time she was in New York we got to know each other a bit. Occasionally we would go out together to have coffee or to go to exhibition openings—

anything that would give us the opportunity to talk about art and work in an informal context. Tamara has a very nice and distinctive accent when she writes, and I often wonder if *her* voice sounds like it looks" (Rubinstein (1996, 132). Surrounding this card are the collected conversation slips between Grigely and Tamara G, placed within an installation entitled *Lo Studio/The Study*, which appeared at the Venice Biennale in 1995. The painterly trope of the "artist's studio" has been retrofitted to include not only the table on which the artist works but the written detritus of actual meetings, conversations, and relationships. Instead of paints, models, and prints, Grigely's studio features wastebaskets, piles of paper, and scotch tape—an allegory, to paraphrase Courbet, of the artist's "real life" among hearing people. As Rubinstein (1996) writes of this exhibition, "Grigely's messy desk installations, which he carefully orchestrates, are not simply replays of scatter art but his fullest attempt to render the complexities of human conversation" (133).

At the core of this complexity is an exploration of metonymy, the way that fragments of conversations point to larger utterances and social occasions. In the absence of a descriptive narrative or full sentence, the viewer must supply contexts. And as an allegory of deaf relations to the hearing world, every written mark instantiates a thwarted relationship to the world that takes speech for granted. The phrase "because you can't," printed on a slip of orange paper, could be a response to a challenge ("Why can't I do such and such?") or a truncation of a larger sentence ("Because you can't do such and such, therefore you must do such and such"). By taking these partial utterances from their communicational conduit and placing them on walls in public spaces, Grigely calls attention to the partial and attenuated nature of deaf/hearing communication when part of the utterance may be completed by lipreading, body language, or other gestures. And since many of these utterances were written on other ready-to-hand documents—museum brochures, menus, matchbook covers—they gesture outward at a larger social nexus where private conversation meets institutional space.[9]

The metonymic character of Grigely's art has an important bearing on what I take to be Grigely's larger critique of audism. Aaron Williamson (1996), speaking of this aspect of Grigely's work, notes that the "writing in the presence of the reader produces a wide variety of reactions which may in themselves abbreviate the communication (for example, a realisation by the speaker that the lack of thought in a casual remark is about to become graphically apparent)" (35). At another level, this metonymic aspect of communication refers to the construction of deafness itself, the marginalization of a population through medical, pedagogical, or eugenic discourses. While there is no direct correlation between marginal texts and marginal identities, there is always the sense that what is left *out* of a given remark ("Is storytelling dying out?" one slip says) is the full presence guaranteed by spoken language—a speech that would, ironically, render such conversation slips unnecessary.

This critical aspect of Grigely's textual work can be seen in a pamphlet called *Deaf and Dumb: A Tale* (1994), which consists of pages from various books and treatises from the late Renaissance to the present, all of which deal with deafness. Like his conversation slips, these pages have been separated from their original codex books, yet there is enough information in each page to indicate what the original book concerns. The pages themselves are facsimiles of actual pages, their antique fonts registering varying periods of print technology, and so have the same rhetorical status as his conversation slips—fragments of actual documents or conversations whose origins have been effaced. The "tale" of the pamphlet's subtitle concerns the ways that deaf persons have been infantilized, pathologized, or demonized throughout history. The cautionary aspect of the pamphlet is illustrated by its homely epigraph: "This little volume, although originally prepared for the Deaf and Dumb, will be found to be equally adapted to the instruction of other children in families, infant schools, common schools, and Sunday schools" (2).

Grigely's mock-serious pamphlet is indeed instructional, but to ends entirely different from the originals. Like Walter Benjamin's Arcades project, Grigely's pamphlet takes historical objects (books and pamphlets) and rubs them the wrong way, exposing racialist and ableist agendas in works with missionary intentions. Several pages are taken from primers in oralist education, including guides for pronunciation and proper elocution. Another text, apparently from an eugenics treatise, warns against the dangers of deaf/hearing intermarriage: "While there is still some doubt as to how large a part heredity plays in deafness, the indications of its influence are clear enough to make a person with a family history of deafness take all possible care to avoid conditions that favor hearing impairment" (24). Many pages offer consoling accounts of deaf people who have been "converted" or "brought over" to the hearing world through oral exercise. Other accounts suggest (wrongly) that deafness coincides with dumbness or muteness and is therefore a sign of insanity or feeble-mindedness. Perhaps the most telling page is drawn from Rousseau, who defines, in brief, the linguistic basis for many subsequent attacks on manual signing: "Still, the speech of beavers and ants is apparently by gesture; i.e., it is only visual. If so, such languages are natural, not acquired. The animals that speak them possess them a-borning: they all have them, and they are everywhere the same. They are entirely unchanging and make not the slightest progress. Conventional language is characteristic of man alone. That is why man makes progress . . . and animals do not" (17).

A last example testifies to the economic marginalization of the deaf by showing plausible trades that they have entered at various "institutions for the deaf and dumb": cabinetmaking, shoemaking, bookbinding, gardening, and printing. In most cases, the page ends midsentence, leaving the fuller context empty. Although *Deaf and Dumb: A Tale* is technically a work of book art, it should be included in Grigely's art installations as a subtle interrogation of the links between textuality and marginalization, what he in his critical work calls "textual eugenics."

It may seem that in describing Joseph Grigely's textual art I have swerved rather far from my initial concerns with Deaf performance. Aaron Williamson may eschew both English and ASL, but there is little doubt that he is "performing" at some level. Grigely's rather quiet installations hardly invite the scrutiny of gesture and orality that is the hallmark of traditional performance artists, but they allow us to return to my use of Henry Louis Gates's idea of "signifyin(g)" as a vernacular act that creates meaning by gesturing at certain received traditions and canons of meaning making. For Grigely to create a textual space based on truncated conversations is to comment on a broken relationship with hearing culture while making art out of that brokenness. By enlisting the hearing viewer in the difficulty of that conversation, Grigely may point to historical fissures that have kept the d/Deaf individual outside, as it were, the gallery and museum—and outside the epistemological discourse of art as a specific kind of knowledge.

As Grigely's art or Aaron Williamson's *Hearing Things* makes evident, alienation from the text—and textuality—is literal: words appear on the ground or museum wall like exotic flora and fauna in some new, cybernetic Eden. Williamson may step on them, point at them, and give them meaning, but he is removed from their production. His nonsemantic roaring, like that of Sarah in *Children of a Lesser God,* is a speech act that challenges the "ordinariness" of ordinary language, making strange not only sounds but the discursive arena in which speech "makes sense." Similarly Flying Words, by treating the sign as a process of community building, reinforces the collective qualities of meaning production on a global scale. Peter Cook's and Kenny Lerner's complex use of sound and sign, far from uniting the two in a gesture of multicultural unity, illustrates the continuing divide between speech-based and Deaf pedagogies. Their metatextual references to both hearing and Deaf audiences challenge the idea that ASL is an invented or iconic language, ancillary to English. Rather, in their hands, it becomes a rich, polyvalent structure, capable of containing the container. The "scandal of speech" in Deaf performance is not that it appears in concert with signing but that its use calls into question the self-evident nature of speech-based communicational models. At the very minimum, such performers make *think-hearing* a phrase that once seen can never be heard the same way twice.

NOTES

1. On the DPN protests, see Brueggemann (1999, 151–200), Christiansen and Barnartt (1995), and Lane (1995).

2. A good introduction to the situation of children of deaf parents can be found in Lennard Davis's memoir *My Sense of Silence: Memoirs of a Childhood with Deafness* (2000). See also his *Enforcing Normalcy: Disability, Deafness and the Body* (1995).

3. Brenda Brueggemann has provided an excellent reading of this performance, as she has of many other ASL poets. I am indebted to her readings of both performances, as well as to videotapes that she and Kenny Lerner lent to me. In the absence of commercially available tapes by Deaf performers, the student of sign literature must rely on a limited set of videos, circulated in an ad hoc manner among friends and colleagues. While this limits the number of performances available for commentary, it points to the limits of video documentation and to the site-specific nature of such performances. The important interactive character of Deaf performance can hardly be rendered in a video.

4. In several of his performances, Williamson utilizes musicians and dancers. In a recent collaboration, Williamson worked with the drummer Craig Astill in what he describes as "a kind of Beckettian reduction of my capacity to hear or sense music. Craig played a frame drum directly into the floor (we insisted on hollow wooden stages only) and I picked up a barefoot vibrational signal from varying distances from the drum, thus stimulating degrees of animation in the improvised performance" (pers. comm., Jan. 18, 2000).

5. Williamson has said that the inspiration for this image came less from an attempt to represent the burden of hearing than from an attempt to impede routinized movement. And to some extent, all of his work involves the imposition of limits to normalized action, constructing a "law of diminishing referentiality" that he shares with a wide range of contemporary performers (class lecture at University of California, San Diego, March 3, 2000).

6. Class lecture at University of California, San Diego, March 3, 2000.

7. Although Derrida does not refer to deaf persons in his various critiques of phonocentrism, he might well consider a population that relies on nonphonetic means to signify and that bases its meaning production on visual rather than audible information. Derrida's "phonocentrism" is usually equated with speech, but Williamson foregrounds "voice" as a multifaceted producer of meaning, not limited to the production of strictly linguistic signs. For further discussion of deafness and Derrida, see Bauman (1997).

8. His book *Textualterity: Art, Theory, and Textual Criticism* (1995) discusses the transformations of cultural texts through various processes of writing, editing, and publishing. Although deafness is not his subject, Grigely does provide a theoretical justification for his creation of installations based on conversation slips and ephemeral notes exchanged between himself and interlocutors. The premise of the book is that "the uniqueness of the unique art object or literary text is constantly undergoing continuous and discontinuous transience as it ages, is altered by editors and conservators, and is resituated or reterritorialized in different publications and exhibition spaces" (1). Translated into Grigely's art installations, such "reterritorialization" would involve the transformation of public spaces where his "conversations with the hearing" take place (bars, cafes, parks) into the art gallery. It would equally involve the ways his art destroys the aura of the unique artwork by its deployment of actual conversations and communications between the deaf and the hearing.

9. This is very much the theme of Grigely's 1998 installation *Barbicon Conversations,* in which his conversation slips appear in various public spaces of London's vast Barbicon Centre. Examples can be found on advertising kiosks, information pamphlets, and docent sheets as well as in the restrooms, bars, and lobbies of the building. Thus Grigely is able to refer to the conversational focus of his work in those spaces where such conversations actually occur.

REFERENCES

Bauman, H-Dirksen L. 1997. "Toward a Poetics of Vision, Space, and the Body: Sign Language and Literary Theory." In *The Disability Studies Reader,* ed. Lennard J. Davis, 315–31. New York: Routledge.

Baynton, Douglas C. 1996. *Forbidden Signs: American Culture and the Campaign against Sign Language.* Chicago: University of Chicago Press.

Brueggemann, Brenda Jo. 1999. *Lend Me Your Ear: Rhetorical Constructions of Deafness.* Washington, DC: Gallaudet University Press.

Children of a Lesser God. 1986. Dir. Randa Haines. With William Hurt and Marlee Matlin.

Christiansen, John B., and Sharon N. Barnartt. 1995. *Deaf President Now! The 1988 Revolution at Gallaudet University.* Washington, DC: Gallaudet University Press.

Davis, Lennard. 1995. *Enforcing Normalcy: Disability, Deafness and the Body.* London: Verso.

———. 2000. *My Sense of Silence: Memoirs of a Childhood with Deafness.* Champaign: University of Illinois Press.

Foucault, Michel. 1988. *Technologies of the Self: A Seminar with Michel Foucault.* Ed. Luther H. Martin, Huck Gutman, and Patrick H. Hutton. Amherst: University of Massachusetts Press.

Gates, Henry Louis. 1988. *The Signifying Monkey: A Theory of African-American Literary Criticism.* New York: Oxford University Press.

Grigely, Joseph. 1994. *Deaf and Dumb: A Tale.* New York: White Columns.

———. 1995. *Textualterity: Art, Theory, and Textual Criticism.* Ann Arbor: University of Michigan Press.

Lane, Harlan. 1995. *The Mask of Benevolence: Disabling the Deaf Community.* New York: Random House.

Medoff, Mark. 1980. *Children of a Lesser God.* Clifton, NJ: James T. White.

Padden, Carol, and Tom Humphries. 1988. *Deaf in America: Voices from a Culture.* Cambridge, MA: Harvard University Press.

Rubinstein, Raphael. 1996. "Visual Voices." Review of Sean Landers, Kenneth Goldsmith, and Joseph Grigely. *Art in America,* April, 100–133.

Williamson, Aaron. 1996. Review of "Joseph Grigely." Anthony d'Offay Gallery, London, March 16–April 20. *Art Monthly,* May, 35–36.

———. 1999. "Hearing Things." *Animated,* Spring, 17–18.

Wrigley, Owen. 1996. *The Politics of Deafness.* Washington, DC: Gallaudet University Press.

AFTERWORD

CAROL A. PADDEN

This is a remarkable collection of essays about American Sign Language (ASL) literature, made more so by the fact that the history of this kind of analysis is so recent. As the authors have detailed so well in this volume, there are many reasons to group poetry, storytelling, and other kinds of signed performance together as a body of literature; they share a certain aesthetic of celebration of the signed form, and collectively they touch on many of the same themes.

The transition to what I call self-conscious sign language performance was rapid. When the National Theatre of the Deaf gave its first performance in 1967, showcasing some of the country's best Deaf actors, their program featured not original but translated poetry. Audree Norton translated, with long and lithe arms, Elizabeth Barrett Browning's "How Do I Love Thee?" ("Let me count the ways . . ."), as Joe Velez "vogued" his way through Lewis Carroll's "Jabberwocky." Bernard Bragg, arguably the most recognizable of Deaf actors at the time, performed the feline "Tyger, Tyger, Burning Bright" (by William Blake). The performers were willing and able but perhaps not yet ready to present on a national stage completely original forms of signed poetry and performance.

As Cynthia Peters explains, it was several seasons later (1971–72) before they offered up an original performance, the outstanding *My Third Eye*. It was vaudevillelike: a collection of skits, demonstrations, a short choreographed sequence, and yes, poetry, linked by sharp humor and a theme of resistance—against the oppression of oral training and denial of sign language that was so much a part of many of the actors' experiences, against demanding family members and teachers asking what was humanly unreasonable, and against an American society that had waited too long before being willing to watch Deaf actors perform on their stages.

It would be foolish to claim that ASL poetry and performance began at this moment because, as Ben Bahan and the editors have argued in this volume, elements of modern ASL poetry can be traced to the earlier kinds of performances in the community. Face to face, and before audiences in all types of venues, Deaf people have been performing imaginatively and with feeling. Predecessors of today's poems and stories, from lyrical signing to compelling narratives, can be found in filmed records as well as in performances passed down from the nineteenth and twentieth centuries. What, then, began with the current generation of ASL poets and performers? What has this particular type of poetry discovered?

The naming of the language as American Sign Language had a great deal to do with the beginnings of ASL poetry. The language of my deaf father's generation was simply "the sign language," but in mine we gave it a name. Once named, the language took on a different position in the community; it became itself an object to behold. Deaf poets and performers became self-conscious, internal, and deliberative and opened themselves to critical study. Clayton Valli began to design poetry that explored the capacity of the handshape and the movement of signs. Dorothy Miles experimented with poetry that would match signs with written English words, in which the two languages would influence each other. Ella Lentz took an experience almost universal to children, that of watching the visual music of telephone wires dipping and swaying while riding in a car, and added the rigorous cadence of number signs to create "Eye Music." Patrick Graybill captured the conflict of longing and loneliness of the deaf child in his haiku about the long drive back to his deaf school in Kansas. The theme was age-old, but it came together with structure in a new aesthetic of sign literature.

Signed narratives took off in new directions too. Sam Supalla brought late-twentieth-century cinematic technique to signed stories. Ben Bahan wove allegory and contemporary imagery into taut narratives. Gilbert Eastman composed an epic poetic narrative in honor of the Deaf President Now movement, stringing together familiar and evocative images from Deaf life. The National Theatre of the Deaf continued to stage more original pieces, not vaudeville but fully formed plays. Don Bangs, Shanny Mow, and Willy Conley mounted original productions and in each explored themes of everyday Deaf lives, from problems with hearing in-laws to tragic deaf education schemes.

At some risk of overgeneralizing, I will offer what I believe are some important characteristics of this new impulse of ASL poetry and performance. It has strong narrative content. Cynthia Peters describes indigenous Deaf American theater as remaining "close to the everyday lives of its viewers." ASL poetry is the same. The stories the performers tell are of resistance, oppression, and deeply felt occupation by others. Whether the piece is Sam Supalla's "Eyeth" or Eugene Bergman and Bernard Bragg's "Tales from a Clubroom" or Ben Bahan's "Bird of a Different Feather," the Other is present, unrelenting, and uncomprehending. Gilbert Eastman's epic poem "Gallaudet Protest" links images of resistance with emblems of nature: as surely as we know that stars appear in the night, a protest will begin. Such pieces tell stories that are personal and familiar to deaf people.

Michael Davidson (in chapter 11 of this volume) describes the project of ASL poetry as essentially a nationalist project because it insists on the uniqueness of the signing poet as someone unlike an English-speaking poet. Furthermore, he observes that ASL poetry is suspicious of "phonocentric models of literature." ASL poetry celebrates the potential of the sign, how lyrical forms can be made out of handshapes and movements. In this sense, ASL poetry not only shows but proclaims a different order, one in which speech and hearing are contested as the only way to organize lives. These themes have been present for a long time in American deaf life—one of the most eloquent calls to resistance was George Veditz's 1913 speech "The Preservation of the Sign Language." As Chris Krentz explains in chapter 3, what marks modern ASL poetry is how it reiterates these themes and imbues them with self-conscious poetic structure. Theme and structure become married; the structure of the poem or narrative is itself an emblem of a new order.

Because he sees the themes of resistance and oppression in ASL poetry as akin to those of the colonial experience as told elsewhere in the world, Michael Davidson proposes that "[a] postcolonial regime is very much under way, and performance is one of its key venues." He is suggesting that we may find useful many nationalist and postcolonial literature projects from around the world, from the Philippines to India and Madagascar, where novel forms of language and performance have risen out of histories of colonial occupation. I would agree. A colleague of mine, Vicente Rafael, has written about the ascendancy of "Taglish," a blending of Tagalog, a Filipino indigenous language, with English for use in popular literature and performance in the Philippines. The blended language reflects the coming together of the Philippines' pre- and postcolonial history, enacted in jokes and cartoons reflecting on the modern problems of the Filipinos.[1]

The unique combination of theme and structure that defines ASL performance can be seen in the poetry and performance of "experimental" sign poets such as Peter Cook and Kenny Lerner. At the start of the performance of their poem "$e = mc^2$" they warn the audience that the piece they are about to perform actually "HAS NO MEANING!" Smiling at their audacity, they specifically tell the audience, "DO NOT TRY TO UNDERSTAND THIS POEM!" The poem is a cleverly lyrical piece combining handshapes and movements that suggest meaning but soon become nonsensical. At the end, the audience cheers at the performance; even though the poem is not a canonical poem with stanzas and a theme it still qualifies as a sign poem because it is so structurally attentive to movement and handshape. The poem's theme is that ASL structure by itself can be lyrical and pleasing. We should also understand that not only poets but their audiences as well have become analytical. Cook and Lerner are performing to well-informed audiences who fully understand their tongue-in-cheek commentary on their own performance. Yet Cook and Lerner also perform poetry that tells of resistance, the best known of which is their "I Am Ordered Now to Talk," which draws on Cook's memories of his oral education as oppressive. Even when they are playful, Cook and Lerner's poems are content-full.

Another way to understand ASL poetry is to view the work of deaf poets working outside ASL, such as Aaron Williamson, a British performance artist who grew up deaf and learned British Sign Language later in life as an adult. As Michael Davidson explains about Williamson's performances, they are whole-body pieces centered on the omnipresence of sound and speech. In one of his more powerful pieces, he carries a heavy plaster model of an ear on his back and portrays deaf people's near-universal experience of confronting again and again the dominance of sound and speaking in every aspect of life. While Williamson celebrates gesture and the visuality of the hands and the body, he does not locate sign language front and center in his acts of resistance. Without sign poetics, he is free to explore the lived world of deaf people—how hands are used to indicate when they are used together with speech, how meaning can be glimpsed with snatches of lipreading and gestures by others. In this sense, it is perhaps deaf poetry. The burden of comprehending others rests on the deaf person, and Williamson enacts this as he carries the heavy plaster ear around on stage.

In contrast, an American work that rails against the omnipresence of the ear, Sam Supalla's "Eyeth," represents the ear not as a plaster object but as a word and a sign ("Ear-th") built into the structure of the signed narrative. Whereas Williamson uses performance to signify, ASL poets and story-tellers use the signs themselves to signify. For this reason, translation is always an issue with ASL literature—the very thing that makes it different also makes it difficult to understand. Whereas Williamson's performance can be understood by watching it, Supalla's cannot without translation. This is why I think postcolonial and nationalist analyses have good potential for understanding ASL literature. ASL literature stands behind the veil of language and is thoroughly steeped in the history of the community.

What comes next, after the self-conscious sign poetry of the late twentieth century? Already there is a new generation of sign performers that blend hip-hop and other urban styles into their signing. Whereas Sam Supalla is careful to articulate his signs as he uses film technique in the "Wildest Whiskey of the West," David Rivera purposely blurs his hand-shapes and cuts short his movements, as if rejecting the precision of "mainstream" sign poetry. He uses television shot structure in his performances as well. His slow-motion piece of a football game mimics the multiple shot angles of television sports shows; the same arm that throws the football appears from several different points of view. His themes are gritty, reflecting his urban experience. His hands form handshapes for signs, but the handshapes are also the street gestures of urban youth. In young ASL poets, we are seeing a movement from a romantically conceived "pure" poetry to a "hip" street poetry.

We are also seeing the internationalization of sign poetry. Italy's sign poetry has seen tremendous growth in the last twenty years. The poetry of the Deaf Italian brother and sister Rosaria and Giuseppe Giuranna uses the closeness of the sibling relationship as a structure for performing stanzas. They alternate lines and even parts of lines in a duet performance that is almost musical. Their lines flow, then build up to a crescendo as the frame of their poetry together becomes larger than each of them individually. Japanese sign narrators use number signs to tell a story, as do Americans, but the numbers run *backwards,* as in one about a fisherman at the end of the day watching a sunset. The poem begins with the number nine and counts down to zero: the fisherman puts down his fishing pole, and when the last sign is reached a zero stands in for a round sun setting. Imagine how many more ways there are of doing sign poetry once we move to the world stage.

The first world celebration of Deaf communities at Deaf Way 1989 brought together an astonishing array of stage performances, sign poetries, music, dance, and visual art. Clearly inspired by it, Deaf Way 2002 featured performances not only from Europe but also from Asia, South America, and Africa. As Deaf people themselves migrate, from Asia to America, from eastern Europe to the Middle East, from Africa to Europe and America, their communities' sign performances travel with them. Already there has been a great deal of borrowing and cross-fertilization of literatures in different sign languages. Perhaps the next volume of ASL literature will not be just about ASL poetry and performance but will be expanded to include world sign literature and will acknowledge the influence of Deaf artists from around the world.

NOTE

1. Vicente L. Rafael, *White Love and Other Events in Filipino History* (Durham, NC: Duke University Press, 2000).

Time Line of ASL Literature Development

It would be impossible to compile an exhaustive time line of the development of ASL literature. Much of the growth of ASL literature has occurred in living rooms, kitchens, dorms, and other vernacular spaces. We have merely attempted to present some of the more public events so that readers may have the broad outlines of the development of ASL literature. We thank Joseph Castronovo, Bernard Bragg, and Ella Mae Lentz for their careful reading and editing of the time line.

1813–17: THOMAS HOPKINS GALLAUDET BEGINS AMERICAN DEAF EDUCATION

- 1813–16—While studying to be a minister in Connecticut, Thomas Hopkins Gallaudet became involved in educating Alice Cogswell, a deaf daughter of his neighbor Mason Cogswell. Gallaudet, sponsored by Cogswell, then traveled to Europe to learn about methods of deaf education. He first went to England but was not well received; the British educators who endorsed oralism were reluctant to share their methods. Fortunately, a French educator of deaf children, the Abbé Sicard, and deaf teachers Jean Massieu and Laurent Clerc, held a public exhibition of their methods of deaf education in London. Clerc and Sicard invited Gallaudet to the deaf school in Paris, which endorsed the manual method. Through observing Sicard and Clerc's work, Gallaudet became committed to the manual method of deaf education and invited Clerc to accompany him to America to found the first school for the deaf.
- 1817—Gallaudet and Clerc founded the first American deaf school, at first called the Connecticut Asylum for the Education and Instruction of Deaf and Dumb Persons and later known as the American School for the Deaf (ASD). The school became the catalyst for the development of a cohesive American Deaf community. For the first time, deaf people from all over the country were brought together, sign was viewed as a legitimate form of communication, and a sign language common to many Deaf

Americans evolved. ASL developed from the blending of French Sign Language, signs from the signing community in Martha's Vineyard, and various home sign languages brought by students to the school. The language was referred to as "the sign language" and "the natural language of signs"; the name *American Sign Language* did not come into use until later in the twentieth century. (For a thorough analysis of development and attitudes toward sign language, see Baynton 1997.)

1817–80: THE "GOLDEN AGE" OF AMERICAN DEAF EDUCATION

This time period has been referred to as the "golden age,"[1] since sign language was encouraged in the classroom, reflecting the manual method of deaf education. Deaf schools using the manual method flourished, as teachers (both Deaf and hearing) and graduates of the residential schools spread ASL to other parts of the country. Use of sign language in the classroom encouraged Deaf adults to become teachers and administrators. At this time linguistics books, in addition to the residential schools, reflected a more bilingual attitude. For example, William Dwight Whitney's 1875 classic *The Life and Growth of Language: An Outline of Linguistic Science* shows a more balanced view of sign language than those presented in later linguistics books. Whitney is very insistent that speech does not equal thought and that complex mental processes can be conveyed in gestures, particularly those used in sign language.

- 1864—The federally funded National Deaf-Mute College in Washington, D.C. (now Gallaudet University) was founded, the first (and, to this day, the only) liberal arts postsecondary institution for Deaf people in the world.
- Mid- to late 1800s—"Prevideotape Period of ASL Literature." Creative uses of ASL began to be explored; the "oral" tradition of ASL became evident in the form of poems, anecdotes, and stories. At this time, however, there was no way to preserve or share this artistry with a wider hearing audience unless the hearing person signed. These artistic forms survived by being passed down manually through successive generations, and they continue to thrive in the Deaf community similarly to the oral traditions of spoken-written languages. In this volume, Ben Bahan (chapter 2) and Christopher Krentz (chapter 3) discuss these oral traditional forms and their relevance to Deaf culture and to notions of literacy. It is important to recognize here that at this time the concept of deaf *literature* could be defined only as deaf people writing and publishing in English (see Panara, Denis, and McFarlane 1960; Batson and Bergman 1987; Gannon 1987). While creative forms of sign language thrived, they could not possibly have been equated with literature because ASL was not considered a "real" language; its utility in the classroom and Deaf community was certainly acknowledged, but primarily in relation to its communication efficacy and assistance in teaching English.

1880–1957: THE "DARK AGE" OF DEAF EDUCATION

- Late nineteenth to early twentieth centuries—Oralism/Manualism Debate. For many years deaf educators around the world were engaged in a conflict over the merits of the oral versus manual methods of teaching. In the United States, Edward Miner Gallaudet advocated the manual method as a superior means to achieve fluency in both sign and reading/writing. Alexander Graham Bell argued just as vehemently for oralism, claiming that sign language alienated deaf people from the rest of society and that full integration required the ability to speak and lip-read.

- 1880—Milan Congress. The advocates of oralism organized the 1880 meeting of the International Conference of Teachers of the Deaf, in Milan, where the members voted to convert all deaf education to oralism, aborting the achievements of sign-based education in Europe. The effects of the Milan Congress eventually spread to America.

- 1880–1960s—As oralism became endorsed across the United States, deaf schools changed drastically. Deaf teachers and administrators were fired, and gradually deaf children knew only hearing teachers who spent day after day drilling them in speech. ASL was forbidden in the classroom but remained strong in the Deaf community.

- Early 1900s—Deaf adults continued to publish written prose and poetry, and a strong deaf presence existed in the silent film world. Noteworthy examples include Albert Ballin, a painter, writer, and actor who published a book in 1930 entitled *The Deaf-Mute Howls;* Lon Chaney, whose success as a silent film actor has often been attributed partially to having parents who were deaf; and the Deaf actor Granville Redmond, who gained recognition in many of Charlie Chaplin's films.[2] See Carol Robinson's chapter in this volume (chapter 10) for more on Redmond and silent film.

- 1913–20—National Association of the Deaf (NAD) ASL Film Project. With the continuing use of oralism in deaf schools, the NAD (founded in 1880) was concerned that the creative use of sign language would be lost. Over a period of seven years the NAD filmed various Deaf individuals making presentations in sign language. Among these were George Veditz, who, in 1913, presented an example of ASL oratory entitled "Preservation of the Sign Language," and John Hotchkiss, who presented "Memories of Old Hartford," a personal narrative about his experiences at the Hartford School (both in *The Preservation of American Sign Language* 1997).[3] These films are the first published recording of ASL literature, the only visual record of ASL used in the early part of the twentieth century. In this volume, chapter 3, by Christopher Krentz, explores in greater depth the significance of this filming, arguing that the impact of film technology (and later videotape) on ASL literacy parallels the impact of the printing press on spoken-written language literacy.

- 1920s to 1950s—Charles Krauel videotaped various Deaf events, literary and otherwise. Some of these films appear in this volume; they can also be found in Ted Supalla's video *Charles Krauel: Portrait of a Deaf Filmmaker* (1994).

- 1930s–40s—Ernest Marshall was a renowned storyteller, celebrating the ASL oral tradition with Deaf audiences for over seventy years. Marshall came from a strong ASL/Deaf heritage, with both Deaf parents and grandparents. See Ben Bahan and Chris Krentz (chapters 2 and 3 of this volume) for more on Marshall.

- 1957—William C. Stokoe began linguistic research on ASL. With his pioneering work in the study of ASL, Stokoe was directly responsible for initiating a new era in Deaf education and, as discussed in chapter 1 of this volume, laying the groundwork for the paradigm shift in conceptions of language and literature. In the 1950s Stokoe, a hearing professor of English, took a position in the English department at Gallaudet College to teach Chaucer. After observing sign language in use by students and Deaf faculty across the campus, he became interested in discovering its linguistic properties. In 1957 the American Council of Learned Societies awarded Stokoe a grant to study ASL, the first research of its kind in the United States.

1960–PRESENT: VIDEO PERIOD OF ASL LITERATURE

· 1960—Stokoe published his first linguistic study of ASL, *Sign Language Structure: An Outline of the Visual Communication Systems of the American Deaf.* This book created a stir in the Deaf community because, while Deaf people had always used sign language among themselves, sign was always considered and accepted as inferior to English. Stokoe's work changed this perception and became a catalyst for linguistic research, research into creative and folkloric uses of ASL, the use of videotape for research, and the beginning of complex literary translations from English to ASL. One of the most well-known literary translations is Eric Malzkuhn's version of Lewis Carroll's "Jabberwocky."

· 1966—Bernard Bragg coined the term *sign-mime* to reflect the differences between the artistic language used in performance and the everyday language of the Deaf community. At the Professional Theatre School of the National Theatre of the Deaf (see below), Bragg used sign-mime to teach translation of poetry and drama and to work with free expression in ASL.

· 1967—Founding of the National Theatre of the Deaf (NTD). NTD began with eight members (Eastman 1980, 24), including Gilbert Eastman, Bernard Bragg, and Lou Fant, with the dual purpose of exposing hearing people to the beauty and power of sign language in performance and providing versatile performance opportunities for Deaf individuals. Early productions consisted of translations of English plays, and, with the exception of a few original ASL pieces, the company remains focused on sign translation to this day. These translations of English literary works exposed Deaf artists and audiences to the creative and artistic possibilities of ASL, paving the way for original ASL texts. Through his work with NTD, Bernard Bragg developed the concept of visual vernacular (VV), a distinguishing feature of ASL that involves the use of filmlike cuts, such as shifting between characters and cutting to show different perspectives of a scene or action. Between 1967 and 1977, Bernard Bragg's home was a frequent gathering place for artists like Ella Mae Lentz, Joseph Castronovo, and Lou Fant to share their work on an informal level and to experiment with the creative possibilities of sign language. Between 1974 and 1976, Lentz and Castronovo in particular explored elements of signed poetry, leading to the development of a poem entitled "Shiva."

· 1967—Gilbert Eastman, a founding member of NTD, offered a course in sign translation for the theater at Gallaudet College, the first course of its kind in the United States (Eastman 1980, 24). The increasing repertoire of NTD and the Gallaudet course demonstrate a growing awareness of the artistry of ASL and its ability to come alive on stage.

- 1971—NTD's production of *My Third Eye.* This play, a collection of personal and group narratives recounting aspects of Deaf culture, was the first original work produced by NTD. The performers created the piece together in ASL, and the hearing actors spoke English translations from ASL, demonstrating the effectiveness of a reverse translation process.

- 1972—With William Stokoe as editor, *Sign Language Studies* was established, the first national journal to focus solely on linguistic, sociological, and cultural research on sign.

- 1973—First performance of *Sign Me Alice,* a play created by Gilbert Eastman (published 1974). This play marks a major turning point in the development of ASL literature. While loosely based on Shaw's *Pygmalion, Sign Me Alice* was created completely in ASL and was the first play to focus on attitudes toward ASL. It explored the experience of being Deaf in a hearing world and being free to choose ASL over English (Eastman 1974, 28–29). Upon its publication, Eastman and William Stokoe created a written script using English glosses of the ASL signs. The published form was thus a printed English transcription of ASL, the first print publication to attempt to come as close as possible to the original ASL.

- 1974—A creative writing course taught by John Canney at Gallaudet University explored the relationship between ASL and poetry. Ella Mae Lentz's work, which began with illustrating ASL on paper and then moved away from paper to the actual presentation of ASL poetry, was influenced by this class.

- 1976—Dorothy Miles's film and book *Gestures.* Miles, a Welsh woman who studied at Gallaudet, became known as one of the first Deaf poets to create works in sign language. *Gestures* is one of the first recorded examples of original, single-authored sign language poetry. Miles's play *A Play of Our Own* was produced in Hartford, Connecticut, in 1975.

- 1978—"Poetry in the Palm of Your Hand" Project, South Bend, Indiana. Funded by the Indiana Committee for the Humanities, this was a year-long project designed to promote ASL as a literary language. Events included a public signed poetry performance and discussion, four workshops, roundtable discussions, and a conference sponsored by Indiana University at South Bend that featured the poet/performers Lou Fant and Ella Mae Lentz and presentations by Lou Fant and John Canney— the first ASL poetry conference in the United States.

- 1979—Publication of *The Signs of Language* by Edward Klima and Ursula Bellugi. This book was groundbreaking in its comprehensive and in-depth linguistic analysis of ASL. It includes what may be the first writing devoted solely to the poetics of ASL.

- 1979—Founding of Sign Media, Inc., the first sign language video publishing company in the United States not affiliated with a postsecondary institution. Other video and CD-ROM publishers founded to publish sign language materials include Gallaudet University Press, DawnSignPress, SignEnhancers, and D.E.A.F. Media, Inc.

- 1980—Sign Media published the videotape *American Sign Language: Tales from the Green Books,* in which a variety of Deaf performers signed classic stories, personal anecdotes, and poems representing Deaf folklore. These works were originally placed at the end of a series of ASL instructional videos called *The Green Books,* but they were so popular among ASL instructors that the works were compiled in their own video. This video presents an example of both the affirmation of Deaf culture and the new technological means to preserve creative and traditional ASL forms.

- 1980—First performance of *Tales from a Clubroom,* by Bernard Bragg and Eugene Bergman (published 1981). This play offered more insights into Deaf culture, taking place in a Deaf club, the center of social activities in many Deaf communities. Though it was written in English, the authors attempted to reflect the rhythm of ASL. They kept the English as neutral and idiom-free as possible to facilitate ease of translation by Deaf theater companies.

- 1984—First ASL poetry course at Gallaudet College. Taught by Clayton Valli, a Deaf poet and professor of linguistics, and Trent Batson, a hearing professor of English, this course was the first time literary analysis, as opposed to linguistic analysis, had been used to study ASL creative forms in the classroom. Valli and Batson took a traditional formalist approach, using written poetic form as a foundation for analyzing ASL poetry. Course content involved the study of videotaped samples of Valli and Lentz's ASL poetry, demonstrating the textual quality of the videotaped signing body.

- 1984—Poetry Workshop at National Technical Institute for the Deaf, sponsored by Jim Cohn. The Deaf poet Robert Panara and the hearing poet Allen Ginsberg led this workshop, which explored shared qualities of form and style in modern American written poetry and ASL poetry, focusing particularly on the power and centrality of the image in both poetic traditions. Present were the poets Patrick Graybill, Debbie Rennie, Peter Cook, and Kenny Lerner. A memorable moment occurred when Graybill spontaneously signed a translation of Ginsberg's poem "Hydrogen Jukebox," cementing the relationship between the two poetic traditions in their exploration of the image.

- 1984—First special session on ASL literature at the annual meeting of the Modern Language Association, organized by Joseph Grigely.

- 1986—"Literature by Deaf Iowans: Linguistic Form and Social Function," PhD dissertation by Jane Frances Kelleher, University of Iowa.

- 1986—Creation of the Flying Words Project (FWP), an ASL performance duo. The Deaf poet Peter Cook and the hearing poet Kenny Lerner developed FWP as a vehicle for exploring the creative possibilities of ASL and as a way to reach both Deaf and hearing audiences through sign language. Beginning in Rochester, New York, Cook and Lerner soon began entertaining and educating audiences across the United States. Their early work frequently involved teaching hearing children to be more expressive with their bodies, beginning first with gesture. Later they led workshops and performed for Deaf audiences. A key development in their work came in 1987, when Jerome Rothenberg invited FWP to perform at a performance poetry conference held at SUNY Binghamton.

- 1986—Publication of Jim Cohn's "The New Deaf Poetics" in *Sign Language Studies.* With the 1984 National Technical Institute for the Deaf (NTID) poetry workshop as the foundation for his analysis, Cohn argued that ASL literature represents the emergence of a new and different poetics—one that is most closely related to the work of hearing image poets like Ginsberg.

- 1987—National Deaf Poetry Conference at NTID. Encouraged by the ideas generated at the 1984 poetry workshop led by Panara and Ginsberg, Jim Cohn hosted a conference devoted solely to ASL poetry. Five poets were featured: Peter Cook, Patrick Graybill, Ella Mae Lentz, Debbie Rennie, and Clayton Valli—the first formal gathering of individuals who identified themselves as ASL poets. The artists performed their works and participated in panel discussions investigating the creative process.
- 1987—Presentation of "The Nature of the Line in ASL Poetry," by Clayton Valli, at the Fourth International Symposium on Sign Language Research; published in 1990. This article made a groundbreaking attempt to identify qualities of ASL poetry that parallel the poetic line of written poetry.
- 1987—"A Study of American Deaf Folklore," PhD dissertation by Susan D. Rutherford, University of California, Berkeley. This dissertation focuses on ASL folklore in the Deaf community and how cultural values and literary uses of ASL are passed from one Deaf person to another via folkloric techniques such as ABC stories and number stories.
- 1988—"Deaf President Now" Movement. When the Gallaudet University Board of Trustees appointed a hearing person to the position of president—passing up two qualified Deaf candidates—the Gallaudet student body responded by shutting down the university, contacting the media, and eventually forcing the board to appoint a Deaf president, the first in Gallaudet's history. The event marked a sense of coming of age for the American Deaf community. In this volume, Kristen Harmon's chapter (chapter 9) examines the epic narrative created by Gilbert Eastman about the event.
- 1988—Publication of "Signers of Tales," by Nancy Frishberg. This article, in *Sign Language Studies,* was one of the first to explore ASL poetry and narrative from the perspective of the oral tradition of spoken languages.
- 1989—Deaf Way Congress, Gallaudet University. This international gathering highlighted aspects of global Deaf culture and featured several ASL poets and storytellers. It was here that the sign for "ASL poetry" first appeared. (See chapter 1 for a description of this development.) After this conference, a book entitled *The Deaf Way* (Erting et al. 1994) was published that included articles based on all presentations.
- 1989—The first national Deaf studies conference was held at Gallaudet University. This conference established Deaf studies as a distinct academic field.
- 1989—W. J. T. Mitchell published "Gesture, Sign, and Play: ASL Poetry and the Deaf Community" in the *MLA Newsletter.* This was one of the earliest recognitions that ASL poetry had wide-ranging implications for literary studies in general.
- 1990—*Poetry in Motion* videotapes published (Graybill 1990; Rennie 1990; Valli 1990b). Sign Media's publishing of this three-videotape volume represents another major turning point in the ASL literary movement because it was the first publication of ASL works in their original form, not glosses or English translations. Featuring the texts of Debbie Rennie, Patrick Graybill, and Clayton Valli, the videotapes are unique because they contain no English translations, either voiced or written. They were the first original ASL poems to be preserved on video *for the Deaf com-*

munity, creating the foundation for a video library of ASL literature that could stand on its own without influence from, or comparison to, English.

- 1991—First National ASL Literature Conference at NTID. This conference featured multiple performances, presentations, and panel discussions exploring key questions concerning how ASL literature is defined, what "counts" as ASL literature, how ASL literature may be analyzed, and how it may be used in deaf education.

- 1991—"Poetic Images" performance at the Herberger Theater Center, Phoenix. This performance was produced and directed by Jaine Richards, then coordinator of Deaf Student Services at Arizona State University, and Heidi Rose, then a doctoral student at the university. The performance featured the storyteller Sam Supalla and Peter Cook and included Deaf students performing works by Clayton Valli, Ella Mae Lentz, and Debbie Rennie. The performance is noteworthy because it was the first time original ASL literature was formally performed by individuals other than the author. Rose discusses some of the implications of these performances in chapter 7 of this volume.

- 1992—Sam Supalla and Ben Bahan's *American Sign Language Literature Series* videotape and workbook published. This video/workbook set was designed to help instructors teach ASL literature and literary analysis. Supalla and Bahan each sign a story and then take the viewer-reader through a step-by-step analysis of form, structure, theme, and style.

- 1992—"A Critical Methodology for Analyzing American Sign Language Literature," PhD dissertation by Heidi M. Rose, Arizona State University. Exploring theories of the body deriving from dance and performance art, the dissertation (1) presents a history of ASL literature, distinguishing between pre- and postvideotape texts; (2) identifies key stylistic features of ASL literature, including bodily rhythm and repetition, modification of conventional ASL signs, visual metaphor, and body-as-camera; and (3) analyzes works by Sam Supalla, Clayton Valli, Peter Cook, and Debbie Rennie.

- 1993—"The Poetics of American Sign Language Poetry," PhD dissertation by Clayton Valli, Union Institute Graduate School. The dissertation delineates a formalist theory of ASL poetry, comparing English and ASL poetics. Valli presents a thorough analysis of the multifaceted rhyming potential of ASL poetry. Valli's work has essentially established the field of ASL poetic analysis.

- 1994—*The Man behind the Mask: An Interview with Bernard Bragg,* a six-volume videotape set published by DawnPictures that contains numerous samples of ASL narrative.

- 1995—*ASL Poetry: Selected Works of Clayton Valli,* a videotape published by Dawn-Pictures. In this collection, the narrator Lon Kuntze introduces viewers to linguistic techniques embedded in Valli's poems. This tape also represents the first ASL publication where performers other than the author recite poems.

- 1995—*The Treasure: Poems by Ella Mae Lentz,* a videotape published by In Motion Press. This collection of Lentz's works explores the role of the camera in making a poem live. Lentz experiments with different camera angles and perspectives, allowing the camera to become part of the text, as opposed to merely recording or preserving the text. Heidi Rose discusses the performative aspects of the video in this volume.

- 1995—Alec Ormsby published "Poetic Cohesion in American Sign Language: Valli's 'Snowflake' and Coleridge's 'Frost at Midnight.'" one of the first articles to offer an in-depth comparative poetics of ASL and English. This same year, Ormsby publishes his doctoral dissertation, "The Poetry and Politics of American Sign Language," from Stanford University.

- 1995—"Fantasies of Deafness, Silence, and Speech," PhD dissertation by Jennifer L. Nelson, University of California at Berkeley. Starting with a theoretical analysis of the phonocentric tradition in classical literature, Nelson argues that this phonocentric literary tradition defines Deaf people in a way that reflects the verbal bias inherent in speech and written representations of speech. Nelson argues for ASL literature as a counterpoint and valid alternative to this tradition. Nelson's chapter in this volume (chapter 6) on the importance of poststructuralist theory in validating ASL as a form of literature (and a form of "writing") equal to spoken and written literature is derived from this dissertation.

- 1996—International ASL Literature Conference at NTID. This conference not only featured the work of a more varied array of American Deaf artists than the 1991 conference but in addition exposed audiences to artists from South Africa and Quebec. A shift in the conceptualizations of ASL literature became apparent as artists and critics demonstrated a more flexible and inclusive definition of sign literature.

- 1996—Modern Language Association reclassification of ASL. The *MLA International Bibliography* had traditionally classified sign languages as invented languages akin to Klingon and Esperanto. With the recognition of this error, the 1996 edition reclassified ASL and other sign languages as equivalent to any spoken language.

- 1996—At Gallaudet University, Ben Bahan first taught the course "Oral Traditions in the Deaf Community," which expands on Bahan's chapter in this volume (chapter 2).

- 1997—Publication of Susan Burch's "Deaf Poets Society: Subverting the Hearing Paradigm" in the online periodical *Literature and Medicine*. Due to Internet technology, this is the first time that a scholarly publication was able to feature ASL poetry on video.

- 1998—"American Sign Language as a Medium for Poetry: A Comparative Poetics of Sign, Speech, and Writing," PhD dissertation by H-Dirksen L. Bauman, State University of New York, Binghamton. Bauman asserts that ASL poetry offers aesthetic potential in its synthesis of visual, spatial, and kinetic modalities that modernist and postmodernist American poetry has been searching for, especially those poets in the tradition of Ezra Pound.

- 1999—Jim Cohn's *Sign Mind* published. This text is a collection of essays on sign poetics and other musings on Deaf poetry and performance.

- 1999 to 2001—ASL Literature Poetry and Storytelling Series, a performance series offered by the Deaf Studies Department at Gallaudet University. Performers such as Joseph Castronovo, Clayton Valli, Ella Lentz, Bernard Bragg, Sam Supalla, and the Flying Words Project were featured.

- 2002—Gallaudet University established a Master of Arts degree in Deaf studies. Curriculum included an integration of cultural studies, critical theory, and ASL literature.

- 2002—Deaf Way II, an extension of the first Deaf Way festival in 1989. Deaf Way II hosted over ten thousand registrants from over one hundred countries. The conference featured presentations on political, educational, social, and artistic aspects of Deaf culture around the world, with a number of presentations focused on sign literature and a wide range of performances of drama, narrative, and poetry. The objective of this conference was to maintain ties within the global Deaf community.
- 2003—*Slope* literary magazine published an online volume focusing on ASL poetry (Rich and Janke 2003). This magazine featured the National ASL Poetry contest, judged by Peter Cook and Kenny Lerner and won by Jeremy Quiroga. This special edition also featured background reading on ASL poetry and Deaf culture.
- 2004—Modern Language Association Forum: American Sign Language. This special forum at the MLA featured three panels that dealt with specific aspects of literary expression through ASL.
- 2004–5—Deaf Poetry Jam: sponsored by CityLore, Inc., and filmmaker Judy Lieff, Deaf Poetry Jam encouraged and trained Deaf high school students from New York City to perform alongside spoken-word poets from the New York area. In May 2005, Deaf high school poets performed with spoken-word poets at the Bowery Poetry Club in New York City.
- 2005—Dutch poets Wim Emmerik and Giselle Meyer teamed with filmmakers Anja Heddinga and Leendert Pot to create *Motioning,* a collection of "film poetry in Dutch Sign Language" (Heddinga and Pot 2005). The highly stylized editing marks a new level in the integration of film language and sign language poetics.

NOTES

1. The terms *Golden Age* and *Dark Ages* are often used to refer to these periods and are not new to this time line.

2. See John Schuchman's *Hollywood Speaks* (1988) for a history of Deaf actors and filmmakers as well as a treatment of Hollywood's portrayal of deafness.

3. These films are available on videotape through Sign Media, Inc., in *The Preservation of American Sign Language—The Complete Historical Collection* (1997).

REFERENCES

American Sign Language: Tales from the Green Books. 1980. Burtonsville, MD: Sign Media.

Bahan, Ben, and Sam Supalla. 1992. *American Sign Language Literature Series.* Videocassette and workbook. San Diego: DawnSignPress.

Ballin, Albert. 1930. *The Deaf-Mute Howls.* Washington, DC: Gallaudet University Press.

Batson, Trenton W., and Eugene Bergman, eds. 1987. *Angels and Outcasts: An Anthology of Deaf Characters in Literature.* 3rd ed. Washington, DC: Gallaudet University Press.

Bauman, H-Dirksen L. 1998. "American Sign Language as a Medium for Poetry: A Comparative Poetics of Sign, Speech, and Writing." PhD diss., State University of New York, Binghamton.

Baynton, Douglas C. 1997. *Forbidden Signs: American Culture and the Campaign against Sign Language*. Chicago: University of Chicago Press.

Bragg, Bernard. 1994. *The Man behind the Mask: An Interview with Bernard Bragg*. Videocassette. San Diego, CA: DawnPictures.

Bragg, Bernard, and Eugene Bergman. 1981. *Tales from a Clubroom*. Washington, DC: Gallaudet College Press.

———. 1991. *Tales from a Clubroom*. Videocassette. Washington, DC: Department of Television, Film and Photography, Gallaudet University.

Burch, Susan. 1997. "Deaf Poets Society: Subverting the Hearing Paradigm." *Literature and Medicine* 16 (Spring): 121–34.

Cohn, Jim. 1986. "The New Deaf Poetics: Visible Poetry." *Sign Language Studies* 52 (Fall): 263–77.

———. 1999. *Sign Mind: Studies in American Sign Language Poetics*. Boulder, CO: Museum of American Poetics.

Eastman, Gilbert C. 1974. *Sign Me Alice*. Washington, DC: Gallaudet College Press.

———. 1980. "From Student to Professional: A Personal Chronicle of Sign Language." In *Sign Language and the Deaf Community: Essays in Honor of William C. Stokoe*, ed. Charlotte Baker and Robbin Battison, 9–32. Silver Springs, MD: National Association of the Deaf.

———. 1983. *Sign Me Alice* and *Sign Me Alice II*. Three videocassettes. Washington, DC: Gallaudet College TV Studio, 1983.

Erting, Carol, Robert Johnson, Dorothy Smith, and Bruce Snider, eds. 1994. *The Deaf Way: Perspectives from the International Conference on Deaf Culture*. Washington, DC: Gallaudet University Press.

Frishberg, Nancy. 1988. "Signers of Tales: The Case for the Literary Status of an Unwritten Language." *Sign Language Studies* 59:149–70.

Gannon, Jack. 1981. *Deaf Heritage: A Narrative History of Deaf America*. Washington, DC: National Association of the Deaf.

Graybill, Patrick.1990. *Poetry in Motion, Original Works in ASL: Patrick Graybill*. Videocassette. Burtonsville, MD: Sign Media.

Hiddinga, Anja, and Lendeert Pot, dirs. 2005. *Motioning*. DVD. Poetry and performances by Wim Emmerik and Giselle Meyer. Amsterdam: Stichten Geelproduckt, Rubenstein Publishers.

Kelleher, Jane Frances. 1986. "Literature by Deaf Iowans: Linguistic Form and Social Function." PhD diss., University of Iowa.

Klima, Edward, and Ursula Bellugi. 1979. *The Signs of Language*. Cambridge, MA: Harvard University Press.

Lentz, Ella Mae. 1995. *The Treasure: Poems by Ella Mae Lentz*. Videocassette. Berkeley: In Motion Press.

Miles, Dorothy. 1976. *Gestures: Poetry by Dorothy Miles*. Book and videocassette. Northridge, CA: Joyce Motion Picture.

Mitchell, W. J. T. 1989. "Gesture, Sign, and Play: ASL Poetry and the Deaf Community." *MLA Newsletter,* Summer, 13–14.

Nelson, Jennifer L. 1995. "Fantasies of Deafness, Silence, and Speech." PhD diss., University of California, Berkeley.

Ormsby, Alec. 1995a. "Poetic Cohesion in American Sign Language: Valli's 'Snowflake' and Coleridge's 'Frost at Midnight.'" *Sign Language Studies* 88:227–44.

———. 1995b. "The Poetry and Politics of American Sign Language." PhD diss., Stanford University.

Panara, Robert F., Taras B. Denis, and James H. McFarlane, eds. 1960. *The Silent Muse: An Anthology of Prose and Poetry by the Deaf.* Washington, DC: Gallaudet College.

The Preservation of American Sign Language: The Complete Historical Collection. 1997. Burtonsville, MD: Sign Media.

Rennie, Debbie. 1990. *Poetry in Motion, Original Works in ASL: Debbie Rennie.* Videocassette. Burtonsville, MD: Sign Media.

Rich, Rita, and Christopher Janke, eds. 2003. "American Sign Language Poetry Special Edition." *Slope.* Retrieved December 24, 2005, from http://slope.org/asl.

Rose, Heidi M. 1992. "A Critical Methodology for Analyzing American Sign Language Literature." PhD diss., Arizona State University.

Rutherford, Susan.1987. "A Study of American Deaf Folklore." PhD diss., University of California, Berkeley.

Schuchman, John S. 1988. *Hollywood Speaks: Deafness and the Film Entertainment History.* Urbana: University of Illinois Press.

Stokoe, William C. 1960. *Sign Language Structure: An Outline of the Visual Communication Systems of the American Deaf.* Silver Spring, MD: Linstok.

Supalla, Ted. *Charles Krauel: A Profile of a Deaf Filmmaker.* Videocassette. San Diego, CA: DawnPictures, 1994.

Valli, Clayton. 1990a. "The Nature of the Line in ASL Poetry." In *SLR '87: Papers from the Fourth International Symposium on Sign Language Research,* ed. W. H. Edmondson and F. Karlsson. Hamburg: Signum.

———. 1990b. *Poetry in Motion, Original Works in ASL: Clayton Valli.* Videocassette. Burtonsville, MD: Sign Media.

———. 1993. "The Poetics of American Sign Language Poetry." PhD diss., Union Institute Graduate School.

———. 1995. *ASL Poetry: Selected Works of Clayton Valli.* Videocassette. San Diego: DawnPictures.

Whitney, William Dwight. 1876. *The Life and Growth of Language: An Outline of Linguistic Science.* New York: D. Appleton.

APPENDIX B

ASL Video References

Bahan, Ben, and Sam Supalla. *American Sign Language Literature Series.* Videocassette. San Diego, CA: DawnPictures, 1992.

Bangs, Don. *Moving Pictures, Moving Hands: The Story of Ernest Marshall.* Videocassette. Studio City, CA: Beyond Sound Productions, 1987.

Bragg, Bernard. *The Man behind the Mask: An Interview with Bernard Bragg.* Videocassette. San Diego, CA: DawnPictures, 1994.

Bragg, Bernard, and Eugene Bergman. *Tales from a Clubroom.* Videocassette. Washington, DC: Department of Television, Film and Photography, Gallaudet University, 1991.

Eastman, Gilbert C. *Live at SMI: Gilbert Eastman.* Videocassette. Burtonsville, MD: Sign Media, 1991.

———. *Sign Me Alice* and *Sign Me Alice II.* Three videocassettes. Washington, DC: Gallaudet College TV Studio, 1983.

Ennis, B. 1993. *Bill Ennis: Live at SMI!* Videocassette. Burtonsville, MD: Sign Media.

Gallaudet University Distance Education Program. 1997. *Telling Tales in ASL: From Literature to Literacy.* Videocassette. Washington, DC: Gallaudet University.

Graybill, Patrick. *Poetry in Motion, Original Works in ASL: Patrick Graybill.* Videocassette. Burtonsville, MD: Sign Media, 1990.

———. *The World According to Pat: Reflections of Residential School Days.* Videocassette. Silver Spring, MD: Sign Media and TJ Publishers, 1986.

Lentz, Ella Mae. *The Treasure: Poems by Ella Mae Lentz.* Videocassette. Berkeley, CA: In Motion Press, 1995.

Lentz, Ella Mae, Ken Mikos, and Cheryl Smith. *Signing Treasures: Excerpts from Signing Naturally Videos.* Videocassette. San Diego, CA: DawnPictures, 1996.

Miles, Dorothy. *Gestures: Poetry by Dorothy Miles.* Book and videocassette. Northridge, CA: Joyce Motion Pictures, 1976.

Miller, Mary Beth. 1992. *Live at SMI: Mary Beth Miller.* Videocassette. Burtonsville, MD: Sign Media.

Mocenigo, R., dir. *American Culture: The Deaf Perspective.* Four videocassettes. San Francisco: San Francisco Public Library.

The Preservation of American Sign Language: The Complete Historical Collection. Videocassette. Burtonsville, MD: Sign Media, 1997.

Rennie, Debbie. *Poetry in Motion, Original Works in ASL: Debbie Rennie.* Videocassette. Burtonsville, MD: Sign Media, 1990.

Supalla, C., and D. Supalla. 1992. *Short Stories in American Sign Language.* Videocassette. Riverside, CA: ASL Vista Project.

Supalla, Ted. *Charles Krauel: A Profile of a Deaf Filmmaker.* Videocassette. San Diego, CA: DawnPictures, 1994.

Valli, Clayton. *ASL Poetry: Selected Works of Clayton Valli.* Hosted by Lon Kuntze. Videocassette. San Diego, CA: DawnPictures, 1995.

———. *Poetry in Motion, Original Works in ASL: Clayton Valli.* Videocassette. Burtonsville, MD: Sign Media, 1990.

CONTRIBUTORS

BEN BAHAN is a Professor and MA Program Director in the Department of American Sign Language and Deaf Studies, Gallaudet University.

H-DIRKSEN L. BAUMAN is a Professor in the Department of American Sign Language and Deaf Studies, Gallaudet University.

MICHAEL DAVIDSON is a Professor in the Department of Literature, University of California, San Diego.

KRISTEN C. HARMON is an Associate Professor in the Department of English, Gallaudet University.

CHRISTOPHER B. KRENTZ is an Assistant Professor of English and Director of the American Sign Language Program in the Department of English, University of Virginia.

W. J. T. MITCHELL is the Gaylord Donnelley Distinguished Service Professor in the Departments of English and Art History, University of Chicago.

JENNIFER L. NELSON is a Professor in the Department of English, Gallaudet University.

CAROL A. PADDEN is a Professor in the Department of Communication, University of California, San Diego.

CYNTHIA PETERS is an Associate Professor in the Department of English, Gallaudet University.

CAROL L. ROBINSON is an Assistant Professor in the Department of English, Kent State University, Trumbull.

HEIDI M. ROSE is an Associate Professor in the Department of Communication, Villanova University.

LIZ WOLTER is a teacher in the English Department of the Lexington School for the Deaf, New York City.

INDEX

Page numbers in italic refer to illustrations or their captions.

218. *See also* Education in sign language; Gallaudet University

on, xvi; Rousseau on, xv, xviii; Saussure on, 122

Language instinct, xviii, 3

Laurel, Stan, 201

Lectures in sign language, 54, 60

Lefebvre, Henri, 72, 87

Leibniz, Gottfried Wilhelm von, 127

Leigh, Michael, 111

Lenis, Kelly, 165n6

Lentz, Ella Mae, 10, 11, 34, 56, 61, 62, 66, 106, 107, 137, 158, 159, 161, 217, 218, 236; as performance artist, 132–33, 135, 141–42

Leonardo da Vinci, 104

Lerner, Kenny, 10, 61, 62, 64, 109, 137, 153; and Flying Words performance, 10, 62, 153, 218–19, *220*, 232, 238

Lexington School for the Deaf, 152, 154, 163, 165nn1,5

Lineation in sign poetry, 95–110, 114–15; and Bragg's work, 104, *105*, 109, 110; cinematic properties of, 109–10; and Flying Words Project, 107–8; and kinetic composition, 107–9; and Lentz's work, 106, 107; and phonocentrism, 98, 99–101; and Valli's work, 95–96, 98, 99, 101, 106; and visual art, 98–99, 104, 105, 108; and visual composition, 104–6; and visual poetry, 101–2, *103–4*

Literature in sign language: academization of, 65; compared to oral literature, 5–7, 21–22, 53, 170–72, 177, 179, 184; and cultural identity, 33; and Derrida's theory of signification, 119–20, 128; and educational practices, 147–65; emergence of, 8–12; and epic form, 170–86; film/video as influence on, 51, 52, 60–65; film/video used for preserving, 56, 147, 148; genre boundaries challenged by, 12; literary criticism of, 9, 12, 65, 69n2; literary practice redefined by, 2–4; marginality of, 5, 6; ownership of, 42–43, 48n24, 132, 135; as performance, 131–44; phonocentrism challenged by, xvii, 3, 4, 5, 217, 218, 237; and utopianism, xvii; voice interpre-

tation of, 218. *See also* Poetry in sign language; Storytelling in sign language

Live at SMI! series, 12, 57, 58, 62

Logocentrism, 126, 224

Logodice, Colleen, 165n5

Lord, Albert, 54, 60, 185

Lukács, Georg, 174–75, 183

Malzkuhn, Brian, 55, 60, 61

Malzkuhn, Eric, 12, 132

Manning, Anita, 67

Marentette, Paula F., 16n3

Marsh, William, 8

Marshall, Ernest, 55

Marshall, Winfield E., 34

Marvel, David, 198

Masten, Jeffrey, 100

Matlin, Marlee, 169, 209, 216

Maucere, John, 72

McGregor, Robert P., 55

McLuhan, Marshall, xviii

Medoff, Mark, 216

Merwin, W. S., 6

Meschonnic, Henri, 99

Miles, Dorothy, 236

Miller, Mary Beth, 12, 57, 62

Milton, John, xvii, xix, 5

Mirzoeff, Nicholas, 196, 198, 199

"Missing Children" (Rennie), 138–40, 141, 161

Mitchell, W. J. T., 3, 15, 102

Modernism, 97

Molière, 47n6

Morris, Garrett, 205, 206

Mow, Shanny, 72, 236

My Third Eye (play), 9, 55, 71, 75–76, 77–78, 79, 82, 83, 84, 85, 88, 235

National Association of the Deaf (NAD), 23, 24, 51, 55, 67

National Fraternal Society of the Deaf, 24

Nationalism, 67, 237, 239

National Technical Institute for the Deaf (NTID), 72, 79–80, 142, 150, 164

National Theatre of the Deaf (NTD), 23, 81–82, 110, 158, 235, 236

Nelson, Jennifer L., 13

Ng, Wilson, 157
Norman, Freda, 35, 42
Norton, Audree, 235

Ohio School for the Deaf, 41
Okpewho, I., 25, 43, 45
Oliver, Mary, 6
Olson, Charles, 11, 224
Ong, Walter J., 51, 53, 56, 173
Oralism, 217, 218, 219, 230
Oral literature, 5–7, 21–22, 52–54; Gal-
 laudet protest epic compared to,
 170–72, 177, 179, 184, 185
Ownership of sign literature, 42–43,
 48n24, 132, 135

Padden, Carol A., 9, 182, 217
Panara, Robert, 79
Parade (NTD production), 71, 82, 85
Peirce, C. C., 197
Pennsylvania School for the Deaf, 163
Percussion signing, 34–36
Pérez Firmat, Gustavo, 80
Performance: body as medium for, 131,
 133–37; and Eastman's protest epic,
 172, 176, 177–78, 182, 184–85; inter-
 preted by non-authorial performers,
 136–40; and Lentz's work, 132–33,
 135; media's impact on, 56–57,
 60–62, 65; ownership of, 132, 135;
 sign poetry as, xvii, 2, 5–7, 10, 13–14,
 131–33, 136–44; textual authority
 problematized in, 135–36, 143–44,
 232n3; video as medium for preserving, 130–36 passim, 145n2. *See also*
 Speech in Deaf performance
Perloff, Marjorie, 99, 132
Peters, Cynthia L., 48n20, 235, 237
Petitto, Laura Ann, 16n3
Philip, Marie, 44
Phonocentrism, xvii, 1, 3, 4, 5, 13, 98,
 99–101, 237; and Derrida's theory of
 signification, 119, 120, 125, 226,
 233n7; and speech in Deaf performance, 217, 218, 224, 226
Photography, 202
Pidgin Sign English (PSE), 147, 165n1,
 214n7

Pinker, Stephen, xvii–xviii
Plato, 16n4
Poetic Images group, 137–40
Poetry: and digital media, 7–8; Emerson
 on, xvi; Goodman on, xvi; ideological determination of, 99–100; and
 lineation, 95, 97–98, 99–101; and
 print medium, 62; revitalization of
 oral, 6; unconventional forms of,
 131–32; visual, 7–8, 101–2, *103–4*, 132
Poetry in sign language: body as medium
 for, xvii, 2, 5, 6, 8, 107, 130–31, 132,
 133; cinematic properties of, 99,
 109–14, 155; compared to oral tradition, 5–7; compared to visual art,
 98–99, 108; and educational practices, 154–55, 156–57, 158; emergence
 of, 9–11, 236; film/video as medium
 for, 51, 52, 60–62, 64, 130; and Gallaudet protest epic, 170, 172; genre
 boundaries challenged by, 12; and
 handshapes, 154–55, 236, 238, 239;
 internationalization of, 239; and
 kinetic composition, 107–9; and lineation, 95–110, 114–15; and linguistic
 classifiers, 152, 155; literary criticism
 of, 69n2; literary practice redefined
 by, 9–10; new sign for, 4; ownership
 of, 132, 135; as performance, xvii, 2,
 5–7, 13–14, 131–33, 136–44; phonocentrism challenged by, xvii, 1–2, 4,
 5, 98, 99–101, 217, 237; and rhymes,
 96, 101, 106, 154; and visuality, 5, 8,
 104–6, *105*; visual vernacular technique in, 10, 11, 110
Poizner, Howard, 122
Political relations: and literary genre,
 173–76; and visual screaming, 196–98
Pope, Alexander, 96
Postcolonialism, 217, 237–38, 239
Postmodernism, 97–98, 226
Pound, Ezra, 11, 108
Print medium: artistic practice influenced
 by, 60–63; and audience-artist relations, 56–57, 59, 63–64; cultural
 accessibility enhanced by, 54–55, 66;
 cultural development promoted by,
 51–52, 68; cultural preservation

enhanced by, 55; language standardized by, 65–66; literacy promoted by, 66; literary criticism biased toward, 202; sign language represented in, 22, 46n2, 48n20, 53, 127–28, 145n4
PSE. *See* Pidgin Sign English
Puppet paws, 209–10

Rafael, Vicente, 237
Ramirez, Sylvia, 165n6
Redden, Laura, 53
Redmond, Granville, 196, 198, 203, *204*, 208
Reich, Maddy, 165n5
Rennie, Debbie, 106, 137–39, 141, 142, 158, 161, 217
Rhyme, 96, 101, 106, 154
Richard, Jaine, 137
Rimbaud, Arthur, 99
Rivera, David, 239
Robinson, Carol L., 14, 128
Robinson, David, 196
Romero, Emerson, 80, 198
Rose, Heidi M., 12–13
Rothenberg, Jerome, 6, 224
Rousseau, Jean-Jacques, xv, xviii, 126, 225, 231
Rubinstein, Raphael, 229
Russell, Mark, 135–36
Rutherford, Susan, 31–32, 41, 47n8, 48n21

Saussure, Ferdinand de, 122, 197, 224
Schneemann, Carolee, 6
Schrag, Calvin O., 134
Schuchman, John S., 196, 198, 203
Shakespeare, William, 82–83, 128, 195
Shange, Ntozake, 6
Sienkewicz, T., 46
Sign language: cultural identity based on, 213n3; as gesture language, xvi–xxii; linguistic classification of, 3; and utopianism, xvii, xix–xx; written forms of, 145n4. *See also* American Sign Language (ASL); British Sign Language; German Sign Language; Pidgin Sign English (PSE)
"Sign /anguish," 195, 207, 213n1
Sign Me Alice (play), 71, 72, 74, 86, 91n36

Sign Media, Inc., 58, 59
Sign-mime, 201, 210
SignRise Cultural Arts, 84, 86, 88
Silent films, 80, 195–204, 205, 207–8, 210, 212–13
Simonides of Keos, 7
Smith, Anna Deavere, 136
Smooth signers, 24–25, 26, 144
Snyder, Gary, 224
Sollars, Werner, 78, 79
Songs in sign language, 33–34, 47n12, 55, 64
Speech, Derrida's theory of, 120, 122, 124–28, 226
Speech in Deaf performance: and audience-performer relations, 219, 224; and biculturalism, 221, 227; and Flying Words' performance, 218–19, *220*, 221, 232; and Joseph Grigely's textual art, 14, 218, 227–31, *228*, 233nn8–9; and phonocentrism, 217, 218, 224, 226; as scandal, 216–17, 226, 232; and "think-hearing" sign, 217, 232; and Aaron Williamson's peformances, 14, 218, 221–22, *223*, 224–26, *225*, 232nn4–5, 233n7, 238
Spilman, Jane, 179, 180
Stallybrass, Peter, 79, 100
Steiner, Wendy, 7
Stern, Carol Simpson, 76
Sternberg, Martin L. A., 165n8
Sterne, Laurence, 62
Stokoe, William, 3, 62, 109, 110, 128
Storytelling in sign language: and ABC stories, 8, 37–38, 40–41, 154; and audience relations, 27–28, 43–45, 57; cinematic technique in, 29–31, 62–63, 109, 150–51, 155, 156, 183, 201–2; compared to oral tradition, 21–22, 170–72, 177, 179, 184; constraints in, 37–42; and cultural identity, 26, 33; at Deaf clubs, 24, 26, 43–44, 48n25; at Deaf schools, 23–24, 26; and educational practices, 150–57; and face-to-face tradition, 11, 13, 21–25, 46; film as influence on, 52; and fingerspelled words, 41–42; and folktales, 31–32; and Gallaudet

Storytelling in sign language *(continued)*
protest, 170–93; genre boundaries
challenged by, 12; handshapes in,
37–42, *39*; literary criticism of, 69n2;
and number stories, 8, 41; and ownership of stories, 42–43, 48n24; paralinguistic elements of, 27–28, 37, 40;
personal experience as subject of, 29;
and "smooth signers," 24–25, 26;
tellers' control of, 26–28; and tellers'
training and development, 25–26;
and translation of printed works,
32–33; venues for, 24, 26, 43–44; and
visual vernacular technique, 151
Subculture, politics of, 173
Supalla, David, 47n12
Supalla, Sam, 11, 31, 33, 57, 63, 65, 137,
236, 237, 239
Supalla, Ted, 56, 65
Swett, William B., 54

Tales from a Clubroom (play), 71, 74
Teaching. *See* Education, oralist; Education in sign language
Television broadcasts, 75, 169, 205. *See also*
Video
Tennyson, Alfred, 99
Textual art, 227–31, *228*, 233nn8–9
Theater, social history of, 72–74
Theater in sign language: at academic
institutions, 71–72, 79–81, 91n36,
92n56; and audience relations,
84–85, 87–88; and Bakhtin's critical
work, 13, 75, 79, 84–85; and carnival,
13, 74, 75, 76, 77, 79, 80, 84–85, 89;
collaboration in, 83–88; and cultural
identity, 78; diversity of, 71–72;
ensemble performance in, 86–87;
heterogeneous structure of, 79–83,
88–89; and inversion, 76–77; social
engagement of, 71, 74; and two-
world condition, 74–75; and vaudeville, 79–81, 83, 87, 88–89; women
in, 90n17. *See also* Fairmount Theatre of the Deaf (FTD); National
Theatre of the Deaf (NTD)
"Think-hearing," sign for, 217, 232
Thomas, Dylan, 81, 89

Translation, 32–33, 34, 47nn12–13, 53, 61,
104, *105*, 182, 183, 235, 239
Twombly, Cy, 227

Utopianism, xvii, xix–xx , 201

Valli, Clayton, 10, 11, 13, 60, 61, 64, 65,
133, 137, 158, 159, 217, 236; and cinematic technique, 112–14; and per-
formance, 140–42, 218; and poetic
lineation, 95–96, 98, 99, 101, 106
Vaudeville, 73, 79–81, 83, 87, 88–89
Veditz, George W., 51, 55, 59, 60, 69, 237
Velez, Joe, 9, 32, 235
Verhoosky, Michele, 72
Vickers, Nancy, 100
Video: ASL culture influenced by, 9, 13,
46, 52, 55, 57–65, 66, 68, 119, 160–61;
ASL instruction using, 58, 59, 66,
147–50; ASL performance preserved
by, 12, 32, 36, 42, 77, 82, 130–36 pas-
sim, 145n2, 147, 148, 174, 232n3; as
ASL "writing," 119, 127, 128
Visual art, 7–8, 98–99, 104, *105*, 108
Visual poetry, 101–2, *103–4*
Visual screaming, 195–98, 200, 203–13
Visual vernacular technique, 10, 11, 110,
151
Voice: and Derrida's theory of significa-
tion, 120, 124, 126, 127; and poetry in
sign language, 130

Walcott, Derek, 173
Waldman, Anne, 6
Weinberg, Louis, 198
White, Allon, 79
Whitman, Walt, 99–100
Williams, William Carlos, 62, 99
Williamson, Aaron, 14, 218, 221–22, *223*,
224–26, *225*, 229, 231, 232nn4–5,
233n7, 238–39
Wolter, Liz, 14
Woolf, Virginia, 202
Wrigley, Owen, 15, 213n3, 221
Writing, Derrida's theory of, 119–22,
124–25, 127–28

Zinser, Elizabeth, 169

Compositor: Sheridan Books, Inc.
Text: 11/14 Adobe Garamond
Display: Perpetua, Adobe Garamond
Indexer: Andrew Joron
Printer/Binder: Sheridan Books, Inc.